African Charter

on Rights & Duties

Enforcement Mechanisms

African Charter
on Rights & Duties

Enforcement Mechanisms

Osita C. Eze

Globethics.net Africa Law No. 10

Globethics.net African Law

Series editor: Prof. Dr. Obiora Ike, Executive Director of Globethics.net in Geneva and Professor of Ethics at the Godfrey Okoye University Enugu/Nigeria.

Globethics.net African Law 10
Osita C. Eze, *Africa Charter on Rights & Duties, Enforcement Mechanisms*
Geneva: Globethics.net, 2017
ISBN 978-2-88931-413-3 (online version)
ISBN 978-2-88931-414-0 (print version)
© 2021 Globethics.net

Managing Editor: Ignace Haaz
Assistant Editor: Nefti Bempong-Ahun

Globethics.net International Secretariat
150 route de Ferney
1211 Geneva 2, Switzerland
Website: *www.globethics.net/publications*
Email: *publications@globethics.net*

All web links in this text have been verified as of June 2021.

TABLE OF CONTENTS

In Memoriam

Grace Ifeyinwa Eze, my late wife

PREFACE

Osita C. Eze former Director General of the Nigerian Institute of International Affairs died in 2012 and left as legacy of his great creative mind a writing for some of us his friends.

Current document is being published posthumously to recognize the intellectual profundity and need for legal and Human Rights instruments for a stable and civilized society. These works remain the life work of Osita Eze. It is time to share it with the reading public.

Permit me to say that Osita Eze is one of the finest legal and jurisprudence experts in Africa. His death some 10 years ago does not close his thought and mind to resonate internationally and to be read everywhere.

Globethics.net Publications has found the work useful in the African Law Series, which intends to present law as the foundation of any society. This booklet shall surely join the relevant and enduring books from the African point of view. Every law student should have a copy.

Prof. Dr Obiora F. Ike
Executive Director of Globethics.net

ACKNOWLEDGEMENTS

This book has taken several years to complete. The first draft was done after I delivered my Chair Lecture as *Ume Umanah Professor of Law* of the University of Uyo on a similar topic. I am, therefore, grateful to the Vice Chancellor Professor Lasisi, who encouraged me to deliver the lecture. As is my practice, my students often provide the testing ground for any work that I intend to embark on. In this regard, I owe a lot of gratitude to my post-graduate students, in International Human Rights Law at the University of Uyo, Abia State University and Rivers State University of Science and Technology, where I taught the subject at different periods.

My lectures on the African Charter at the European Institute of Human Rights at Strasbourg, France (2004), offered me yet another opportunity to put final touches to the manuscript.

Remarkably, the title of the book was finally decided upon at the tail end of the work. There have been some works whose titles simply followed the title of the African Charter on Human and Peoples Rights. It was thought that a title that reflected the essence rather than the form would be preferred. Hence, *African Charter on Rights and Duties and Enforcement Mechanisms* is emphasizing the aspect of actualisation of rights. In this regard, I am grateful to my old schoolmate and friend Mr. Alexander Peter Egom who helped to shape the new title. Mr. Joseph Ajiboye Oni of the Nigerian Institute of International Affairs deserves special recognition for his dedicated and untiring effort in putting together the bibliography and index of the book. Finally, I owe a debt of gratitude to my daughters *Nnenna* and *Chisom* who had to contend with my immersion in the work.

1

INTRODUCTION

1.1 General

The African Charter on Human and Peoples' Rights—the African Charter—represents a positive step forward in the promotion and protection of rights on a continental basis. The African Charter which was adopted by the Assembly of Heads of State and Government in June 1981 and came into force in 1986[1,2]. It is remarkable in its coverage of rights and duties whether of states, individuals or peoples. The substantive human and peoples' rights provisions embrace civil and political rights (first generation rights), the socio-economic and cultural rights (second generation rights), and peoples' or solidarity rights (third

---

[1] Addis Ababa, CAB/LEG/67/Rev. 3, 1981.

[2] As at January 1992 the following 41 countries had ratified or adhered to the Charter; Algeria, Angola, Benin, Botswana, Burundi, Burkina Faso, Cameroon, Cape Verde, Central African Republic, Chad, Comoros, Congo, Cote d'Ivoire, Djibouti, Democratic Republic of Congo, Egypt, Equatorial Guinea, Eritrea, Ethiopia, Gabon, Gambia, Ghana, Guinea, Guinea-Bissau, Kenya, Libya, Lesotho, Liberia, Madagascar, Malawi, Mali, Mauritania, Mozambique, Mauritius, Namibia, Niger, Nigeria, Rwanda, South Africa, Sahrawi Arab Democratic Republic, Sao Tome and Principe, Senegal, Seychelles, Sierra Leone, Somalia, Sudan, Swaziland, Togo, Tunisia, Tanzania, Uganda, Zambia, Zimbabwe, (see "How to Address a Communication to the African Commission on Human and Peoples' Rights", International Commission of Jurists, Jan.1992 Annex 1). The number has since increased to 53.

generation rights). The duty provisions cover those for individuals, peoples and states.[3]

An African Commission on Human and Peoples' Rights, (the Commission) is established. Inaugurated in 1986 it has been in business since 1987. It is an institution of the Organisation of Arfrican Unity (OAU) charged with the primary responsibility of, *inter alia,* promoting and ensuring the protection of human rights and peoples' rights.[4] The African Court, advocated earlier by some jurists came much later.[5] The Protocol to the African Charter on the establishment of an African Court on Human and Peoples' Rights came into force in March 2004, thirty days after the 15th ratification as required [Article 34(2)]. The Court is to complement and reinforce the functions of the African Commission.

The African Charter, which presumes the pre-eminence of the Rule of Law and popular participation in government,[6] may be well regarded as a 'Charter of Demands' for the respect of the dignity inherent in the human person, of human and peoples' freedoms and liberties, as well as, their social, material and cultural rights. It may also serve as a liberalising and liberating covenant in which African States recognizing the primacy of the human condition have agreed not only to bring their laws, policies and practices in line with the philosophy and aims and objectives of the African Charter but also[7] to shift from their rigid adherence to the so-called 'national jurisdiction clause' which purports to reserve to the state matters allegedly within its exclusive domestic

---

[3] See *infra.*

[4] Article 30.

[5] T. O. Elias, Background paper for the UN Seminar on the Establishment of Regional Commission on Human Rights with special Reference to African (Monrovia: Liberia 10-12 September, 1979), p. 8.

[6] Article 3 (equality before the law and equal protection of the law) and 7 (right to fair hearing) in particular, as well as Article 13 (participatory rights).

[7] Article 1.

jurisdiction.[8] The Constitutive Act of the African Union, AU, the successor to the OAU, while insisting on the principle of non-interference in the internal affairs of a state moderates it with the principle of respect for democratic principles, human rights and the rule of law [Article 4(g) and (m)].[9] The subject matter of this book is relevant and timely. This is because it gives us an opportunity to assess the possible impact (after just over two decades of the Charter coming into force) of the continental regime on national records on the promotion and protection of human rights in the context of the new near unipolar world order (with the United States of America as the declared leader and co-ordinator) dominated by the philosophy of free enterprise with its emphasis on the dominance of the market and respect for civil and political rights, with little space for the right of freedom from want. Also, there have emerged in Africa since the 90s movements for democracy aimed at overthrowing authoritarian regimes, whether military or civilian, in which mass and popular organisations, trade unions and non-governmental organisations (NGOs) play a major role. Thirdly, the crisis of socialism, and the triumph of capitalism require a re-examination of the theories underlying both socialism and capitalism with a view to appreciating their continuing relevance to the problematics of human and peoples' rights. And finally the 1994 seminar on managing the protection of human rights organised by the British Council at Abuja, by raising conceptual issues and addressing political problems relative to human and peoples' rights, the Rule of law and democracy, the problematics of Human rights enforcement under the African Charter as well as some practical issues on how to enhance

---

[8] See *infra.*

[9] The Act came into force in 2002.

effective actualization of human and peoples' rights – what works?[10] – further stimulated the desire to revisit[11] this very important area of our being as *Homo Sapiens* in order to assess the possibilities and constraints for human and peoples' rights promotion and enforcement, as well as contribute in creating greater awareness of rights guaranteed and duties imposed.

But the evaluation of the possible impact of the African Charter can only make sense if considered in the light of national regimes on human and peoples' rights. Prior to the Charter, various legal and institutional frameworks existed (and still exist) for the promotion and protection of human rights at the national level. In the context of underdevelopment and preponderance of regimes of liberal persuasion, emphasis was placed on civil and political rights to the near total neglect of socio-economic and cultural rights, except the right to private property and that of association.[12] In recent times, in line with the spirit of the African Charter and development, within the United Nations and elsewhere, some African constitutions now include ECOSOC rights.[13]

And even these rights, because of the concrete material conditions underscored by the prevalent modes of production – integration of the pre-capitalist modes of production into the global economy with its

---

[10] The British Council in West African, *Managing the Protection of Human Rights*, Document from an International Seminar held in Abuja, Nigeria 28 February - 4 March 1994.

[11] At the seminar on *Managing the Protection of Human Rights*, the author presented a paper, titled "The place of the African Charter in the Enforcement of Rights" (see pp. 89 - 97).

[12] Before the crisis of socialism, constitutions of countries like, Algeria, Burkina Faso, Benin, etc. had in line with the socialist tradition (being socialist oriented states,) tended to undermine capitalism and, had in varying degrees, sought to promote socio-economic rights. See Osita C. Eze, "The Organisation of African Unity and Human Rights; Twenty-five Years After", N.J.I.A. Vol.14, number 1, 1988, p.158.

[13] See *infra.*

impoverished and alienated majority of African Peoples remained mostly illusive. In particular, there were frequent violations of these rights where they have not been circumscribed by limitations in the interest of public safety, public order and national security which, more often than not, translate into the survival of the government of the day. Since the 1980s with first stagnation and then regression and increasing development of underdevelopment, impoverishment of the majority, increasing repression and declining capacity of African governments to take autonomous decisions in matters of development, human rights to the extent that they exist remain precarious.[14]

It is in context of these developments and particularly the growing penetration and domination of Africa's political economy by the IMF, the World Bank and more recently the World Trade Organisation, WTO, all of which collaborate[15] as well as the Transnational Corporations (TNCS), that one has to assess the relevance of the African Charter and role of African Governments, in the post African Charter era, in the promotion and protection of human rights in all its manifestations – civil, political, social, economic and cultural. The question then arises if the African governments, which have the primary responsibility to guarantee human rights within their domains, have fallen below the mark, whether the AU can provide the needed respite? Can the African Charter provide the basis and the means to enhance continental promotion and protection and at the same time progressively influence national performance in the field of human rights?

Can the AU's limited success in the field of refugee protection be improved in the regime envisaged under the Banjul Charter? Since

---

[14] *Ibid*; Osita C. Eze "Theoretical perspectives and problematic" In *Society and The Rule of Law,* Osita C. Eze ed (Owerri: Totan Publishers Ltd. 1987), p. 24 *et seq;* Marx/Engels, *Selected Correspondence* (Moscow 1986), p500; J. Farrar, *Introduction to legal method,* (London, Sweet & Maxwell, 1977) pp. 62-63.

[15] See *infra.*

human rights are primarily concerned with how society is organised, who rules, with what intent and restraints and in whose interest the issue arises as to the place of the poor, who form the majority and who are invariably victims of rights abuses, in the scheme of Banjul Charter? In effect, the acid test for the contribution of the African Charter in the field of human rights, goes beyond efforts of the OAU/AU in the field of the fight against colonialism, racism and apartheid, which are matters normally regarded as being outside the domestic jurisdiction of member states and should concern itself with the extent to which it has influenced and will continue to have impact on the fundamental functions of government, that is those of law making, interpretation and enforcement of human rights laws and the creation of the socio-economic conditions that give them substance. These are the challenges which confront the African Union, the successor to the OAU, from its inception.

1.2 Methodology and Conceptual Framework

We have argued elsewhere that analysis of social reality ultimately depends on the methodological preference of the author. The author may make his methodological/conceptual framework explicit or leave it to be inferred from the work. We prefer the former since it attempts to state, as clearly as possible, the theoretical and conceptual framework for explaining and analyzing social phenomena, minimizes the danger of semanticism and focuses the attention of the reader on salient rather than ephemeral issues.[16]

Our basic position is that law and human rights guaranteed thereunder are essentially dependent variables. Just like law, morality, social, political and ideological values are parts of the superstructure even when they have influenced and continue to have impact on the

---

[16] P.E. Ollawa, *Participatory Democracy in Zambia: The Political Economy of National Development,* Elmscourt, Arthor H. Stockwell, Ltd., 1979, Chapter 2.

socio-economic system which gives essence and substance to human rights. The role of the State, the most important aspect of the superstructure, is ultimately determined by this reality. Put differently, we intend to emphasize the ultimate determinant role played by the dominant mode of production that determines the nature of the state and the character of the ruling class and the ends which state power serves both within its jurisdiction and in its external relations. The state is not seen as a creature of nature, denuded of its historically determined material conditions, a neutral umpire outside and above classes, simply moderating conflicts, seeking to redress rather than perpetuate inequalities that provide the motive force for the struggle for human rights.[17]

This approach, in our view, rejects the idealist approach that places cognition before matter on which the former depends; the metaphysical approach that is not rooted in material existence, 'pure' or raw empiricism that pretends the absence of values and is obsessed with the collection of facts while being bereft of conceptual or theoretical insight relevant to understanding and analyzing social phenomena,[18] the eclectic approach that is *a priori* determined deriving justification from whatever argument is available; and the fragmented approach that is either oblivious of or unwilling to see the dialectical relations and the interconnectedness and interdependence between various facets of our material and social existence regarding them as separate or at best tangentially related.

Yet, any serious scientific enquiry into a social phenomenon, of which law and human rights are a part, will reveal

---

[17] I. Nzimoro "The Crisis in the Social Sciences: the Nigerian situation "*The World forum (occasional Paper, No. 2* pp.31-32; Osita Eze "Theoretical Perspectives and problematics *op cit*; pp.22-23.

[18] P. E. Ollawa, *Loc cit.*

> "That the seemingly autonomous, disparate and disjointed morsels of social existence – literature, art, politics, the economic order, science, the cultural and psychic condition of people – can all be understood (and influenced) only if they are clearly visualized as parts of a comprehensive totality (not disjointed) morsels of the historical process".[19]

In the divide between those who drive and benefit mostly from the globalization process and more than half the world's population that is left out of it, is a reflection of the inequity of the new global economic order. This new order has serious implications for the actualization of human and peoples' rights.[20]

We shall thus adopt the dialectical method which examines the relevance of forces of production, nature and character of state or public power and their relevance to relations within the state forces, and in relations between states, alienation, division of labour, fetishes etc. in their onward movement, placing pre-eminence on matter over cognition and analyzing the contradictory elements and their resolution. The dialectical method proceeds by thesis, anti-thesis and synthesis and is eminently suited to an incisive understanding of the struggle for human rights[21]. By hindsight, this approach explains much of the confusion inherent in the naturalist, positivistic and normativistic conceptions of human rights that have remained with us in various forms today.[22] It also explains the inadequacy of the sociological school that has proved

---

[19] F. Barran, "The commitment of the intellectual" in his *The longer view* (New York, Monthly Review, 1966), p.8.

[20] See *infra.*

[21] *Human Rights Studies in Universities,* by J.E. Mc Carthy, J.B. Marrie, S.P. Marks and I. Sirois, under the supervision of Karel Vasak (Paris, UNESCO, 1973), p.82.

[22] A Hunt, *The Sociological Movement in Law.* (London, Macmillian Press Ltd. 1978). pp. 150-151.

itself incapable of freeing itself, to some extent, from the positivistic tradition of Anglo-American Jurisprudence. In the words of Hunt[23]

"The plea for the sociology of law is not for sociology of law conceived of as a specialist subdivision within sociology: rather it has been the intention to demonstrate that questions about law involve major questions that confront contemporary society. As such law presents itself as an important area of inquiry for social theory and sociology in general. This central importance of law revolves around its contribution to a participation in the social processes whereby modern capitalist society is sustained. These processes are constituted through complex interaction of the state and political structures of capitalist society. It is these questions to which the general and pervasive tradition of the sociological movement in law has failed to address it".

We hope to expose these inadequacies in what follows.

Our approach, therefore, rejects the technojuristic conception of law and human rights, which emphasizes perception through juridical lenses that serve as blinkers which prevent penetration of the material and social conditions that give character and substance to law and human rights.[24]

With respect to the rural areas where most of the population lives, it is important to indicate our rejection of the simplistic and fragmented theory of dualism between urban and rural sectors. The rural sector may be neglected in many areas of human rights, but it is in many respects

---

[23] *Ibid.*

[24] Osita C. Eze "Legal Structures for the Resolution of International Problems in the Domain of Private Foreign Investments: a Third World Perspective Now and in the Future". GAJ Intland Comp. L vol.9 Issue 3, 1979 p. 535. I have used the expression "technojuristic" to designate a jurist who confines himself/herself to purely legal aspects of a social phenomenon to the detriment of other basic meta-legal factors.

organically linked to the urban centres which it primarily serves. The underdevelopment and therefore denial of human rights in the rural sectors is a direct consequence of the organic but unequal and exploitative relations between them which derive from the ideology of ruling class that is mostly urban biased and based.[25]

Selective emphasis on urban growth, the almost near absence of basic infrastructure – health-care, water, education, facilities for upgrading rural skills – not only deprives the rural population of the opportunity for self-fulfillment, but inhibits migration of those who are technically competent to assist to the rural areas. In most African countries over 70 percent of the population lives in the rural areas and, except in countries which have adopted people oriented policies, they are left out of the benefits of human rights movement. Our conception of human rights points not only to the inadequacies of human rights in the urban centres for the urban poor, but by implication its penury in the rural areas.

Finally, we intend to examine the dimensions of the conception of human rights at the international level. It is worth noting, however, that as with the domestic scene, human rights are primarily a function of power politics based on economic and coercive (military) power. This explains why slave trade and colonialism which were sanctioned by international law became subsequently illegal and contrary to the principles of international law and in particular international human rights law. The altered balance of forces, particularly as a result of the emergence of the socialist system opposed to capitalism, and the independence of erstwhile colonies also led to challenges and erosion of

---

[25] I Roxborough, *Theories of Underdevelopment,* (London: The Macmillan Press Ltd., 1979) P.17; J.S. Saul and P. Woods, "African Peasantries", in *Political Economy of African Selected Readings.* D.L. Cohen and J. Daniel Ed (London: Longman Group Ltd. 1981), p. 113 *et seq.* A.L. Mabogunje. *The Development Perspective: A Spatial Perspective,* (London: Hutchinson University Library 1980) pp.78-79.

Eurocentric international law and its implications for human rights.[26] This has also led to the emergence and concretization of such core rights, as those of self-determination and development.

Experience shows that development at the international level seems to be ahead of development at the national level. Bridging this gap poses a challenge for states which feel that the standards so set might prove difficult to meet. Progressive regional conventions can, nevertheless, play a positive role, in the long run, in the promotion and protection of human rights.

In examining the place of the African Charter in the promotion and protection of human rights, we shall analyze the relevant conventions, the sources of their legal validity, as well as the institutions and machinery for their promotion and enforcement. These include those established   by the African Charter and by the Commission as they faced challenges of carrying out their mandate[27]. It will become evident from our discussion that while continental agreements establish the framework for promotion and protection, they assign some roles to the state governments, their courts and tribunals.[28] And there is evidence that some regional courts, such as those of the East African Community and the Economic Community of West African States (ECOWAS),

---

[26] O.C. Eze, "Crisis of Public International law and Regulation of Private Foreign Investment: The Quest for a New Legal Order" *Nigerian Journal of International Studies,* Vol. 5 & 6, 1981-82 G. Schwarzenberger, *Frontiers of International Law.* (London: Stevens and Sons, 1962) p.53; A. Nussbaum, *A Concise History of the Law of Nations,* New York: Macmillan, 1954, Revised Edition). P. 193; Seaton and Maliti, *Tanzania Treaty Practice.* (London: Oxford University Press 1973) A Bokor-Szego, New *States and International Law;* (Budapest, Akedemiai Kiado 1970); Abdalla, "Heterogeneity and Differentiation - The End of the Third World" Development *Dialogue* II (1978).

[27] See *infra.*

[28] See *infra.*

have competence in matters of human rights. Where do such courts fit into the scheme of the African Charter?

1.3 Scope and Objective

As is evident from our discourse on methodology, the primary concern of this work is to examine enforcement of rights whether individual or peoples as well as duties in the context of Africa's political economy. This has to be done with due regard to factors that may enhance or inhibit their actualization. Beyond this there are certain specific areas that should be of special concern to us such as:

1. Whose rights are guaranteed under the Charter and in particular the meaning of 'peoples' under the African Charter;

2. Who or what may infringe the rights guaranteed under the Charter.

3. The import of duties and how and by whom they are to be enforced;

4. The relevance of national law to and the role of national institutions and agents of law enforcement in the management of human and peoples' rights

5. The place of regional courts in the scheme of the African Charter

6. The mandate of the Commission on Human and Peoples' Rights, its promotional and enforcement functions and the national jurisdiction clause

7. The mandate of the Court on Human and Peoples Rights,[29] its promotional and enforcement functions and the national jurisdiction clause

---

[29] See Protocol to the African Charter on Human and People's Rights on the establishment of an African Court on Human and People's Rights, Annex I.

8.   The adequacy and efficacy of the procedural right of enforcement and who and what may exercise the right and on what basis; and

9.   The legal import of 'determinations' by the Commission and decisions of the Court relative to guaranteed rights and the related matters of remedies available to victims and the issue of ensuring compliance.

It is our intention, therefore, to examine the African Charter both from conceptual/theoretical and practical perspectives in order to contribute to the raising awareness, deepening of consciousness and understanding of human and peoples' rights and duties, expanding the frontiers of human rights and in particular promoting more effective protection and thereby ensuring the enthronement of responsible and responsive government ever conscious that its primary responsibility is the security and welfare of the citizens and an enlightened and ever vigilant civil society insistent that state power be exercised within the bounds of the law and in proportion to and in accordance with its delegated authority.

2

AFRICAN CONCEPT OF HUMAN RIGHTS LINKING THE PAST TO THE PRESENT

2.1 General

African societies in their process of development have evolved ideas of right and duty, right and wrong, as well as, notions of justice and fairness. These ideas and notions, as in other societies, formed the foundations of what subsequently came to be known as human rights in western jurisprudence which provided the framework for their conceptualization and doctrinal development[30].

The issue is not, therefore, whether in its relative isolation, before contact with external forces, Africa had ideas and notions akin to human rights, but that of ascertaining their nature, scope and underlying philosophy at the various stages of its history and socio-economic development. If before recorded history in most of Africa these ideas had to be deduced from the way African societies were organised and the total political culture, there is no doubt that in recent history African and non-African scholars, judicial institutions, and politicians in particular, have sought to develop African jurisprudence and provide a

---

[30] See generally, M. Gluckman, Judicial Process Among the Barotse of Northern Rhodesia, 2nd enlarged edition, Manchester University Press, 1967, T.O. Elias, *The Nature of African Customary Law* 2nd Impression, Manchester University Press 1962, L.P. Mair, *Native Politics in Africa*, London Routledge, 1936.

theoretical and conceptual framework for the understanding of African ideas of human rights.

If by African concept of human rights we postulate that there are human rights, or aspects of them, which are uniquely African, contacts with Europe and in particular colonialism have had a decisive impact on African notion(s) of human rights rooted in her history, tradition and specific condition. Colonialism meant that the African ruling elites lost their capacity to govern and make laws for their peoples. Thenceforth, the ultimate source of legal authority laid in the colonial authorities whose laws and policies determined the validity and ethical underpinnings of local laws[31].

The options opened up by the independence of the colonized territories offered opportunities for laws and human rights rooted in the liberal, socialist and religious and cultural traditions[32]. Thus African concept of human rights is not static but dynamic and has been subject to various influences both internal and external, which have influenced and continue to a certain degree, to shape its essence and content. In order, therefore, to fully appreciate African philosophy of human rights it is necessary to:

1. locate it in the context of its history spanning from pre-colonial precapitalist - formations to the present day;

2. examine the dynamics of its internal evolution before and, after contact with external forces, which had a decisive impact on it, bearing in mind the pervasive influence of African and imported religions with their tendency towards

---

[31] P.F. Gonidec *Les Droits Africans: Evolution et Source,* Paris R. Pichon and R. Durand-Auzias, 1968 p.7; Osita C. Eze *Human Rights in Africa: Some select-ed Problems, Lagos* N.I.I.A. in Cooperation with Macmillan Nigeria Publishers Ltd. 1984 Chapter 1.

[32] *Ibid,* pp. 24-27.

        fostering mythical and naturalist conceptions of human rights.

3.   Take due account of the process of universalisation of the principles, and to a lesser extent, the contents of human rights, since Africa as part of an increasingly integrated and shrinking world system influences and is in turn influenced by world currents;

4.   determine whether in view of the overwhelming impact of external variables on Africa's socio-economic and political formations and the resultant acculturation, whether we can seriously maintain that there is much left of the 'traditional' African concept of human rights, and

5.   finally, ascertain, given the heterogeneity of African societies whether there existed and still exist a sufficient degree of homogeneity, to justify the assertion of the existence of a Pan African notion of human rights particularly if account is taken of their different patterns of evolution into modern states, levels of development, socio-economic and political organisations and the underlying divergent ideological orientations; which had greater impact before the crisis of socialism and the dominance of the market in which the World Trade Organisation, WTO plays a dominant role and whether the compromise that underscored the African Charter has resolved the issue of heterogeneity[33].

2.2 Meaning, Scope, Problematics

Irrespective of where and when human rights are discussed there is hardly any agreement as to their meaning or scope. What is clear is that

---

[33] See *infra*.

human rights, as legal rights, are those guaranteed by positive law within a given legal system creating enforceable rights and obligations within the law. But there also exist moral or social rights which when not guaranteed by law are not strictly legal rights. Refusal to accept this distinction has led to confusion between the so called fundamental human rights which *in her* in individual *qua human* beings and are often regarded as rights even when not guaranteed by law. This approach often leads to a distinction between human rights such as the right to life and social rights such as the right to education. Yet it is evident that no matter how fundamental a right may be unless it is guaranteed under a given legal system as a positive right it has no juridical leg to stand upon. This is why I defined human rights as representing "demands or claims which individuals or groups make on society, some of which are protected by law and have become part of *lex lata* while others remain aspirations to be attained in the future". In either case it is the moral, social and economic values, incorporated into the law in response to these demands or claims that give or will give law its essence[34].

Increasingly, literature on human rights has tended to distinguish between individual rights on the one hand and group rights on the other hand. There are also emergent state rights such as the right to development which may be interwoven with the individual's right to development. The assertion that group rights dominate in African societies raises the issues as to whether any right can be conceived outside the framework of society and therefore, the legal significance of 'group', peoples' or otherwise solidarity rights.

Furthermore, there is the question as to what extent the universalisation of human rights principles has impinged on the Africanness of certain human rights. For example 'all societies accept that the right to life is fundamental. But for some that right simply

---

[34] Osita C. Eze, Human Rights in Africa *op cit,* p.5, See also L. Henken, "Human Rights" in R. Benhardt (Ed), Encyclopedia of International Law.

means proscription of the taking of life otherwise than in accordance with the law or due process while for others it signifies in addition the legal guarantee of the means – food, shelter, health care etc – needed to sustain life. The question then arises as to whether universalisation refers primarily to the principles as opposed to the contents or both or even whether in some cases there can be some universal minimum content? There is also the problem of identifying those rights which are rooted in certain forms of socio-economic organisation which are to be found in all societies at similar stages of development. For instance, the right to participate in government is determined by the nature of the social system whether it is slave owning, feudal or capitalist without geographical boundaries[35]. The question may also be posed as to whether all rights and are inalienable?

Finally, given that until recently African history was, apart from societies of Islamic tradition which had longer periods of recorded history, by way of oral tradition, the problem of sources of the history of African societies, including that of its institutions is posed. Furthermore, and deriving from what has been said above, there arises the issue of periodisation of African history during the pre-colonial period. These factors should caution us against romanticism in dealing with matters of human rights in Africa prior to colonial imposition for otherwise there may arise a problem of interpreting the foundations of human rights in 'traditional' precapitalist Africa on which accurate assessment of subsequent developments depend.

It is for these reasons that we have drawn the attention of human rights scholars to the fact that:

"Legal research in the field of human rights protection in pre-colonial Africa would, therefore, have to (i) depend on scanty material available in the legal field, (ii) deduce from non-legal

---

[35] See section 2 of this Chapter.

materials that depict the level of socio-economic formation and consequently the level of the evolution and development of Africa's legal systems and (iii) derive the degree and actual contents of human rights in Africa by looking at and analysing colonial legislations and practices that either confirmed or abrogated practices that existed before and during colonial domination of Africa. Legal research is further compounded because apart from African societies which had come under Islamic influence where the laws had assumed a written form, African customary law was mostly handed down by oral tradition"[36].

Consequently, it is our considered position that, given the problems already enunciated, the methodology and conceptual framework chosen may aid or impede our examination of the African concept of human rights. In order however to better appreciate the dynamics of the evolution of Africa's idea(s) of rights, it is necessary to locate them in their appropriate historical epochs.

2.3 Periodisation of African History and Evolution of Concepts of Human Rights

2.3.1 *General*

Without any pretensions as to the final division of African history into periods of identifiable stages of development, we intend to adopt a classification which represents stages of her socio-economic development:

1.   Communal mode or primitive communalism
2.   Slave owning
3.   Feudal and
4.   Independence and afterwards

---

[36] Osita C. Eze *Human Rights in Africa,* op. cit p.9.

This classification is not rigid in the sense that the various stages must take into account the specificities of Africa and the variations occasioned thereby in some cases. And we must bear in mind that when capitalist oriented structures dominated from the time of colonial rule through the post independence period there were some African states that opted, even though with limited successes, for socialist oriented development. Nor should we forget the emergence of Islamic states in some parts of the continent[37].

The reason why this approach is adopted is rooted in the political economy approach which by examining how economic foundations of a society are organised informs us not only of the social relations within that society but also of its customs, culture, politics, the structure and nature of the state as well as its legal system. This approach minimises the confusion which results from simply dividing African history into the 'traditional' and modern[38], for as will become evident African concept of human rights includes those rights which had their roots in pre-capitalist formations (including both customary and Islamic ones) that have been further developed as well as those that developed with the imposition of liberal democracies and those that became incorporated into African law and practices as a result of world movements in the field of Human Rights particularly since the founding of the United Nations.

2.3.2 *African Traditional Society*

The term "African traditional society" generally refers to pre-capitalist Africa (pre-colonial) comprising the primitive communal stage, the slave mode and feudal modes elements of which have survived to the present day. Apart from the primitive communal stages which were common to all human societies, the other modes vary in

---

[37] Libya combines both Islamic and 'socialist' traditions.

[38] See *infra.*

relation to Africa. But if African tradition is conceptualised in a dynamic sense to mean the manner, particularly the uniquely African way, in which African societies are organised and conduct their daily affairs then it would embrace modern African "tradition". This in our view is the main meaning which makes sense in the light of our present work.

Early Western sociological thought[39] would have us believe that traditional societies are those that possess little or no capitalist value - that is to say that they lack equality, individualism, personal freedom, rational, scientific and pragmatic orientations rather they

> "act according to sacral - religious orientations, they tend to do things not simply because it is useful but because tradition sanctions it, their life chances are determined by circumstances of birth, so are their relations".[40]

Ultimately what matters is the primary group rather than the individual. [41] We shall examine the reasons for persistence of 'primary groups' and group or peoples' rights in the African context and why this is so.

For our purposes it is sufficient to state that the so called elements of traditional society are not fully lacking in capitalist societies. These 'irrationalities' co-exist with the 'rationality' of the capitalist society. The main differentiating factors between the traditional society and the capitalist one are the mode of production, the level of development of the productive forces and the nature of social relations that exist at each stage of socio-economic development that ultimately determine its politics, belief system, laws, and the nature of its institutions. It is to these that we shall turn.

---

[39] Claude Ake, *Social Science as Imperialism: The theory of Political Development,* (Ibadan University Press, 1979) p.115.

[40] *Ibid.*

[41] *Ibid.*

2.3.3 *Communal Mode*

All human societies, including those in Africa, have gone through a stage, when because of the very low level of the development of productive forces, collective ownership of the means of production, collective labour and equal distribution of the fruits of labour were necessary for subsistence. There was no possibility of private accumulation and, therefore no classes and consequently neither the need for a state nor law existed[42] - law making being one of the fundamental functions of states the other functions being those of the judiciary and the executive.

Whatever rules of conduct that existed could at best be described as non-legal, even if 'binding' usages and rules of custom. The adage that *'ubi societas ubi ius'* - where there is a human society there is law - could not have applied to this stage of development for society here could only properly refer to states at various stages of development that could more appropriately refer to classical slave societies as existed in Europe and Asia as well as feudal societies. In our view law properly so called existed with the emergence of private property and the state. In Africa, states began to emerge before 1500 B.C. with transition in most cases from the communal mode to feudalism which many never reached.[43]

---

[42] "The Origin of the Family Private, Property and the State" in Marx Engels, Selected Works (Moscow Progress Publishers, 1982) pp. 461 – 556; P. Wilmot, *Sociology: A New Introduction* (London: Collins International Text Books, 1985) Chapter 4: Osita C. Eze "Theoretical Perspectives and Problematics" in *Society And The Rule of Law,* Osita C. Eze., (Owerri Totan Publishers Ltd. 1987) Chapter 1.

[43] W. Rodney, *How Europe Underdeveloped Africa,* (Tanzania publishing House, 1972), p.46.

2.3.4. Slave Mode and Transition to Feudalism

Even though there existed pockets of slave owning societies particularly in North African Countries and other Moslem societies in pre-colonial Africa, most of Africa did not pass through classical slave mode of production as was the case in Europe and Asia.[44] What is clear, however, is that the emergence of slave owning societies signaled both the emergence of private property and social inequality and to the extent that human rights existed, they must have been indeed very limited as they could only have been relevant to the free men. It may, however, be stated that ownership of human beings which emerged towards the last stage of communalism and co-existed with it, was not as dehumanising or exploitative as Euro-Asian slavery for in Africa slaves rapidly became free men and enjoyed whatever rights that attached to free men.[45]

It has been ably argued that pre-1500 Africa was in a transitional stage between the practice of Agriculture (plus fishing and herding) in family communities and the practice of some activities within the state and societies comparable to feudalism, a stage which, except for countries like Ethiopia most did not reach. In many cases feudal relations did not take the classical form but was based on allegiance, and taxes and labour extracted from the ordinary people. Nevertheless, the transition to feudalism led to social stratification, particularly in the hierarchical societies and the emergence of antagonistic classes even when elements of communalism persisted as they in fact do to the present day. In the so called atomized and republican societies, such as the Igbo of Eastern Nigeria, the family and clan heads, who had the right

---

[44] *Ibid p.45.*

[45] *Ibid.*

to the labour of the family or the clans extracted surpluses, built up wealth and became a class of its own.[46]

There began to emerge the concept that certain families were entitled to rule and even if there were checks on the powers of the rulers particularly in the hierarchical societies of the Hausa-Fulani and Yoruba type of Northern and Western Nigeria respectively, they were provided by the same ruling class which did not say much for the human rights of the ordinary people. Typically the power to make laws, interpret and enforce them were centralized in the ruler whether he is an Emir or a Chief.

Writing about the annexation of *Bechuanaland* located in South Africa, in the 18th century *Schapera* maintained that:

"The territory thus annexed was then divided into districts, each being placed under the control of an "overseer" (*modisa*) who was either a senior noble or one of the chief's trusted retainers (*batlhanka*). The inhabitants of each district became the serfs (*malata*) of the local overseer. He made them herd his cattle and cultivate his fields, and usually also brought some of them into the capital to do the menial job in his home. In addition, he could appropriate whatever property they acquired. This referred especially to such hunting spoils as ivory, ostrich feathers, and the skins of wild animals, all of which he claimed for himself, leaving them only meat… Serfs remained permanently attached to the family of their master and after his death were inherited by his children. They were apparently seldom, if ever, bought or sold, though their master could give or lend them to other men, and they often formed part of a daughter's dowry, but they themselves were never free to seek work with anybody else or to move away from their district. If oppressed, as they often were,

---

[46] Afigbo, Ropes of Sand: Studies in Igbo History and Culture, Ibadan and London: University Press and Oxford University Press, 1981 (1984).

they had no access to the tribal courts and should they run away they might be followed up and brought back by force. They lacked many other civic rights, including participation in political assemblies, and were not admitted into membership of age regiments, nor were they allowed to possess livestock of their own."

This graphic picture painted by *Schapera* of a feudal type society contrasts vividly with the human rights performance in traditional Africa as romanticized by *M'baye.*[47]

M'baye's[48] argument that pre-colonial Africa knew of human rights adapted to the political and social situations existing in that epoch cannot be faulted except that, as already indicated, human rights properly so called could not have existed at the period of primitive communalism. According to him these rights were recognised and protected, but must be looked at in the context of societies that were atomized and hierarchical by the caste system and at the same time unified by mythological beliefs. The object of law was to maintain society in the state in which it was handed down by the ancestors. The European concept of human rights, that is to say, the amalgam of principles essentially favouring individuals against groups to whom they are opposed was not found in traditional African societies. The African was absorbed in the group. African society was humanist and socialist. It could not have failed to pay attention to the human being and all that appertains to him, particularly his rights. This type of humanism led as a

---

[47] Schapera, Government In Politics In Tribal Societies, (London: C.A. Watts and Co. Ltd.) 1963, p.218 cite in Prince E.K. Quashigah, Human Rights In Traditional and Modern Africa: An Analytical And Comparative Study, Ph.D. Thesis in Law for the Faculty of Law University of Nigeria, 1989, pp.102-103.

[48] See *infra.*

consequence, to a scrupulous mutual respect and recognition of the rights and liberties for each individual and for the group.[49]

M'baye then proceeds to list the human rights that existed and were protected in Africa. These were the right to life, freedom of expression, freedom of religion, freedom of association, freedom of movement, the right to work and the right to education. The right to life could be said to have existed during the period since African mythology and culture regarded life as sacrosanct and the African societies were prepared to impose and enforce sanctions for unlawful taking away of life which they considered a very serious offence punishable by death, banishment or other forms of penalties depending on the gravity of the offence. But this did not prevent human sacrifice, the burying of the dead with human beings, including wives with their husbands in certain cultures as well as the killing of twins. Nor at this stage was there a legal obligation on society to provide the means of sustenance to the indigent except to some extent in societies that shared the Islamic tradition. Freedom of expression to the extent that it existed could not have authorised challenges to the nascent feudal societies even though it was by and large practised in the non-hierarchical societies through the council of elders and the age grades. Nor could the freedom of association relate to participation in government either directly or indirectly at least in the mature hierarchical societies of the feudal type where a few families had assumed the hereditary and divine right to rule.

While *Schapera's* rendering of feudal type of African society depicted exclusion and non-participation of serfs in the political process the possibility was there that in less 'developed' similar societies there might be limited participation as *Green* pointed out;

---

[49] "Organisation de L'Unité Africaine" in : *Les Dimensions Internationales des Drots de l'Homme* (Paris UNESCO, 1978) pp. 650-652.

According to him:

"Many pre-colonial African politics were participatory to a substantial extent. In some at least particular interest groups or subclasses were self-organised and had spokesmen within the political process. (That others were excluded – e.g. slaves and women – demonstrates limits on pluralism but not its total absence, many organisations e.g. age groups (often parallel but separate ones for females and or males), religious bodies, economic groupings existed, had powers and functions of their own and were to some degree accountable. The hereditary principle was in practice by no means totally inconsistent with participation and accountability. The selection in most cases had a range of candidates who could be picked without being seen to violate the hereditary principle, further recall – fairly draconian form of accountability – was frequently institutionalised, e.g. 'destooling and for political leadership the hereditary principle was far from universal - e.g. it did not appear to have applied to age groups"[50]

Green's position, which we do not oppose, simply indicates that even within the framework of a particular mode of production variations may exist.

As to the right to work, it would seem more like forced labour as the extraction of taxes and dues from the subjects compelled them to work. In the not so hierarchical societies, however, collective work on self-help basis, a remnant of the communal mode, for the benefit of the participants, and not for appropriation by the rulers, represented an instance of the right to work.

Lest we are misunderstood, the argument is not that human rights were not recognized or protected in pre-colonial Africa. Our position is

---

[50] R.H. Green "Participatory Pluralism and Pervasive Poverty: Some Reflections "*Third World Legal Studies,* 1989, p.23.

that the categories of rights protected as well as their scope and ultimately who enjoys any of these rights are in the end determined by the nature and character of the society that is being examined. It is evident that human rights protection evolved stage by stage as societies developed and consequently it differed depending on whether we are concerned with, the slave mode, feudal mode, or nascent capitalism that followed in the wake of colonial rule. And at any given time variations existed raising the issue as to the real scope of African conception of human rights.

2.3.5. Colonial Period

We have tried to demonstrate that one should take with caution the nostalgia about human rights protection and the democratic character of our 'traditional' institutions, in the same vein we cannot assume that participation was assured and excesses of the governors checked while ignoring the structural limitations imposed by the nature of the socio-economic and political systems and the very limited and negligible role played by the majority, whether directly or indirectly, in governance. Of significant importance is their inability to satisfy their material and spiritual needs (human rights) in the context of scarcity and inequality.

By the time of colonization of Africa, the societies that now form Africa countries, which were at various stages of evolution, had gone through a gradual but 'violent' process of unequal trade and slave trade and finally conquest, all of which led to the incorporation of African countries into the world capitalist system as junior 'partners', introducing yet another dimension to the evolution of human rights concept and protection.

The imperatives of colonialism whether by direct or indirect rule were predominantly economic. The Europeans were no longer interested in dealing with the middlemen (rulers). It became necessary because of the demands and consequences of the industrial revolution and nascent capitalism to take direct control. From then on the capacity of the rulers to make laws for their own people passed into the hands of the colonialist who not only began to establish rudimentary dependent capitalist structures but also imposed for their legitimating a corresponding legal superstructure that increasingly emphasized private property and representative government even when the local elite were belatedly incorporated into the machinery of government. The foundation was already laid for the contradictory pre-eminence given to private property side by side with civil and political rights, even when the basic material and political inequality between the colonialists and locals ensured that there was discrimination in the manner in which the laws were applied.[51]

Thenceforth, the pervasive and dominant influence of Judaeo-Christian jurisprudence gained ground. Even when native law and custom as well as Islamic law could generally be enforced, it could not be observed or enforced if it was repugnant to natural justice, equity and good conscience, or incompatible, either in form or by necessary implication with any Ordinance or any rule, regulation, order, proclamation or bye-law made under any Ordinance for the time being in force, in the Territory. But the standards of natural justice, equity and good conscience and the laws, orders etc. by which they were to be judged were of colonial origin. It was under this provision that the *Osu* system, the killing of twins, and human sacrifice were abolished.[52]

Despite these apparent gains and the nostalgia expressed in some quarters that even the colonial constitutions contained provisions on human rights, (civil and political rights) it was clear that alien rule was a negation of fundamental human right of self-determination. It encouraged ethnic and class differentiation, and even if it could be construed as a higher level of development than the feudal-slave systems which it co-existed, and progressively displaced, it was essentially

---

[51] J.S Read" Bills of Rights in "The Third World", Some Commonwealth Experiences" in *Verfassung and Recht in Ubersse*, I. Heft, I. Quartal 1973.

[52] Elias, Nature of African Customary Law op.cit.

inegalitarian and anti-ethical to human rights. The colonial economy was primarily intended to serve colonial interest. No serious foundations were laid for national development. The basis was already laid for dependent underdevelopment of the post-colonial era, a condition inherited and sustained by and large by most of the post-colonial ruling classes.

Having set the stage, it remains to examine what progress, if any, has been made in human rights promotion and protection since independence and the prospect for further development of human rights in Africa.

2.3.6 Post Colonial Period

Bill of Rights in African Constitutions

African tradition could not have ended with the pre-colonial period. It persists to the present day and incorporates all the developments since then including the impact of external variables, discussed above which have been incorporated into it. Thus when we talk of African jurisprudence we do not only mean the jurisprudence of Africa en route to feudalism or resulting from increasing class differentiation but also the jurisprudence as it evolved under the early implantation of Christianity and Islam, colonialism and the post-independence era. In effect we mean the dominant role which Judaeo-Christian jurisprudence came to play and the penetrative role of religion - Christianity and Islam which became established in some parts of Africa from the earliest times long before the first contact with Europe. The same argument applies with equal force to the various modes of government, whether pre-capitalist or non-capitalist as well as to the modes of production and forms of social relations.

An examination of African constitutions, particularly those that embodied bills of right will reveal to what extent the essentially African traditional conception of human rights were subverted only to be retrieved to a large extent by the African Charter.[53] Even when many of these constitutionally guaranteed rights share the same underlying principles, as those that existed in Africa, their contents were markedly different. All share in varying degrees the principle of 'participation' in government yet contrary to the practice in traditional African political institutions which did not allow for opposition the right to participate as envisaged in most constitutions allowed for multi-party systems and, therefore, opposition. Discrimination or institutional practices which excluded certain categories of persons such as slaves, women and strangers to the community from participating in the political process would have been faulted on the principle of universal adult suffrage. There are also other examples.[54]

Suffice it to state that most of the countries of 'liberal' persuasion adopted bills of rights modeled on the Universal Declaration of the Human Rights which placed emphasis on civil and political rights even when the implementation of the socio-economic and cultural rights included therein were 'optional'[25a]. Constitutions of most of the Francophone countries referred in their preambles to the French Declaration of the Rights of Men and Citizens while yet countries of socialist persuasion adopted constitutions similar in many aspects to the socialist constitutions of the Eastern Europe with emphasis on socio-economic and cultural rights. These bills of rights became dominant and by and large determined the limits of legitimate human rights.[55]

Even up to date these bills of rights are still in force in most of these countries even when many of them have not only signed but ratified the African Charter which is now in force and binding on the parties thereto. Admittedly, the civil and political rights contained in these constitutions

---

[53] See Osita C. Eze, *Human Rights in Africa...* op.cit. pp.20-21.

[54] See *infra.*

[25a] See *infra.*

[55] See Schapera and Green *op.cit.*

have found their way in the African Charter which also includes socio-economic and cultural rights. New African constitutions such as those of Ghana, Uganda and South Africa include justifiable ECOSOC rights.[56] Are these rights not, therefore, part of the African Concept of Human Rights?

2.3.7 Conclusion

It is evident that the periodization of African history, based on some recognizable indices such as the various stages of her socio-economic development, is necessary if we are to avoid treating pre-capitalist Africa as a continuum without identifiable landmarks. Africa has a history and its peoples made it in the process of trying to subdue the environment through various techniques and forms of social organisations. For most of Africa, even though the pre-capitalist, pre-colonial period knew only of oral tradition, sociological and anthropological studies have contributed immensely in unraveling Africa's past. Consequently, one is better informed about the modes of production, the nature of its political systems, laws and local belief system during this period. For the colonial period and, in particular, the independence era, with written and documented history, greater opportunities opened up for a more scientific analysis of African tradition in its dynamic sense.

Based on available information, we hasten to state that African concept of Human Rights, both in the historical and contemporary sense embraces those:

1. that evolved from within and from its womb without external influences - the extended family system; as well as certain notions of justice such not being a judge in ones cause and hearing the other party (even

---

[56] See Chapter 6.

> though these co-existed with conflicting practices of trial by ordeal or divination);

2.   that are similar to (i) above but have been influenced by world current- right to life and property;

3.   that were incorporated and adapted to the African environment–democratic pluralism and the right to participate in government, and

4.   that were imported without much of adaptation - the adversary methods of settlement of disputes with their underlying checks and balances.

To the extent that the laws reflect our total culture rights protected there under represent to a greater or lesser extent the African concept of human rights and the African Charter is without doubt the most authoritative rendering of the African tradition even when by its philosophy it is not expected to develop in isolation of world movements in the field of human rights.

The African Commission and Court in their task of finding a jurisprudence suitable to the African condition have an arduous task, particularly given the sources - both primary and subsidiary, and the implicit repugnancy doctrine relative to international law norms that should inform their interpretation of the African Charter. The Commission and the Court have in particular to be imaginative in interpreting the concept of "people" given that the African Charter does not include any definition of the term and the rather general provisions on rights (with equally general limitations on some of the rights) and duties. The Commission and the Court can through setting standards for local legislations, interpretation and application of the Charter give it life or stifle it. In the end the African governments and, in particular, African peoples can transform this historic document into a living one that addresses issue of basic concern to African peoples - peace, development and respect for and protection of human and peoples' rights thereby enhancing the legitimacy and wider acceptance of the African conception of human rights.

3

BACKGROUND TO THE AFRICAN CHARTER

To better appreciate the dynamics that ultimately led to the adoption of the African Charter and to a great degree shaped its contents, it will be necessary to examine, as appropriate, the precedents set by the United Nations and other regional human rights organisations in Europe and America, as well as the catalytic role played by the OAU in that process. [57] And it should not be forgotten that most African countries adopted at independence, constitutions that embodied bills of rights that were influenced to a large extent by development within the UN system.

3.1 From the Beginning

The OAU had since inception remained the focal point for human rights in Africa. Admittedly, before the adoption of the African Charter, its role in this regard was rather limited.[58] In this regard, it has either acted alone or in collaboration with other international organisations such as the UN and its agency the Economic Commission for Africa

---

[57] This section is culled mostly from Osita C. Eze, "The Organisation of African Unity and Human Rights: Twenty Five Years After" *op. cit*; p.158 et seq. It has been adapted to the needs of this book.

[58] See *Infra.*

(E.C.A.). It is, therefore, pertinent to assess their contributions in this direction.

If the Organisation of African Unity represented a concrete achievement of the Pan-African movement, some of the major advocates of Pan-Africanism, Kwame Nkrumah, George Padmore and Jomo Kenyatta, long before any black African country, except Liberia and Ethiopia, became independent had shown concern for human rights. At the Fifth Pan-African Congress held in Manchester in 1945, where the first conscious effort was made to establish a link between human rights and the fight against colonialism on the one hand and between Pan-Africanism and human rights on the other, they called *inter alia*, for the abolition of all racial discrimination, for freedom of expression, of the press and assembly and free compulsory education up to the age of sixteen.[59]

Although, these rights are among those sought to be protected in in-dependent African states, they could only have been pursued at the par-ticular epoch in order to facilitate the struggle against colonialism. These rights were typically denied to the colonized peoples.[60]

In the meantime, the adoption of the Charter of the United Nations which had as one of its primary objectives the protection of human rights gave[61] further impetus to the universal protection of human rights. The work of the United Nations in the field of human rights, essentially

---

[59] Karel Vasak "Problems Concerning the Setting Up of Regional Commissions on Human Rights, With special Reference to Africa" Background paper for the United Nations Seminar on the Establishment of Regional Commissions on human rights with Special reference to Africa, Cairo 2-15 Sept. 1969. 50216/3(17) 1969, p.11.

[60] James Read, "Bills of Righs in "The Third World' Some Commonwealth Experiences" In Varfassung und *Right in Ubersee* ed. Prof. Dr. Herbert Kruger 1 Heft 1 Quartal, 1973, p.29.

[61] See UN Charter, the preamble, Articles 1(2) SS, 68 as well as chapters XI and XII.

carried out by its Human Rights Division, a subsidiary organ of ECOSOC, lead in 1948 to the adoption of the Universal Declaration of Human Rights.[62]

It took just over one decade after the adoption of the Universal Declaration for some interest to be shown for regional protection of human rights in Africa. Indeed, the founding fathers of the O.A.U were persuaded that

> "The Charter of the United Nations and the Universal Declaration of Human Rights, to the principles of which we reaffirm our adherence, provide a solid foundation for peaceful and positive co-operation among states."

Before the adoption of the OAU Charter in 1963, the first Congress of African Jurists which took place in Lagos from 3 - 7 January 1961, when many more African colonies had regained their independence adopted a resolution on human rights that was to lay down the basis for future efforts for the establishment of rules and mechanisms for regional promotion and protection of human rights in Africa. The Congress stated that in order to give full effect to the Universal Declaration of Human Rights, a suitable tribunal should be set up to which all persons within the jurisdiction of African states should have recourse. To that end, an African Convention on Human Rights was needed since that alone would permit the realization of the dual aspirations of independent Africa, namely liberty and unity.[63] While emphasis was placed on liberty from external domination, the internal dimensions of liberty were not forgotten.

These then were the antecedents to the Charter of the Organisation of African Unity. The OAU Charter adopted in Addis Ababa in May 1963

---

[62] The declaration was adopted and proclaimed by General Assembly resolution 217 A (III) of 10th December, 1948.

[63] See the *Rule of law and Human Rights, Principles and Definitions.* (International Commission of Jurists, Geneva 1966), Appendix D.

has certain provisions which, while not directly alluding to human rights and might not have been envisaged by the drafters of the Charter as much, do in fact constitute material and social conditions for the enjoyment of other human rights such as those enumerated in the Universal Declaration of Human Rights. It must be emphasized, however, at the onset that three issues dominated the Addis Ababa Conference: African Unity, decolonization and the elimination of racism. These together constitute what has been termed the 'spirit of Addis'.[64]

The preamble to the OAU Charter is replete with references to human rights. The Heads of African State and Government assembled in Addis Ababa were convinced that it is the inalienable right of all peoples to control their own destiny and being conscious of the fact that freedom, equality, justice and dignity are essential objectives for the achievement of the legitimate aspirations of the African peoples were determined to safeguard and consolidate their hard-won independence as well as the sovereignty and territorial integrity of their states and to fight against neo-colonialism in all its forms. Foundations were already laid at the regional level for the twin rights of self-determination and development.[65] References to the desire to harness the natural and human resources of the continent for the total advancement of their peoples in all spheres of human endeavour; the determination to transcend ethnic and national differences; and dedication to common progress of African could in fact be interpreted to provide a frame of action in the domain of human rights, particularly when viewed in the context of the rights of self-determination and development.[66] We are aware that preambular provisions whether in treaties or domestic legislations are not normally

---

[64] Z. Cervenka. *The Organization of African Unity and Its Charter*, (London C Hurst & Co 1968) p.13.

[65] See *infra*.

[66] Charter of the Organisation of African Unity, (Addis Ababa: May 1963), preamble. See *also infra*.

regarded as legally binding, especially since their wordings lack enough specificity to allow for juridical interpretation. The preamble does, however, set a general tone for the dispositive provisions that might subsequently be embodied in the relevant instrument. This line of reasoning is in fact reinforced because it was on the basis of the intentions of the Heads of African State and Government as set out in the preamble they "agreed to the present Charter."

What has been said of the juridical nature of the preamble applies with equal force to references to the United Nations Charter and the Universal Declaration of Human Rights. In other words, members of the OAU have not, by adopting the preambular provisions, imposed upon themselves any obligation. With reference to the UN Charter, their obligations arise because they are parties to that convention. With respect to the Universal Declaration of Human Rights, the Declaration by itself, is not a legally binding instrument, even though it has in fact paved the way for generalization of certain normative rules on human rights and to the adoption of certain international conventions, particularly the two UN Covenants of 1966.[67]

Certain provisions of the 'purposes' are also consecrated to human rights. Like the preamble the 'purposes' are not normally regarded as imposing any legal obligations on parties to a treaty. The language tends, however, to be more specific. The 'purposes' of the OAU Charter not only set the goals of the member states of the OAU, but also stipulate, albeit in a rather general fashion, how they should be achieved.

The relevant provisions include the co-ordination and intensification of the co-operation and efforts of members of the OAU in order to achieve a better life for the peoples of Africa; the defence of their independence; the eradication of all forms of colonialism from Africa and the promotion of international co-operation, having regard to the

---

[67] These are the interventional Covenants on Civil and Political Rights and Economic, Social and Cultural Rights.

Charter of the United Nations and Universal Declaration of Human Rights[68]. It is odd that no reference was made to the eradication of neo-colonialism, bearing in mind that the preamble already envisaged a determination to fights against *inter alia* neo-colonialism. It is arguable that opposition to neo-colonialism could be subsumed under the defence of independence of African States since, in strict terminology, neocolonialism, being a change in the pattern of foreign domination that undermines the right to self-determination, conflicts with the notion of veritable as opposed to flag-independence.

In order to achieve the goals which the members of the OAU had set for themselves, they undertook to co-ordinate and harmonize their general policies especially in the following fields.

1. Political and diplomatic co-operation;
2. Economic co-operation, including transport and communications
3. Educational and cultural co-operation
4. Scientific and technical co-operation; and
5. Co-operation for defence and security.[69]

---

[68] Charter of the Organisation of African Unity, Article 11(2).

[69] See Z. Cervenka. *The Organisation of African Unity* p.68 et seq, See also B. Ndiaye. "La place des Droits de l'home dans la Chatre de L'Organization de L'Unite fricane, 'danlla Charter de L'Organization de l Unite Africaine), *in less dimentions internationals des droits de l'homme,* ed, by Kerel Va sak (Paris: UNESCO, 1978) pp. 671-672; See also Elias, background paper for the UN Seminar on the Establishment of Regional Commission on Human rights with Special Reference to Africa, (Monrovia, Liberia), 10-12 September 1979), p.8 who pointed out that one of the principal objectives of the commission was to study African Political institutions and legal ideas with particular reference to the promotion of the rule of law and the observance and protection of fundamental human rights throughout the continent.

While political and diplomatic co-operation as well as co-operation for defence and security could aid in the defence of the independence of member states as well as in the fight against neo-colonialism, cooperation in the fields of education, culture, health, sanitation and nutrition has a direct bearing, by providing the material, social and cultural basis, if not immediately on the protection of human rights, at least on their promotion.

In fact, in order to give teeth to these objectives, Article XX of O.A.U, requires the Assembly of Heads of State and Government to establish the following specialized commissions: (1) Economic and Social Commission: (2) Education and Cultural Commission (3) Health, Sanitation and Nutrition Commission: (4) Defence Commission; and (5) Scientific, Technical and Research Commission.

Even though the commissions adopted various impressive programmes of action, very many of which did not materialize, they, nevertheless, provided useful framework for making concrete contributions to the promotion of certain socio-economic rights in Africa.

In addition to the above named commissions, a sixth specialized commission, the Commission of Jurists, was established and consequent upon the approval of the recommendation of the OAU Council of Ministers, it became a specialized Commission.[70]

Preparatory work for the creation of the commission started off with a Conference of African Jurists which took place in Lagos August 1963 and with an inaugural Conference of the commission also held in 1964.

It is surprising that the Charter of the Commission for Jurists did not make specific references, safe in relation to the development of the concept of justice, in its Article 1 of 'purposes', to human rights. It was, in

---

[70] Z. Cervenka. *The Organization of African Unity, op cit.*

any event, dissolved in 1966, since it could not, like many other commissions, function for lack of quorum.[71]

Admittedly, some institutions were created to deal with some of the goals which members had set for themselves under Article 11 of the OAU Charter. Given also our liberal interpretation of the provisions of the Charter relative to human rights promotion and protection, a close look at how these goals were to be achieved would reveal their somewhat restrictive nature. The article, in fact, enumerates all the activities of a modern state, except those that concern the fundamental functions of a state that is those that concern matters of constitution, administration of justice and police. And these are matters that deal directly with human rights promotion and protection. In effect, African States, at the time of the adoption of the Charter, were not prepared to allow other than domestic organs to deal with matters that touched on the protection of human rights.[72]

Indeed, Article III(2) which, as we shall demonstrate later, imposed legal obligations on the parties, proscribed interference in the internal affairs of states. A similar provision in the UN Charter had given rise to a lot of controversy. Article 2. para. 7 of the UN Charter states

> "Nothing contained in the present Charter shall authorize the United Nations to intervene in matters which are essentially within the domestic jurisdiction of state."

While the possible interpretations of a corresponding provision of the UN Charter may serve to indicate the possible attitude of states with respect to the internationalization of matters that may generally be con-

---

[71] See Osita C. Eze, "OAU Faces Rhodesia": The African Review, Vol. 5 No. 1 1975, pp.51-54 M.H. Fargal African Unity and Liberation (M.A. Thesis, University of Dar-es Salaam, 1968). Chapter 6: A Gupta, "The Rhodesia Crisis and the Organisation of African unity", International Studies, (New Delhi), vol. 9.1 (July 1967), p.458.

[72] See *infra*.

sidered to be within the sphere of their domestic jurisdiction, they are of limited utility in so far as the provisions of the OAU Charter is concerned. This is because there are two material differences in the wordings of the two provisions. Firstly, the UN Charter forbids 'interventions', a formulation that is much narrower than the expression 'interference' used in the OAU Charter. Secondly, while the UN Charter reserves to the states matters essentially, within their domestic jurisdiction, the OAU Charter, without any qualification, reserves to states matters within the ambit of their internal affairs. Thus, on two scores, the OAU Charter covers a much wider scope than the UN Charter. It is unlikely that the choice of words in the OAU Charter was a matter of accident since its drafters were familiars with the corresponding provisions of the UN Charter and the controversies surrounding its interpretation. It would seem, therefore, that the drafting was a reflection of the basic concerns of the founding fathers of the OAU that no outside body should deal with matters within their domestic jurisdiction. Human right questions would appear to fall within this. This explains, in part, why most African governments stood aloof when fundamental human rights were breached with impunity under the regimes of Idi Amin of Uganda and Bokassa of Central African Republic. Since most African governments were in *pari delicto* with respect to breaches of human rights, it was not surprising that the domestic jurisdiction clause was so broadly phrased. This being the case, human rights promotion and protection were limited to inter-state co-operation. This position has changed somewhat as the interventions in Liberia, Sierra Leone and elsewhere has shown. The Adoption of the African Charter on Human and Peoples Rights, the Constitutive Instrument of the African Union as well as the Human Rights Conventions continue to nibble at the domestic jurisdiction clause.

Article III of the principles consecrates certain provisions of human rights, such as respect for the inalienable right to independent existence, peaceful settlement of disputes, and decolonization of the rest of Africa still under colonial rule. These provisions create concrete legal obligations for the states as underlined by Article VI of the Charter which provides that "Member States pledge themselves to observe scrupulously the principles enumerated in Article III..." It is surprising that no mention was made of apartheid and racism. With respect to liberation of African territories, the obligation undertaken by states found concrete expression in the creation of the OAU Liberation Committee and support for liberation movements that have led to the independence of African States.

One of the earliest achievements of the OAU was the adoption of the Convention concerning the Specific Aspects of Refugee Problems in Africa (1969). The Convention adds to the 1951 UN Convention on Refugees as amended by the Protocol of 1967, which is regarded as the "basic and universal instrument relating to the status of refugees..." It broadens the definition of refugees to include

> "every person who owing to, external aggression, occupation, foreign domination or events seriously disturbing public order in either part or the whole of his country of origin or nationality, is compelled to leave his country of habitual residence as a result of such events in order to seek refuge in another place outside his country of origin or nationality"[Article 1(2)].

Many of the conditions described can be understood in the context of colonialism even though many may now be present in independent African States. The main spirit behind the convention, which to a large extent is reflected in the African Charter on Human and Peoples Rights is captured in the preamble provision in which the states parties were "convinced that all the problems of our continent must be solved in the

Spirit of the Charter of the Organisation of African Unity and in the African context". Yet the convention recognizes the 'basic' and universal character of the UN refugee convention which reflects the deep concern of states for refugees and their desire to establish common standards for their treatment" [preamble, paragraphs 8 and 9].[73]

The Economic Commission for Africa, a subsidiary organ of the Economic and Social Council established in April 29, 1958, is primarily concerned as a body with assisting African countries in their quest for social and economic development. In resolution 671 (XXV) establishing the Commission it is provided that "The Economic Commission for Africa, acting within the policies of the United Nations and subject to the general supervision of the Economic and Social Council, shall, provided that the Commission takes no action with respect to any country without the agreement of the government of that country, "(a) initiate and participate in measures for facilitating concerted action for the economic development of Africa, including its social aspects, with a view to raising the level of economic activity and levels of living in Africa, and for maintaining and strengthening the economic relations of countries and territories of Africa both among themselves and with other countries of the world." The activities of the ECA embrace such fields as training of personnel, trade, monetary and fiscal affairs, transport and communications, natural resources and development planning in general.

The ECA has played an active role in the promotion of the rights of African women and has collaborated with the OAU in the formulation and implementation of the Lagos Plan of Action, adopted in 1980, a manifesto for the transformation and liberation of African Economies.[74]

---

[73] See *infra.*

[74] K.Y. Amoako Perspectives on African Development, United Nations Economic Commission for Africa, UN, New York, 2000, pp. 62 et seq.

By 1971 in response to the demands of African women for gender equality. The ECA launched its first formal programme for women in development.

More specifically it is observed that there remain serious problems in the area of human rights for women. Such problems are to be found in serious discrepancies between national legislation and the provisions of international instruments on human rights, including major discrepancies between statutory law customary and religious laws.[75] The pressing need for law reform has been aptly put thus.

While it may be maintained that the Commission is not conceived as an institution for the protection of human rights, its activities in the various fields, if properly conceived and given acceptance by the various African governments, could be promotional. Since ultimately policies or programmes drawn up by the Commission can only be translated into action to the extent that they correspond to national policies and objectives, the states themselves remain the ultimate determinant of the extent to which they can contribute in this direction.

Attempts to directly involve the ECA in human rights protection seem to have been rejected by most African states. A draft resolution introduced by Nigeria, which was co-sponsored by several other states requesting the Economic and Social Council to invite the regional economic commissions to study ways and means by which they would contribute to the promotion and protection of human rights and even envisaging the inclusion of this activity in its terms of reference, was withdrawn in the face of opposition by several states. While the principle of regional human rights arrangements was accepted by the General Assembly, reference to regional commissions was avoided.[76]

---

[75] *Ibid.*

[76] E/CN.4/L.907 Rev.I;4322 pp. 84-88J. Blaustein Regional Promotion and Protection of Human Rights' Commission to study Organisation of Peace (40th Anniversary Year, Appendices, 1979). pp 38 et seq.

The Nigerian draft and initiative notwithstanding, the 1976 ECOSOC resolution confirmed the original terms of reference of the regional commissions as agents for social and economic development which called for "all the organisations and agencies in the system to work closely with the regional commissions to achieve the overall economic and social development objectives at the regional level. [77]

It is not surprising that states are reluctant to enlarge the competence of the ECA, a subsidiary organ of the UN, to cover human rights protection at the regional level. African states, as we shall demonstrate later, prefer an organisation that is endogenous to the continent over which they have control.

It would seem, however, that the changing environment in Africa has led to the realization that the ECA could play a greater and more effective role in the promotion of human rights. The draft Report of the 1979 Monrovia seminar felt that a useful role could be played by the Economic Commission for Africa in the promotion of human rights, particularly in connection with economic, social and cultural rights. It was, therefore, recommended that the Economic Commission for Africa should adopt measures, programmes and policies to promote the realization of human rights. The Economic Commission for Africa, it was stated, could be particularly useful in the dissemination of information about human rights faculty within its secretariat.

It was evident that what was envisaged was not a regional commission for the protection of human rights which the seminar considered to be the proper function of the OAU

Our discussions so far show that apart from colonialism and racism which fall outside the ambit of their national jurisdiction African countries, were only prepared to accept some limited regional obligation with respect to refugees. We have already alluded to the call by African jurists assembled in Lagos in 1961 for the creation of an international

---

[77] ECOSOC Res. 2043 (LXI), 5 August, 1976.

machinery for the protection of human rights. Similar calls were made at several of the seminars on human rights organised by the United Nations Organisation. [78]

The Dakar Colloquium, a private venture between the International Commission of Jurists and the Senegalese Bar Association, emphasizing that economic and social development was a human right, recommended the establishment of a human rights commission as one of the means of tackling the fundamental and urgent problems of human rights in Africa.

Despite these developments, it was not until 1979 that the Conference of OAU Heads of State and Government held in Monrovia passed a resolution calling upon the Secretary General of the OAU to "organize as soon as possible in an African Capital, a restricted meeting of highly qualified experts to prepare preliminary draft of an African Charter on human rights".

Before the OAU had settled down to working out ways and means of establishing a regional commission or drafting a convention on human rights the UN Seminar on the Establishment of Regional Commission on Human Rights with special reference to Africa held in Monrovia from 10 - 12 September, 1979 had come out with a proposal for the establishment of a commission which shall have the functions of promoting and protecting human rights. [79]

It is note worthy that, after several years of hesitation, indecision and indeed opposition, the African governments have accepted the impera-

---

[78] Hr/Liberia/1979/D Rep. 2 Chapter 1 para 20 See also ST/SAD/HR/38, paras 40-55. For other conferences which   urged protection of other spectrum of human rights and the establishment of a regional organ see E. G. Bello, "The African Charter on Human and People's Rights; A legal Analysis" Extract from *Recueil de cours*, vol. 194 (1985), p. 21 etc.

[79] For the text of the UN Monrovia Proposals for the setting up of an African Commission on Human Rights. See Osita C. Eze, Human Rights in Africa, *op cit*, Appendix Two.

tive of establishing a regional organ for the promotion and protection of human rights.

The Heads of State and Government in Monrovia were motivated by their faith in fundamental human rights, in the dignity and worth of the human person and in the equal rights of men and women and of nations, large and small, and the need to establish conditions under which justice and respect for the obligations arising from treaties and other sources of international law can be maintained and to promote social progress and better standards of life in large freedom. They reaffirmed their commitment to the Charter of the OAU in which they accepted that the Charter of the United Nations and the Universal Declaration of Human Rights provide a solid foundation for peace and positive co-operation among states and reiterated their pledge in the OAU Charter to promote international co-operation with due consideration of the Charter of the United Nations and the Universal Declaration of Human Rights. They further stressed that African peoples have always attached respect to human dignity and fundamental human rights bearing in mind that human rights are not confined to civil and political rights but cover economic, social and cultural problems.

This resolution, in fact, confirms our earlier position that the UN Charter, as well as other international instruments generalizing human rights principles, have had a positive effect on African's acceptance of a regional human rights organ.

3.2 From Monrovia to Nairobi

While the UN Monrovia draft provided a useful precedent, it was the OAU Charter on Human and Peoples' Rights that dealt in a more comprehensive manner with regional promotion and protection of human rights in Africa.

The Draft African Charter on Human and People's Rights was drafted in implementation of Decision 115 (XVI) Rev. I, by which the Assembly of Heads of State and Government requested the Secretary General of the OAU at its Sixteenth Ordinary Session held in Monrovia (Liberia) from 17 – 20th July, 1979 to organize as soon as possible in an African Capital a restricted meeting of highly qualified experts to prepare a preliminary draft of an 'African Charter on Human and Peoples' Rights, providing *inter alia* for the establishment of bodies to promote and protect human and peoples' rights. The restricted meeting of experts met in Dakar (Senegal) from 28th November to 7th December, 1979 and prepared a preliminary draft.[80]

The Charter which with some modifications was adopted by the OAU Council of Ministers in Banjul (Gambia) in January 1981, has since been adopted by the Assembly of Heads of State and Government and has since come into force, having been ratified by a simple majority of the member states of the OAU.[81]

Recent developments in the continent would seem to reinforce the objectives of the African Charter. The Treaty for African Economic Community signed in Abuja, Nigeria, in 1991, the Khartoum Declaration and the African Charter for Popular Participation in Development (1990) The New Partnership For African Development (2002) all recognize the need for respect for human rights and for popular participation in both the politics and economic processes. The ECOWAS Treaty (1993), the treaty establishing the East African Community (EAC), the courts of both ECOWAS and EAC have jurisdiction in human rights matters,[82] as well as the Constitutive Act of the AU make provision for parliaments to serve each of them.[83] Most significantly, the Protocol

---

[80] Doc. CAB/LEG/67/REV.1, p 1.

[81] Article 63(3) of the African Charter.

[82] For further discussion of these developments see *Infra.*

[83] See chapter 10 *Infra.*

establishing the African Court on Human and Peoples' Rights is now in force.[84]

---

[84] *Ibid.*

4

SCOPE AND NATURE OF RIGHTS GUARANTEED AND DUTIES IMPOSED

4.1 Preamble

At this point it is necessary to examine the provisions of the Charter on human and peoples' rights and duties. The African Charter, as is the general practice with other conventions, begins with the preamble or 'preliminary recitations' indicating *inter alia* the object of the Charter, the philosophy underlying it and the general direction in which the jurisprudence of the Human Rights Commission and Court should evolve. States parties to the African Charter reaffirm their undertaking under the OAU Charter "in accordance with which 'freedom', equality, justice and dignity are essential objectives for the achievement of the legitimate aspirations of the African peoples, (para. 3); the pledge they solemnly made in Article 2 of the said Charter to eradicate all forms of colonialism from Africa, to promote international co-operation having due regard to the Charter of the United Nations and the Universal Declaration of Human Rights contained in the declarations, conventions and other instruments adopted by the OAU, the United Nations and the Movement of the Non-Aligned countries (para. 8).

Paragraph 11 of the preamble not only reaffirms the commitment of the founding fathers of the OAU, as a measure of safeguarding and consolidating their hard won independence as well as their sovereignty and territorial integrity, to fight colonialism and neo-colonialism in all its forms as well as racism, but has also extended it to their duty to achieve the total liberation of Africa which would apparently involve the elimination of Zionism, the dismantling of aggressive foreign military bases and all forms of discrimination particularly those based on race, ethnic groups, colour, sex, language, religion or political opinion.

On the philosophy and jurisprudence of African Charter, emphasis is placed on the virtues of their historical tradition and the values of African civilization which should inspire and characterise their reflection of the conception of human rights (para. 5); the essential importance traditionally attached in Africa to human and peoples' rights and freedoms (para. 7); the right to development and the satisfaction of economic, social and cultural rights which constitute the guarantee of civil and political rights[85] – a philosophical shift from the previous situation which tended to emphasize civil and political rights to the near exclusion of economic, social and cultural rights and which is sought to be imposed by the born again democrats in the post crisis of socialism and Gulf War World Order[86], (para.9); and the understanding that the enjoyment of rights and freedoms also implies the performance of duties on the part of every one (para. 10). Furthermore paragraph 6 recaptures in a rather less assertive manner, the naturalist theory that there are certain rights – the rights of man – which in her in an individual *qua human* being such as the civil liberties and freedoms and perhaps the right to property when it states that fundamental human rights stem from the attributes of human beings.

But given the integrated conception of human rights adopted in the Charter, it may well be argued that each category of rights is

---

[85] Other international conventions and human rights instruments seem to accept the interdependence and interconnectedness between civil and political rights on the one hand and economic, social and cultural rights on the other but fall short of elevating them to the status of enforceable rights. See the Universal Declaration of Human Rights (1948) Article 22.

[86] see *infra* There appears to be increasing general acceptance of the relevance of economic, social and cultural rights.

fundamental and therefore, inherent, given that in the words of the charter

"Civil and political rights cannot be dissociated from economic, social and cultural rights in their conception as well as universality and that the satisfaction of economic, social and cultural rights is a guarantee for the enjoyment of civil and political rights".

While it recognizes that international protection is justified, it is aware that it is above all the reality and respect of peoples' rights which effectively guarantee human rights.

As can be seen, the preamble or 'preliminary recitations' are a form of introduction indicating in a general way why the parties entered into the treaty (object and purpose) and the philosophy underlying it. It generally sets the tone for what follows. In terms of the structure of a treaty it is one of the principal parts of the treaty.[87] Even then, because of the very general nature of the language employed and because it normally precedes what is often considered as the substantive or dispositive provisions of the treaty which are normally considered as creating rights and obligations – they are usually regarded as not creating rights and obligations for the parties.

The preamble is, however, not without any legal significance. One of the accepted rules of treaty interpretation is that which prays in aid of the object and context of the treaty. This customary rule of international law is restated in Article 3, of the Vienna Convention on the law of Treaties (1969)[88] which stipulates:

---

[87] *Starke, Introduction to International Law*, 9th Edition, (London: Buttter-worths, 1984) p.439. see also supra.

[88] For the text of the Vienna Convention on the Law of Treaties, see D. J. Harris, Cases and Materials on *International Law,* 9th edition (London: Sweet and Maxwell, 2983). pp 565 *et seq.*

1. A treaty shall be interpreted in good faith in accordance with the ordinary meaning given to the terms of the treaty in their context and in the light of its object and purpose.

2. The context for the purpose of the interpretation of treaty shall comprise in addition to the text, including its preamble and annexes..."

On two scores it can be said that the preamble to the African Charter qualifies as an aid to interpretation. Firstly, it indicates the object of Charter – namely the respect for, promotion and protection of human and peoples' rights and ensuring the performance of duties enumerated in the Charter. Secondly, as part of the Charter, it forms part of the 'context' which may be relevant in interpreting particular words or phrases whose meaning is doubtful. Some arbitral practice supports reference to the preamble as an aid to interpretation. This was the case in the (*Beagle Channel Arbitration of 1977, Argentina V. Chile*)[89] in which the Court of Arbitration had regard to the preamble of 1881 Boundary Treaty.

Both the Objectives and Principles Provision of the African Union (AU) which is the successor of the OAU affirm commitment to promotion and protection of human and peoples' rights. Some of the objectives of the African Union are: to promote international cooperation taking due account of the Charter of United Nations and the Universal Declaration of Human Rights, to promote democratic principles and institutions, popular participation and good governance, and promote and protect human and peoples' rights in accordance with the African Charter on Human and Peoples' Rights and other relevant instruments [Article 3(e), (g), (h)]. Among the principles are those of participation of African peoples in the activities of the Union, promotion of gender equality, respect for democratic principles, human rights, the rule of law and good governance, respect for the sanctity of human life,

---

[89] I.L.M. 634 (1978). Starke *op cit,* p.457.

promotion of social justice as well as condemnation and rejection of unconstitutional changes of government, and the right to live in peace and security [Article 4(c), (l), (m), (h) (o), (p)].

Emphasis on peace and development is promotional of material and social conditions for the actualization of rights. And The Constitutive Act of the AU has in defence of rights given the Assembly of Heads of State and Government, power to decide on intervention, as a qualification to the non interference provision, in a Member State 'in respect of grave circumstances namely; war crimes, genocide and crimes against humanity' all of which fall within the province of human rights [Article 4(h) and 7].

4.2 Dispositive Provisions

Unlike the preamble, dispositive or otherwise substantive provisions, of a treaty create rights and obligations, impose duties, and establish organs with various competences to perform assigned functions. For the purposes of this work this area is subdivided into:

1. Provisions having general import,
2. Civil and political rights,
3. Economic, social and cultural rights,
4. Peoples' rights, and
5. Duties

4.2.1 *Provisions Having General Import*

4.2.1.1 *The Import of Article I*

This section is concerned with Article 1 which deals with the under-taking by states parties to the African Charter to recognize, the rights, duties and freedoms enshrined therein and their pledge to adopt and secure them within their jurisdiction by legislative and other measures.

The section also deals with non-discrimination (Article 2), equality before the law and equal protection of the law (Article 3).

The former raises the issue as to the legal consequences of a treaty validly entered into by a state for domestic law and executive acts. It is an accepted general rule of international law that a state which has entered into a valid treaty is bound to carry out its obligations therein in good faith *(pacta sunt servanda)*. It is equally a well settled rule of international law that a state cannot rely on the defects in or inadequacies of its municipal law to avoid its international obligations. In the *Alabama Claims Arbitration*,[90] the British Government's argument that because its constitutional law was not such as to provide it with the power to interfere with the private construction and sailing of ships concerned Great Britain had not violated its obligations as a neutral in the United States Civil war by allowing the construction and sailing to occur was rejected by the tribunal. In the words of the Tribunal

"... the government of Her Britannic Majesty cannot justify itself for a failure in due diligence on the plea of insufficiency of the legal means of which it possessed".[91] Seen from this perspective Article 1 of the African Charter would seem superfluous as it simply confirms the obligation of states under customary international law to honour their treaty obligations in good faith. This line of reasoning is in agreement with the Advisory Opinion of the Permanent Court of International Justice (PCIJ) in Exchange of Greek and Turkish *Population case.*[92] In that case, the court having examined Article 18 of the Treaty of modifications as may be necessary with a view to ensuring the execution of the present convention, advised that

---

[90] Moore, I. Int. Arb. 493 p.656 (1972); D.J. Harris, *op cit*, p.58.

[91] *Ibid.*

[92] *Advisory opinion*, P.C.I.J. Reports, Series B, No 10 p.20 (1925).

"This clause merely lays stress on the principle which is self-evident, according to which a state which has contracted valid international obligations is bound to make in its legislation such modification as may be necessary to ensure the fulfillment of the obligations undertaken".

In Sir Dawda K. Jawara v. The Gambia[93] the complainant alleged *inter alia* violation of rights resulting from acts of the military regime in suspending the Bill of Rights as contained in the 1970 Gambian Constitution by Military Decree No 30/31, extra judicial killings and ouster of courts' jurisdiction. On Article I the Commission held:

Article I gives the Charter the legally binding character always attributed to international treaties of this sort. Therefore a violation of any provision of the Charter automatically means a violation of Article 1. If a State party to the Charter fails to recognize the provisions of the same, there is no doubt that it is in violation of this Article. Its violation, therefore, goes to the root of the Charter.

The Republic of the Gambia ratified the Charter on 6 June 1983. in its first periodic report to the Commission in 1992, the Gambian government asserted that "Most of the rights set out in the Charter have been provided for in Chapter 3, Sections 13 to 30 of the 1970 Constitution... The Constitution predicts the Gambian accession to the covenants, but in fact gave legal effect to some of the provisions of the Charter". This therefore means that the Gambian government gave recognition to some of the provisions of the Charter (i.e. those contained in chapter 3 of its Constitution), and incorporated them into its domestic law.

By suspending Chapter 3, (the Bills of Rights), the government therefore restricted the enjoyment of the rights guaranteed therein, and by implication, the rights enshrined in the Charter.

---

[93] 147/95 and 149/96.

It should however be stated that the suspension of the Bill of Rights does not *ipso facto* mean the suspension of the domestic effect of the Charter. In Communication 129/94, the Commission held that the obligation of … a government remains unaffected by the purported revocation of the domestic effect of the Charter.

The suspension of the Bill of Rights and consequently the application of the Charter was not only a violation of Article 1 but also a restriction on the enjoyment of the rights and freedoms enshrined in the Charter, thus violating the Charter as well".[94]

While the Commission in the instant case affirms the rule of customary international law, it fails to explicitly indicate the implication of the recognition of some of the rights. The implication is however, clear from the interpretation of the legal significance of Article 1 of the Charter that selective recognition is not allowed.

Whether or not the mere existence of domestic laws which are in conflict with international law obligations amounts to violation or whether, such laws must be implemented before violation can take place is not settled. Fitzmaurice an eminent jurist seems to equivocate in his consideration of this matter when on the one hand he argues that

> "the supremacy of international law in the international field simply means that if nothing can be done or is done, the state will on the international plane have committed a breach of international law obligations, for which it will be internationally responsible, and in respect of which it cannot plead the[95] condition of its domestic law by way of resolution"

---

[94] *Ibid.*

[95] "The General Principles of International Law considered From the Standpoint of the Rule of Law "92 Hague *Recueil*5 at pp.70-80 (1957 11).

and on the other hand that if a state in the application of its domestic law acts contrary to international law.. it will commit a breach of its international obligations.[96] In the former it would seem referring to what "can be done" that the mere existence of laws in conflict with international law obligations is violative of international law and referring to 'what is done' – that actual implementation is violative of international law obligations. The latter reaffirms only the second limb of the former that implementation/ application of domestic law contrary to international law is a breach. The Commission seems to have adopted these two limbs of the argument when it in effect held that any violation of any provision of the Charter automatically means a violation of Article 1 as well as that if a State party to the Charter fails to recognize the provisions of the same, it is in violation.[97]

Nigeria has in conformity with its constitutional requirements adopted an enabling law which brought the African Charter into force in Nigeria.[98] Several matters fall to be considered as a result of this singular act. The Nigerian constitution is supreme over all other laws.[99] The enabling law has transformed the African Charter into a domestic legislation.

---

[96] *Ibid.*

[97] see *Supra*

[98] 1979 Constitution of the Federal Republic of Nigeria S.12 (1) which provides that treaty between the Federation and any other country shall not have the Force of Law except to the extent to which any such treaty has been enacted into law by the National Assembly" see also s.1(1) & (2) and para. 29 of second schedule to the 1979 constitution see U.O. Umuzurike "Nigeria's Ratification of the African Charter on Human and Peoples' Rights – implications and consequences" The *Calabar Law Journal*, vol. 2, 1988, pp. 19-20. The 1999 Constitution of Nigeria contains identical provision. See Art 12(1) and corresponding provisions of the 2nd Schedule to the 1999 Constitution.

[99] S.1 (1) & (2).

Except where domestic law gives pre-eminence to international law, including treaty law, the general practice is that domestic courts uphold the supremacy of domestic law, even when they may interpret domestic law so as not to conflict with international law. Where the constitution is the supreme law, as is the case in Nigeria,[100] then it will hold sway over a conflicting treaty transformed into domestic law. Where there is conflict between an enactment and a treaty transformed into domestic law, the rules of interpretation stipulating that the later in time, except where the contrary is provided, shall override the earlier law to the extent of inconsistency will apply. [Sani Abacha v Gani Fawehinmi (2000) 6 NWLR Pt 660, 177 – 359], this celebrated case gave opportunity for the Nigerian Supreme Court to decide on the status of the African Charter under Nigerian Law. The apex court found *inter alia* that:

"Where, however, the treaty is enacted into law by the National Assembly, as was the case with the African Charter which is incorporated into our municipal (i.e. domestic) law by the African Charter on Human and Peoples' Rights (Ratification and Enforcement) Act Cap. 10 Laws of the Federation of Nigeria 1990 (hereinafter referred to simply as Cap. 10), it becomes binding and our courts must give effect to it like all other laws falling within the judicial powers of the courts. By Cap. 10 the African Charter is now part of the laws of Nigeria and like all other laws the courts must uphold it. The Charter gives to citizens of member states of the Organization of African Unity rights and obligations, which rights and obligations are to be enforced by our courts, if they must have any meaning. It is interesting to note that the rights and obligations contained in the Charter are not new to Nigeria as most of the rights and obligations are already enshrined in our Constitution. See

---

[100] See *Supra.*

Chapter IV on the 1979 and 1999 Constitutions. No doubt Cap.10 is a statute with international flavour. Being so, therefore, I would think that if there is a conflict between it and another statute its provisions will prevail over those of that other statute for the reason that it is presumed that the legislature does not intend to breach an international obligation. To this extent I agree with their Lordships of the Court below that the Charter possesses "a greater vigour and strength" than any other domestic statute, but that is not to say that the Charter is superior to the Constitution as erroneously, with respect, was submitted by Mr. Adegboruwa, learned counsel for the respondent. Nor can its international flavour prevent the National Assembly, or the Federal Military Government before it removes it from our body of municipal laws by simply repealing Cap. 10. Nor also is the validity of another statute be necessarily affected by the mere fact that it violates the African Charter or any other treaty, for that matter – see: *Chae Chin Ping v United States,* 130 US. 181 where it was held that Treaties are of no higher dignity than acts of Congress, and may be modified or repealed by Congress in like manner; and whether such modification or repeal is wise or just is not a judicial question".[101]

The practice at the international level holds that in case of conflict between international law obligations and domestic law, an international tribunal is bound to give primacy to international law.

In effect whatever the practice may be at the national level in the end it is the supremacy of international law that holds sway.[102] It is im-

---

[101] See also Osita C. Eze, *"Application of International Human Rights Law in Nigeria"* paper presented at a seminar on Domestic Application of Human Rights Law held in Banjul the Gambia, 29th – 30th July 2000.

[102] See, The *Republic v. Charles Okunda Mushiyi, The Republic v. Donald Mechack Ombisis* (Kenya) I. LM, vol. IX No. 3, May 1970, pp. 556-566;

portant to emphasize this point because in some of the local cases in which reliance was placed on some provisions of the African Charter, it would seem that the courts have held the view that they were not applicable.[103] As the spate of human rights petitions which relied on the relevant

provisions of the African Charter increased in response to massive violations of human freedoms and liberties – right to liberty, freedom of movement, and of expression and even the right of access to ordinary courts under the military[104], it was reported through the electronic media that a decree had been issued ousting the application of the African Charter by the Nigerian Courts. In view of our earlier discussion on the relationship between international law and domestic law, the decree would have been of no avail in so far as the obligations of Nigeria under the African Charter were concerned. Indeed it is quite clear given the dichotomy which the 1979 and 1999 constitutions created between civil and political rights which are justiceable and economic, social and

---

German Interests in Polish Upper Silesia, P.C.I.J. (merits) (m.26), Ser. A. No. 7, *Greeco Communities cases,* P.C.I.J. Ser. B, No. 17, 32, *Costa v. ENEL (1964-65) Common Market Law Review,* pp. 197-201; s. Ross "The Common market Tribunal – The Solution to the conflict between Municipal law and International Law in East Africa" I.C.L.Q. vol. Part 2, April 1972, pp. 361-374, FXN Jenga" Contrast Between the Effect of the Laws of the European Community and the East African Community in the constituent territories" *East African Law Journal,* 1968 pp. 150-151; Osita C. Eze, *The Legal status of foreign investments in the east African common* Market, Leiden; ijthoff, 1975 pp. 30 -31.

[103] The cases one by Nigerian Civil Liberties Organisation (CLO) relating to ejections of individuals from areas which they had made their homes and other by Constitutional Rights Project (CRP) concerning the detention of a person were apparently thrown out because the matter were still in court. See U.O. Umozurike' Five Years of the African Commission on Human and Peoples Rights," NSIA lecture Series No. 2 1992, p.14. Need this be so even where the court's jurisdiction has been ousted?

[104] See *infra.*

cultural rights which are non-justiceable and the enforceability of civil, political, social, economic and cultural rights as well as peoples rights under the African Charter, that Nigeria had an obligation once it ratified the charter both under general international law and Article 1 of the African Charter to brig the constitution in line with the latter where one adopted the position that the mere existence of domestic law which contradicts international law obligations amounts to a breach. It finally did.

4.2.1.2 Non-Discrimination

We start this section by giving a general meaning of 'discrimination'. For this purpose we adopt and adapt the definition of discrimination as stated in Article 1(1) of the International Convention on the Elimination of All Forms of Racial Discrimination, (1965). Accordingly 'discrimination' means any distinction, exclusion, restriction or preference which has the purpose or effect of nullifying or impairing the recognition, enjoyment or exercise, on an equal footing, of human rights, fundamental freedoms and peoples' rights in the civil, political, economic, social and cultural or any other field of public or where appropriate private life.

The basis on which discrimination may be proscribed may vary depending on the aims and objectives of the instrument or convention in question. The African Charter attempts a broad coverage of the grounds on which discrimination is prohibited.

Article 2 of the African Charter – the non-discrimination provision stipulates that: "Every person shall be entitled to the enjoyment of the rights and freedoms recognized and guaranteed in the present Charter without distinction of any kind such as race, ethnic group, colour, sex, language, religion, political or any other opinion, national and social origin, fortune, birth or other status."

The modern foundation for the non-discrimination provisions which have become parts of increasing number of conventions and declarations[105] on human rights can be traced to the Charter of the United Nations where the peoples of the United Nations, in the very first paragraph of the preamble to the Charter, reaffirmed their faith in fundamental human rights, in the dignity and worth of the human person and in the equal rights of men and women. The equality of rights principle also imports the notion of non-discrimination.

Prior to the Charter of the United Nations and under the League, the Permanent Court of International Justice had to deal with the issue of equality in treaties concerning minority protection. The Court pronounced on the essence of such treaties:

> "the idea underlying the treaties for the protection of minorities is to secure for certain elements incorporated in a state, the population of which differs from them in race, language or religion, the possibility of living peaceably alongside that population and co-operating amicably with it, while at the same time preserving the characteristics which distinguish them from the majority and satisfying the ensuing needs".[106]

As we have shown elsewhere, in order to attain this objective two things were regarded as particularly necessary, and have formed the subject of provisions in these treaties.

The first is to ensure that nationals belonging to racial, religious or linguistic minorities shall be placed in every respect on a footing of perfect equality with the other nationals of the state.

The second is to ensure for the minority elements suitable means for the preservation of their racial peculiarities, and their national characteristics.

---

[105] The Universal Declaration of Human Rights, Article 2; International Covenant on Economic, Social and Cultural Rights, Article 2(2); International Covenant on Civil and Political Rights, Article 2 (1); European Convention on Human Rights, Article 14; American Convention on Human Rights, Article 1.

[106] *The Minority Schools in Albania,* (1935). Ser. A/B, No. 64, p.17.

These two requirements are indeed closely interlocked, for there would be no true equality between a majority and a minority if the latter were deprived of its own institutions and were consequently compelled to renounce that which constitutes the very essence of its being a minority. [107]

There is a striking similarity between the problems the minority protection treaties were intended to solve and the problems now facing many independent African states. Not only are most of the states composed of various nationalities, sometimes belonging to different racial groups having different cultural and religious values as well as languages, but there are exists also the arduous task of welding these heterogeneous societies into nation states without, at the same time, destroying, in the words of the court, 'that which constitutes the very essence of its being a minority', and one may add of being one of the competing nationalities. [108] The African Charter on Human and Peoples Rights has creatively responded to this aspect of Africa's political economy, especially in its provisions on peoples rights supplemented by ECOSOC rights and duties.

In the *Belgian Linguistic Case (merits)* [109] The European Court of Human Rights interpreted the non-discrimination provision in Article 14 of the European Convention for the Protection of Human Rights and Fundamental Freedoms (1950). Article 14, which but for a few differences, is identical with Article 1 of the African Charter stipulates as follows:

"The enjoyment of rights and freedoms set forth in this convention shall be secured without discrimination on any

---

[107] *ibid* see also Osita C. Eze, *Human Rights in Africa; Some selected Problems*, Lagos, N.I.I.A./Macmillan Nigerian Publishers 1984, pp.72-73.

[108] *Ibid.*

[109] Eur. Court. HR Series A Vol. 6 Judgement of July 23 1968 Harris *op.cit*, pp. 526-528.

ground such as sex, race, colour, language, religion, political or other opinion, national or social origin, association with a national minority, property, birth, or other status".

The facts of the case were as follows: For the purpose of determining the language of instruction in its state and state supported schools, Belgium is divided territorially by law into unilingual and bi-lingual areas. In the former which consist of Dutch, French and German speaking areas, the predominant language of the region is the language of instruction. In the latter including six communes surrounding Brussels, special arrangements exist. The Court held by eight votes to seven that the system does not comply with the first sentence of Article 2 of the protocol in so far as it prevents certain children solely on *bases of the residence* of their parents, from having access to the French language schools existing in the six communes on the periphery of Brussels invested with a special status…"

The court also found/held that:

1. Article 14 does not have an independent existence since it relates solely to "rights and freedoms set forth in the convention"

2. A measure which in itself is in conformity with the requirements of the Article enshrining the right or freedom in question may, however infringe this Article when read in conjunction with Article 14 – as though Article 14 formed an integral part of each of the Articles laying down rights and freedoms.

3. Following the principles which may be extracted from the legal practice of the larger number of democratic states, the principle of equality of treatment is violated (since Article 14 does not forbid every difference in the treatment of persons in the exercise of rights and freedoms recognized) if

the distinction has no objective and reasonable justification the existence of which must be assessed in relation to the aim and effects of the measure under consideration regard being had to principles which normally prevail in democratic societies, and

4. A difference of treatment in the exercise of a right laid down in the convention must not only pursue a legitimate aim, Article 14 is likewise violated when it is clearly established that there is no reasonable relationship of proportionality between the means employed and the aim sought to be realized. This would be the case where as in one situation in the Belgium Linguistics case, "it would have been possible to have devised another language instruction scheme for the region concerned that placed lesser burden on the minority language children.

Three aspects of the findings of the court are instructive and will no doubt, be relevant to the enforcement function of the African Commission and Court namely, that the non-discrimination provision applied to and should be read in conjunction with other provisions on rights and freedoms; that despite its appearance of guaranteeing "absolute" equality of treatment (French versions *sans distinction aucune*) it admits of differential treatment based on a legitimate aim and that the proportionality test (reasonable relationship of proportionality) between the means employed and the aim sought to be realized must be met. The non-discrimination provision in the African Charter speaks only of rights and freedoms. Even though duties are not expressly covered there under, the right to equality before the law and equal protection of the law, which itself not only imports non discrimination but is also subject to the non-discrimination clause, brings it within the ambit of non-discrimination [Article 3].

Finally, it needs to be stated that the court's interpretation was informed by principles which normally prevail in democratic societies: The issues of non-discrimination and equality principle are, as we shall see later, also the subject of specific regulation under the peoples' rights provisions of the African Charter.

The African Commission had on several occasions made determinations with respect to alleged violations of Article 2 of the Charter on non-discrimination. In Recontre Africaine pour la Defense des Droits de l'Homme/Zambia[110] in which 517 West Africans were expelled from Zambia in 1992 on grounds of being in Zambia illegally the Commission found that even though Zambia had the right to deport illegal aliens it had to do so in accordance with Articles 2 and 12 the later proscribing mass expulsion of aliens defined as that which is aimed at national racial, ethnic or religious group. The exclusion of the nationals of immediate neighbours of Zambia, namely Tanzania and Zaire offended both Articles. In another petition by Association of Members of the Episcopal Conference/Sudan of East Africa, the Commission determined that there was discrimination against Christians in the matters of conscience and religion by reading Articles 2 and 8 (on freedom of religion) together.[111]

The petition brought against the Mauritanian government by a number of NGOs on account of predominantly Moorish (Beidanes) government against the blacks who live in South including Sonike, Wolofs and the Hal Pulaar was concerned with discrimination based on race. The blacks had accused the then governments (1986 and 1992) of marginalizing them. The commission determined:

"Article 2 of the Charter lays down a principle that is essential to the spirit of this convention, one of whose goals is the elimination of all forms of discrimination and to ensure equality among all human beings. The same objective under-pins the

---

[110] 71/92.

[111] 89/93.

Declaration of the Rights of People Belonging to National, Ethnic, Religious or Linguistic Minorities adopted by the General Assembly of the United Nations in resolution 47/135 of 18 December 1992. Article 1(1) of this document indeed stipulates: "States shall protect the existence and national or ethnic, cultural, religious or linguistic identity of the minorities within their respective territories and shall stimulate the establishment of conditions conducive to the promotion of such identity". From the foregoing, it is apparent that international human rights law and the community of States accord a certain importance to the eradication of discrimination in all its guises. Various texts adopted at the global and regional levels have indeed affirmed this repeatedly. Consequently, for a country to subject its own indigenes to discriminatory treatment only because of the colour of skin is an unacceptable discriminatory attitude and a violation of the very spirit of the African Charter and of the letter of its Article 2."[112]

Not only was the Commission outright in condemning racial discrimination, which it found violative of Article 2, it freely drew inspiration from international human rights standards by praying in aid of 'instruments' (Article 60) as well as subsidiary measures-reliance on customary international law and general principle of international law (Article 61) for non-discrimination is both a principle of international law and a rule of customary international law being supported by overwhelming state practice.

Furthermore, by insisting that one of the goals of the Convention is the elimination of all forms of discrimination not only does it indicate that the grounds listed are not exhaustive but also that despite the

---

[112] See fn. 28 *infra.*

statecentric architecture of the Charter that[113] discrimination by non state entities such as natural and juridical persons may also be covered. Some of the UN Conventions, the International Convention on the Elimination of All Forms of Racial Discrimination (1965) and Convention on the Elimination of all forms of Discrimination Against Women (CEDAW) (1976) unlike the African Charter are explicit on imposing on States Parties the duty to eliminate discrimination by persons, groups or

organisations.[114]

More recent African constitutions except that of Nigeria which is rather statecentric in its rendition of the non-discrimination clause cover discrimination by non state entities. And even in the Nigerian case, judicial practice which has progressively recognized the individual as a violator of rights would seem to extend its scope beyond acts or omissions directly attributed to the State or its organs.[115] Under the 1992 Constitution of Ghana[116], the non-discrimination clause is applicable not only to government and its agencies but also 'all natural and legal persons in Ghana' where applicable to them [Article 12(1)]. The 1995

---

[113] 54/91 Malawi African Association /Mauritania, 61/91 Amnesty International /Mauritania, 98/93 Ms Sarr Diop, Union Interafricaine des Droits del'homme and RADDHO/ Mauritania, 164/97 a 196/977 Collectif de Veures et Ayants-droitt Mauritania, 210/98 Association Mauritanienne de Droits de l'Homme/Mauritania. All these petitions we considered together at the 16th Session held in March 1994.

[114] Article 21(d) and Article 2(e) of CEDAW is formulated in terms of 'discrimination by any person, organisation or enterprise'. For the texts of the Two Conventions see Human Rights A Compilation of International Instruments, Volume 1(First Part) Universal Instruments, New York United Nations 1993 pp.150 - 163 and pp. 66-79.

[115] Constitution of the Republic of Nigeria, Lagos, Government Printer, 1999, s.42.

[116] Constitution of the Republic of Ghana 1992.

Constitution of the Republic of Uganda[117] equally covers both categories of potential violators (Article 20). The 1996 Constitution of South Africa[118] is peculiar in its formulation, this being a product of its history and the need to create a peaceful multiracial/multicultural society. The Bill of Rights applies to both State and non State entities (natural and juristic persons) (Article 8). More specifically it is provided that neither the state nor natural or juristic person may unfairly discriminate against any one on the grounds stated [Article 9(4) and (5)].

Finally as already indicated when considering Article 1 (on states undertaking to recognize Charter rights and freedoms) in Sir Dawda K Jawara/The Gambia, The Commission found that "The suspension of the Bill of Rights and consequently the application of the Charter was not only a violation of the Article but also a restriction of the enjoyment of rights and freedoms enshrined in the, Charter, thus violating Article 2 of the Charter as well."[119]

It therefore is evident from the 'broad' source of the jurisprudence of the Commission and possibly the Court that national decisions and regional jurisprudence will enrich and be in turn enriched by both the continental and global currents in this very fundamental area of the law.

4.2.1.3 Equality before the Law and Equal Protection of the Law (Art. 3)

Article 3 of the African Charter provides that – "Every individual shall be equal before the law; every individual shall be entitled to an equal protection of the law."

---

[117] Constitution of the Republic of Uganda 1995.

[118] Constitution of the Republic of South Africa, Government Gazette, Cape Town 18 Dec, 1996, No. 17678. See also Osita C. Eze "Economic and Social Rights in a New Constitution" paper presented at a Review Meeting on the Position of the CFCR to be Submitted on the Review of the 1999 Constitution, 2001.

[119] 147/95 and 149/96.

In a sense the equality provision, as already indicated, raises the issue as to whether formal and/or substantive equality is intended. It also raises the issue as to whether only judicial conduct is the matter or whether in addition executive and legislative acts may be impugned for non-compliance.

With respect to the former it is quite clear that when read in the context of other reinforcing rights guaranteed by the Charter – the right to education, the right to work or social security, and the right of access to courts etc. - that the formal guarantee of equality before the law or equal protection of the law will be of little avail to the majority who neither have knowledge of the rights guaranteed nor the means of pursuing their claims, in the absence of comprehensive legal aid scheme as is the case in most developing countries, before courts that may be neither independent nor impartial.

For these people a Bill of Rights and even more so an international convention on human rights would seem rather esoteric and some arbiter or a commission (the African Commission) located in a place called Banjul, in Gambia appear rather remote. The local courts are except where increasingly NGOs take up the cases of victims of violations of human and peoples' rights nearly inaccessible to them. and the majority of cases which are resolved before customary institutions, that are not part of the formal judicial systems, may settle matters involving human rights – right to fair hearing, that no one should be a judge in his case – without following strict rules of procedure or evidence and being concerned primarily that substantive justice is done in the particular case.

The UN Human Rights Committee's interpretation of a similar, even if somewhat more elaborate provision in the UN Covenant on Civil and Political Rights, is instructive on the import of the equality before the law provision, Article 26 of the covenant provides:

"All persons are equal before the law and are entitled without any discrimination to the equal protection of the law. In this respect, the law shall prohibit any discrimination and guarantee to all persons equal and effective protection against discrimination on any ground such as race, colour, sex, age, language, religion, political or other opinion, national or social origin, property, birth or other status".

Article 26 the UN Covenant went beyond prescribing equality before the law and equal protection of the law. It affirmed that equality in this context imports non-discrimination. Whether this addition is necessary in view of the "apex" non-discrimination clause which applies to all rights and freedoms is another matter[120].

In the case of *Zwaan de Vriez vs the Netherlands (182/84)*[121] the Committee having found that the law granting social security rights treated men and women differently came to the conclusion that the question at issue was not whether the Covenant on civil and Political Rights imposed an obligation on states to provide social security, but whether, where a state decided to institute a system of security, it could do so in breach of Articles. 2(1) non-discrimination clause, Article 3 – equality of men and women provision and Article 26 read together. The Committee found, in effect, that Article 26 imposed an obligation on the state whether in the exercise of its legislative, administrative or judicial activity.

The African Commission has had occasion to interpret the equality provisions of the Charter. In Legal Resources Foundation /Zambia the Commission held that the Zambian Constitution (Amendment) Act 1996 which provided *inter alia* that anyone who wanted to contest the Office of the President must prove that both his/her parents were Zambians was

---

[120] See *Supra.*

[121] Justice Lallah, "International Human Rights Norms" in *Judicial Colloquium in Bangalore op cit* p.19.

violative of Article 3 of the Charter on equality before the law and equal protection of the law.[122] In yet another petition the Commission found that the selective manner in which rehabilitation measures, intended to address the consequences of the suspensions, dismissals and retirements of Magistrates that took place on June 10 1987 by the 'Conseil National de la Revolution' which ruled Burkina Faso from 1983 – 1987, was applied was violative of Article of the Charter.[123] It has also made a finding that the rampant arrest and detention of the petitioner by the Nigerian Security officials which eventually led to his going into hiding for fear of his life has deprived him of his right to equal protection of the law guaranteed under Article 3.[124] It has also been held that the denial of the right of a citizen to leave and enter his country and to participate in politics was in violation of Article 3(2).[125] One might ask why if the equality provision is used also to connote non-discrimination whether its inclusion is not superfluous. It is our considered position that this is not the case for two reasons: firstly its broad formulation is not limited by the categorization of the grounds on which inequality, as in the case of non-discrimination, is proscribed; secondly while the non discrimination clause relates to rights and freedoms guaranteed in the Charter, the equality before the law provision goes beyond these to capture other laws, policies of government that do not necessarily fall within the ambit of human rights.

In *Broeks V. Netherlands (1987) 2 selected Decisions HRC 196,* the Committee held that the circumstances in which Mrs. Broeks found herself at the material time and the application of the then valid Netherlands law made her a victim of violation based on sex, of Article 26 of

---

[122] 211/98.

[123] Movement Burkinabe des Droits de l'Homme et des Peoples 204/97.

[124] Kazeem Aminu/Nigeria 205/97. See also Media Rights Agenda/Nigeria 224/98.

[125] John K. Modise/Botswana 97/93.

the International Covenant on Civil and Political[126] Rights, because she was denied a social security benefit on an equal footing with men.

In the *Belgian Linguistic Case* the European court having found that Article 6 of the European Convention, which guarantees the right to fair and public hearing does not compel states to institute a system of appeal court held, that however, it would violate that Article, read in conjunction with Article 14, were it to debar certain persons from these remedies without a legitimate reason while making them available to others in respect of the same type of action".

It can thus be seen that while non-discrimination and provisions share the same basic principles, the context in which they are employed might define their specific scope and content. They may also in certain contexts be used interchangeably.

---

[126] See also Avellanal v Peru, HRC, GAOR, 44th Session supp 40, p.146(1989), Danning v. Netherlands (1987) 2 Selected Decisions HRC 209, See Harris J. op cit pp.681-683.

5

CIVIL AND POLITICAL RIGHTS

5.1 Introduction

Civil and political rights (first generation rights) are provided for in Articles 4 – 13. Together with the right to property and the freedom of association, (i.e. with respect to trade unions which are of earlier pedigree than the second generation rights, and are part of the economic and social rights), these rights are invariably guaranteed in constitutions of countries of liberal persuasion. Generally also these rights and freedoms tend to impose limitations on the exercise of state power. In certain contexts they are categorized as rights that guarantee freedom from fear as opposed to ECOSOC rights that guarantee our freedom from want. Group or peoples rights encompass these two categories in that they guarantee our freedom from both fear and want. We shall now consider these rights.

5.2 Right to Life

5.2.1 Introduction

Compared to the form of guarantee of human rights in other international instruments on human rights the African Charter seems to have adopted an economy of words. With respect to the right to life, it simply provides that:

"Human beings are inviolable. Every human being shall be entitled to respect for his life and the integrity of his person. No one may be arbitrarily deprived of this right".

The Article apart from guaranteeing respect for life and proscribing its arbitrary deprivation makes provision for the inviolability and respect for the human person. It is not quite clear what the affirmation of the inviolability of the human person imports save that arbitrary deprivation of life might, violate that norm. The relationship between respect for integrity and human life is less obvious. But the right to life is part of what has been classified as 'physical integrity'[127] which includes liberty, security, arrest, detention, torture and other ill treatment, standard of living, health, work, and social security and welfare. To the extent that their non actualization undermines the right to life there is a violation of the right to the integrity of the human person even when the particular right is not guaranteed as a legal right.

5.3 Other Legal Experiences

An analysis of these two aspects will be facilitated by comparing them with similar provisions in some other international instruments. Article 6(I) of the International Covenant on Civil and Political Rights provides that "Every human being has the inherent right to life. This right shall be protected by law. No one shall be arbitrarily deprived of his life".

Non arbitrary deprivation of life seems to be the core limitation of the inviolability of human life yet what is its significance? Where a dictatorship whether military or civilian, imposes itself on the governed can its laws not properly be regarded as arbitrary not being based on popular consent? And even assuming that laws restrictive of the right to

---

[127] P. Sieghart, International Law of Human Rights, Oxford University Press, 1985, p. 128 *et seque.*

life are passed by a constitutional government are there other grounds, apart from the defect that may be occasioned by arbitrariness, on which they could be challenged? The UN Committee on Civil and Political Rights has determined that; the Article imposes an obligation on the states parties to reduce infant mortality, to eliminate malnutrition, to prevent epidemics and to abolish weapons of mass destruction. And this is so even though these issues may not ordinarily be justiceable.[128]

The rationale seems to be that in addition to the proscription relating to the taking of life, the state has an obligation to protect life.

While the approach of the UN Human Rights Committee may be guided by the scope of rights guaranteed under the Covenant, the African Commission has the possibility of adopting a much more expansive interpretation of the right to life. The Charter[129] guarantees the right to work, to enjoy the best attainable state of physical and mental health, the right to peace and to a general satisfactory environment which are necessary if the right to life is to transcend, as it is found in the Nigerian constitution, its very restricted meaning. Article 33 of the 1999 Republican Constitution of Nigeria stipulates *inter alia* that:

"Every person has the right to life, and no one shall be deprived intentionally of his life save in execution of the sentence of a court in respect of a criminal offence of which he has been found guilty in Nigeria"(s.33 (1).

"Intentional deprivation" replaces "arbitrary deprivation" found in both the UN Covenant and the African Charter. It would seem that arbitrary deprivation would involve some element of intent but an intentional act may be either arbitrary or non-arbitrary.

---

[128] Lallah, *op cit* p.15. Cf Osita Eze "Legal Aspects of Reparation; Arguments for and Against" Forthcoming; Harris *op cit,* p.374, Lauterpacht, *Private Law Sources and Analogies of International law* (1927) pp. 135-143.
[129] See *infra.*

International law jurisprudence does not seem to require 'culpa' or 'dolus' in all delicts and even international law rules on criminal responsibility seem unsettled.[130] In appropriate cases, therefore, international organs charged with human rights enforcement may be influenced by domestic judicial practice in the interpretation of the relevant provisions on the right to life.[131]

Unlike the African Charter and the UN Covenant, the 1999 Nigerian Constitution imposes limitations on the right to life. S33(2) provides that:

"A person shall not be regarded as having been deprived of his life in contravention of this section, if he dies as a result of the use, to such extent and in such circumstances as are permitted by law, of such force as is reasonably necessary; a) for the defence of any person from unlawful violence or for the defence of property; b) in order to effect a lawful arrest or to prevent the escape of a   person lawfully detained or; c) For the purpose of suppressing a riot or insurrection or mutiny".

But the formulation and interpretation of these provisions have tended to be technistic and given the fact that what would have amounted to a guarantee of economic, social, and cultural rights, have been declared by the constitution to be non-justiceable, they may not lend themselves

---

[130] See *Infra.*

[131] Supreme Court per Nnamani and Nnaemeka Agu J.J.S.C. in *Ananaba Obuke v The State.* 1988 INWLR, 539 – where they held that mechanical computation of the appellants right of appeal would amount to a violation of his right of appeal and consequently his right to life. See also *Bello v Attorney General of Oyo State,* (1986) 12 SC.1 where the deceased right even though similarly construed was abrogated by his execution during the pendency of his appeal in the Court of Appeal. See also C. Okpaluba, Judicial Approach to Constitutional Interpretation in Nigeria, Enugu, Matt Madek & Co., 1992, pp. 263-264.

to as broad an interpretation as is possible under the African Charter. Furthermore it is curious that defence of property provides a justification for deprivation of life. And even though it is required that the use of force must be reasonably necessary in, the circumstances and to such extent as is permitted by law, it is the National Assembly which has power to pass such laws.[132]

Section 13 of the 1992 Republican Constitution of Ghana, which guarantees the right to life is in substance, the same as S.33 of the Nigerian Constitution. It may, however, given the provisions of S.33(5) lend itself to a wider interpretation S.33(5) of the 1992 constitution of the Republic of Ghana, provides that the rights, duties, declarations and guarantees relating to the fundamental human rights and freedoms specifically mentioned in this chapter shall not be regarded as excluding others not specifically mentioned which are considered to be inherent in a democracy and intended to secure the freedom and dignity of man". This is apart from the fact that the constitution as already indicated guarantees ECOSOC rights.

The Indian Case of Olga Tellis v. Bombay Municipal Corporation

(1986) AIR 180 SC, represents an instance of creative interpretation of the right to life. It concerned the eviction of slum dwellers who alleged deprivation of their right to life under Article 21 of the Indian Constitution.

---

[132] Even though S.318 of the 1999 constitution defines 'Law' to mean 'a law enacted by a House of Assembly' the word 'law' as used in s.33 would seem to refer to law made by the National Assembly and possibly the state House of Assembly. If the matter relates to the alteration of the constitution, or mutiny and the police powers. Competence resides only in the National Assembly of Art 11 (3) where the word 'laws' is used to describe enactment by the National Assembly.

Article 21 stipulates:

"Protection of life and personal liberty – no person shall be deprived of life and liberty except by procedure established by law".

The Supreme Court held *inter alia* that:

1.   The scope of Article 21 is wide and far-reaching, and includes, as an equally important facet, the right to livelihood because no person can live without the means of living.

2.   Other provisions of the Constitution, being Directive Principles of State Policy not enforceable in the courts, provide that the state shall direct its policies towards ensuring that citizens have the right to an adequate means of livelihood and employment.

3.   If there is an obligation upon the state to secure to citizens an adequate means of livelihood and the right to work, it would be sheer pedantry to exclude the right to livelihood from the content of the right to life. The state may not, by affirmative action, be compelled to provide adequate means or work to citizens. But any person, who is deprived of his right to livelihood except according to a just and fair procedure established by law, can challenge the deprivation as offending the right to life conferred by Article 21.[133]

The Supreme Court's decision in *Olga Tellis case* is very instructive and could provide some inspiration for interpreting constitutions such as those of Nigeria with similar structures.

The African Charter does not specifically deal with the issue as to whether death penalty is permissible or not. It may, however, be main-

---

[133] See *Judicial Colloquium in Bangalore. op cit,* p.225.

tained, given the rule of interpretation of treaties which tends to be hesitant, except where the intention to do so is clear, to restrict state sovereignty that no obligation to abolish death penalty is imposed. By way of contrast it is clear from a reading of the relevant provisions of the UN Covenant on Civil and Political Rights, that, the death penalty which is not proscribed and which does not require states parties to abolish it nevertheless requires that its use be restricted to the most serious crimes. It is possible that the relevant provisions of the African Charter (as well as other international instruments on the subject which prescribe humane and civil treatment) if read together with the provision guaranteeing human rights may import an interpretation restricting occasions on which death penalty could be imposed.

Article 4 of the American Convention on Human Rights which guarantees the right to life is instructive in many respects. It broaches but does not finally determine from what moment life begins by protecting that right" in general, from the moment of conception". The death penalty is not to be re-established in states that have abolished it" [Article 4(3)]. Capital punishment shall in no case be inflicted for political offences or related common crimes [Article 4(4)]. And capital punishment shall not be imposed upon persons who, at the time the crime was committed were under 18 years of age or over 70 years of age nor applied to pregnant women [Article 4(5)].[134] The American Convention shares[135]

---

[134] For controversy surrounding the desirability of the death penalty with respect to drug trafficking see C.O. Okonkwo "Death Penalty: Myth or Reality" who argues in favour of death penalty and A.A. Adeyemi "Death Penalty in Nigeria: Criminology Perspectives" Isabella Okagbue "The Death Penalty As An Effective Deterrent To Drug Abuse and Drug Trafficking" who argued against. All in Narcotics Law and Policy in Nigeria, eds, A. Kalu and Y. Osinbanjo, Lagos, Federal Ministry of Justice, Vol. 8, pp. 260-279, 280-314, 315-341.

[135] American Convention on Human Rights Article 4(1).

with the UN Covenant[136] the guarantee of the right of every condemned person to apply for amnesty, pardon or commutation of sentence.

5.4 Right to the Respect of the Dignity Inherent In a Human Being

Article 5 of the African Charter guarantees the right to the respect of the dignity inherent in a human being. Accordingly all forms of exploitation and degradation of man/woman particularly slavery, slave trade, torture, cruel, inhuman or degrading punishment and treatment are prohibited. The rational for this provision would seem to be that as special species there are certain treatment to which persons should not be subjected since such treatment would serve to reduce them to the status of sub-person. Apart from those listed, infliction of corporal punishment, obliging an alleged traffic offender, without due trial, to jump like a frog, and even the imposition of rulership either by force of arms or by subverting the electoral process by rigging elections or mindless annulment of election results, without due process, as was carried out by Babangida can be encompassed within the framework of inhuman and degrading treatment.

Human trafficking[137] has become increasingly of special concern as it directly confronts the right to the dignity of the human person it has taken new forms from the traditional slavery or slave trade, and embraces analogous practices and activities. Various jurisdictions offer different definitions of human trafficking. But the United Nations Protocol to Prevent, Suppress and Punish Trafficking in Persons especially Women and Children, supplementing the United Nations Convention against Transnational Organised Crime (2001) defines trafficking in person as:

- "the recruitment, transportation, transfer, harbouring or receipt of persons, by means of the threat or use of force or other forms of

---

[136] Article 6(5) of the Covenant on Civil and Political Rights.
[137] Article 4(6).

coercion, of abduction, of fraud, of deception, of the abuse of power or of a position of vulnerability or of the giving or receiving of payments or benefits to achieve the consent of a person having control over another person, for the purpose of exploitation. Exploitation shall include, at a minimum, the exploitation of the prostitution of others or other forms of sexual exploitation, forced labour or services, slavery or practices similar to slavery, servitude or the removal of organs

- The consent of a victim of trafficking in persons to the intended exploitation set forth in subparagraph (a) of this article shall be irrelevant where any of the means set forth in subparagraph (a) have been used;
- The recruitment, transportation, transfer, harbouring or receipt of a child for the purpose of exploitation shall be considered "trafficking in persons" even if this does not involve any of the means set forth in subparagraph (a) of this article;
- "Child" shall mean any person under eighteen years of age. [Article 3].

This definition is made clearer by identifying its key elements:

- the action of recruitment, transportation, transfer, harbouring, or receipt of persons;
- by means of the threat or use of force, coercion, abduction, fraud, deception, abuse of power or vulnerability, or giving payments or benefits to a person in control of the victim;
- for the purpose of exploitation, which includes exploiting the prostitution of others, sexual exploitation, forced labour, slavery or similar practices, and the removal of organs.(Protocol Art 3(a)

- Consent of the victim is irrelevant where illicit means are established but criminal law defenses are preserved. (Protocol Art. 3(b), Convention Art. 11(6))[138].

Article 3 of the Protocol against the Smuggling of Migrants by Land, Sea and Air supplementing the United Nations Convention against Transnational Organized Crime, stipulates that "smuggling of migrants" shall mean the procurement, in order to obtain, directly or indirectly a financial or other material benefits, of the illegal entry of a person into a State party of which the person is not a national or permanent resident".[139]

Smuggling comprises the following elements:

- procurement of illegal entry;
- for financial or other material gain;
- Across a border into another State

This differs from human trafficking. The difference between the two offences is that trafficking in persons is often smuggling *plus* coercion or deception at the beginning of the process and exploitation at the end. As the practical problem of differentiating the two has been amply put

"this means that it is often difficult to know whether a particular case falls under the definition of smuggling of migrants or trafficking in human beings. Consequently, in investigation and prosecution it is sometimes necessary to rely on measures against smuggling until the investigators or prosecutors discover the additional elements of trafficking. For this reason it is important that law enforcement personnel as well as judiciary who work in trafficking are familiar with both concepts. The provisions of the

---

[138] See United Nations, Training Manual, Projects of the Governments of Benin, Nigeria and Togo, United Nations Office on Drugs and Crime (undated), p.14.
[139] For the text of the Protocol see op cit. pp. 174-184.

two Protocols that concern border controls and travel documents are the same, which demonstrates that smuggling and trafficking in persons share some activities"[140]

While the Protocol deals only with trafficking across national boundaries, it does not preclude trafficking in humans within national boundaries as some national legislations provide (Trafficking in Persons (Prohibition) Law Enforcement and Administration Act, 2003, Federal Republic of Nigeria Official Gazette No. 89, Vol 90, 2003)[141] It is to be noted, however, that the Protocol requires states to criminalize trafficking in persons. It therefore reinforces the human rights regime under which individuals and groups have the right of petition, provides for compensation of victims of human trafficking, and may indeed be invoked against African countries parties to the African Charter before the Commission and the Court[142].

Zimbabwean case of *Ncube, Tshuma and Ndhlove V. The State*[143] *Supreme Court of Zimbabwe, Judgment, No Sc. 156/87* gives some insight into judicial attitude to inhuman and degrading treatment, with special reference to corporal punishment. The three appellants having been found guilty of rape were sentenced to *inter alia* whipping of six strokes each. The appeal by the appellants was allowed in respect of the part of the sentences ordering them to be whipped. The decision of the supreme court rested on the interpretation of s.15(1) of the Declaration of Rights of Zimbabwe which provides:

"No person shall be subject to torture or inhuman or degrading punishment or other such treatment". Gubbay, J.A. held that:

---

[140] op cit, p. 22.

[141] See Federal Republic of Nigeria Official Gazette, No. 89, Vol. 90, A411-427, Lagos, 6th October 2003.

[142] See Supra.

[143] Cited in *Judicial Colloquium in Bangalore, op. cit,* pp.229-230.

> "S.15 (1) is not confined to punishments which are "grossly dis-proportionate"; those which are inhuman or degrading in their disproportional to the seriousness of the offence, in that no one could possibly have thought that the particular offence would have attracted such a penalty – punishment being so excessive as to shock or outrage contemporary standards of decency"

Citing with approval the European Court's decision in

Tyrer v. United Kingdom, delivered on the 25th April 1978 [2EHHR.1.1] which was directly concerned with Article 3 of the European Convention of Human Rights- a provision worded virtually identically to section 15(1) of the constitution of Zimbabwe"

Gubbay also held that:

"The whipping which each appellant was ordered to receive breaches section 15(1) of the constitution of Zimbabwe as constituting a punishment which in its very nature is both inhuman and degrading"

The Court drew from international practice as well as placed reliance upon some adverse features which were inherent in the infliction of whipping:

- The manner in which it is administered
- By its very nature it treats members of the human race as non-humans
- It is a procedure easily subject to abuse
- It is degrading to both the punished and the punisher alike"

The practice in some African countries might not be supportive of this line of reasoning. In the family corporal punishment is seen as necessary for proper upbringing of the child. And in criminal matters, the law prescribes corporal punishment for certain offences. But with the adoption of special conventions on women and children it would seem that some foundation has been laid for a slow but sure movement away from this tradition.

In effect distinction can be made between punishments that are inherently inhuman and degrading and those which become so because they could not meet the proportionality test.

The African Commission has on several occasions ruled on various forms of inhuman and degrading treatment as well as torture. In petition 232/99 – John O. Ouko/Kenya – the Commission found that denying the complainant bathroom facilities throughout the period of his detention of 10 months violated Article 5. The Commission held, however, that the allegation of torture was not substantiated and therefore failed.[144] Increasingly great attention is being paid to torture as an inhuman, cruel and degrading treatment, particularly as law enforcement agents employ it to extort money or extract confession. A standard and authoritative definition of torture is to be found in the 1975 United Nations Declaration Against Torture:

> "For the purpose of this Declaration, torture means any act by which severe pain or suffering whether physical or mental, is intentionally inflicted by or at the instigation of a public official on a person for such purposes as obtaining from him or a third person information or confession, punishing him for an act he has committed or intimidating him or other persons. It does not include pain or suffering arising only from, inherent in or inci-

---

[144] 151/96 Civil Liberties Organisation/Nigeria-deprivation of the right to see ones family, and of light, insufficient food, lack of access to medical care constitute a violation of Article 5; 224/98 Media Rights Agenda/Nigeria the Commission upholding that the conditions of the detention of the complainant were inhuman, cited with approval Principles 1 and 6 For the Protection of All Persons under Any Form of Detention or Imprisonment, 225/98 Huri-Laws/Nigeria, 143/95, 150/ 96 Constitutional Rights Projects and Civil Liberties Organisation/Nigeria.

dental to lawful sanctions to the extent consistent with the standard minimum rules for the Treatment of prisoners".[145]

The UN Convention Against Torture adopted by the General Assembly on December, 10, 1984, adopts a similar but more elaborate definition than that of the 1975 Declaration.[146]

Article 1 of the Convention provides:

" For the purposes of this Convention, torture means any act by which severe pain or suffering, whether physical or mental, is intentionally inflicted on a person for such purposes as obtaining from him or a third person information or a confession, punishing him for an act he or a third person has committed or is suspected of having committed, or intimidating or coercing him or a third person, or for any reason based on discrimination of any kind when such pain or suffering is inflicted by or at the instigation of or with the consent or acquiescence of a public official or other person acting in an official capacity. It does not include pain or suffering arising only from, inherent in or incidental to lawful sanctions". The convention is concerned with the prevention and punishment of torture committed by government officials. Under the convention an order from a superior officer or a public authority may not be invoked as a justification of torture (Article 2(3)).[147] And no exceptional circumstance whatsoever, whether a

---

[145] A. J. Jongman "Torture Definition and Legal Instruments" In PIOOM – *The Politics of Pain Torturers and Their Masters* R.D. Crelinsten and A.P. Schmid eds (1993) Appendix R.P. 161; see also *The United Nations And Human Rights*, New York, 1984, pp.58-59.

[146] Jongman, *loc.cit.*

[147] *ibid.* For the text of the Convention against Torture and Other Cruel, Inhuman or Degrading Treatment or Punishment, 1984, see *Human Rights In International Law Collected Texts – 2nd Edition*, Strasbourg, Council of Europe Publishing 2000, pp.156-168.

state of war or a threat of war, internal political instability or any other public emergency may be invoked as a justification of torture (Article 2(2)). Equally important is the undertaking by States Parties to criminalize torture, attempt to commit torture, and an act by any person which constitutes complicity or participation in torture, in their domestic law. Such offences shall be punishable by appropriate penalties which take into account their grave nature (Article 4(1) and (2)).

There have in recent years, been adopted a number of codes or principles which seek to deal with torture by law enforcement officers and medical doctors. Article 5 of the code of conduct for law enforcement official adopted by the United Nations General Assembly on December 1979, states that no law enforcement officials may inflict; instigate treatment or punishment, nor may any law enforcement official invoke superior orders or exceptional circumstances such as war, or a threat of war, a threat to national security, internal political instability or any other public emergency as a justification for torture or other cruel, inhuman or degrading treatment or punishment".[148]

In 1975 the World Medical Association issued the guidelines for Medical Doctors concerning torture. The Tokyo Declaration forbade doctors to condone or participate in any acts related to torture or to other cruel, inhuman and degrading punishment. Again the Principles of Medical Ethics, adopted by the General Assembly on December 18, 1982, stipulates that it is a gross violation of medical ethics for health personnel to engage actively in, or attempt to commit torture on any grounds including public emergency.[149]

---

[148] Jongman, op.cit.

[149] *Ibid.*

It is realized that despite the progressive steps taken in the proscription of torture that effective enforcement is far from being realized as parties to the relevant conventions, declarations and codes have tended to perpetrate torture. These developments, which relate to attempts to ensure a more effective enforcement are however worth mentioning.

The meeting of lawyers and doctors from 23 countries in Norway in June 1990 recommended that a standing international Tribunal is expected, where a doctor is found guilty, to report the erring doctor to the national licensing body and medical association of its findings in order to carry out disciplinary action.[150]

In order to ensure compliance and prevent abuses a draft optional protocol to be adopted by the UN Convention obliges a state party to permit visits, as provided in the protocol, to any place within its jurisdiction where persons deprived of their liberty are held with a view to strengthening, if necessary, the protection of such persons from torture and from other cruel, inhuman or degrading treatment or punishment in accordance with international standards (Art.1). A sub-committee for the prevention of torture and other inhuman or Degrading treatment is to be established.

The committee's functions are essentially preventive. It is to carry out fact finding missions which may be the basis of the recommendations.

Since Article 5 of the African Charter does not expressly impose any limitations on the rights guaranteed therein and does not allow for dero-

---

[150] *ibid* See also the Vienna Declaration and Programme of Action on Human Rights, 1993, para, 55 where it is stated that one of the most atrocious violations against human dignity is the act of torture, the result of which destroys the dignity and impairs the capability of victims to continue their lives and their activities". For the text of the Vienna Declaration see Human Rights in International Law.Collected Texts – 2nd ed, op cit. pp. 199-226.

gations the African Commission, will be justified if in its interpretation of the Article, it adopts an expansive approach which encompasses the absolute nature of the protection against torture as well as other inhuman and degrading treatment. If this is accepted then national Legislation of parties to the African Charter would have to be modified to conform with this understanding of the import of Article 5.

Finally on inhuman and degrading treatment, it should be noted that the state of prisons and police cells in most, if not all African countries, fall far below the UN standards in terms of sanitation, availability of potable water, access to medical care, food, space etc. Efforts should be made to correct this situation since having been denied of their liberty (and are therefore not in a position to provide for themselves) the prisoners may not be justifiably denied of their rights which, just like freemen, they are entitled to. The inadequacies of prisons and police cells enumerated above can individually or collectively cause death - denial of the right to life, as well as violate other social rights viz, the right to health guaranteed under the Charter[151].

A number of cases decided by the African Commission on torture are not very illuminating 215/98 Rights International/Nigeria where the allegation that the complainant Mr. Wiwa was horse-whipped and subjected to various forms of torture was upheld by the Commission. The petition by the[152] Chairman of the Movement Burkinabe des Droits de

---

[151] Osita C. Eze. "The Police, Rule of Law and Human Right-public perspective" *Forthcoming in Policing Nigeria Project.*

[152] See also 225/98 Huri-Laws Nigeria Supra; in 205/97 Kazeem Aminu/Nigeria the allegation of torture did not succeed because it was not substantiated. See also 27/89, 46/91, 99/93 – conditions of detentions in which children, women and aged were held in Rwanda violated Article 5, 25/89, 47/90, 56/91, 100/93 (Joined) Free Legal Assistance Group, Lawyers Committee for Human Rights, Union InterAfricaine des Droits de l'Homme, Les Temoins de Jehovah/Zaire-found that the torture of 15 persons by a military unit violates Article 5.

l'Homme et des Peuples (MBDHP) an NGO provided occasions for the Commission to elaborate on the import of Article 5. It held:

"Article 5 of the Charter guarantees respect for the dignity inherent in the human person and the recognition of his legal status. This text further prohibits all forms of exploitation and degradation of man, particularly slavery, slave trade, torture, cruel, inhuman or degrading punishment and treatment. The guarantee of the physical integrity and security of the person is also enshrined in Article 6 of the African Charter, as well as in the Declaration on the Protection of all Persons against Forced Disappearances, adopted by the General Assembly of the United Nations in Resolution 47/133 of 18 December 1992, which stipulates in Article 1(2): "Any act leading to forced disappearance excludes the victim from the protection of the law and causes grave suffering to the victim and his family.

It constitutes a violation of the rules of international law, especially those that guarantee to all the right to the recognition of their legal status, the right to freedom and security of their person and the right not to be subjected to torture or any other inhuman or degrading punishment or treatment. It also violates the right to life or seriously imperils it". The disappearance of persons suspected or accused of plotting against the instituted authorities, including the arrests carried out by the presidential guard and subsequent disappearance in May 1990 of Mr. Guillame Sessouma and a medical student, Dabo Boukary, constitute a violation of the above-cited texts and principles. In this last case, the Commission notes the submission of a complaint on 16 October 2000".

5.5 The Right to Liberty and to the Security of His/Her Person

Article 6 of the African Charter guarantees the right to liberty and to the security of the individual. No one may be deprived of his freedom except for reasons and conditions previously laid down by law. And, in particular, no one may be arbitrarily arrested or detained.

The Commission has determined a number of cases on arbitrary deprivation of liberty particularly where due process was not followed.[153] The Commission has held elaborating on the substance of Article 6 that it guaranteed the 'physical integrity and security of the person (204/97 Movement Burkinabe de Droits des l'Homme et des Peuples/Burkina Faso).

Both the European and American conventions on human rights make similar provisions for the liberty and security of the individual. So do several of the commonwealth constitutions. In all these cases, rather than adopt a general provision permissive of limitations attempt is made to specify possible limitations to the right to liberty and security of the individual.

Article 5(1) of the European Convention provides: Everyone has the right to liberty and security of person. No one shall be deprived of his liberty save in the following cases and in accordance with a procedure prescribed by law:

---

[153] 232/99- John D Ouko/Kenya; 225/98 Huri-Laws/Nigeria 224/98 Media Rights Agenda/Nigeria, 213/98 Rights International/Nigeria, 64/92 Krishna Achathan (on behalf of Aleke Banda) Malawi in this petition the Commission held that "the massive and arbitrary arrests of office workers, trade unionists and Roman Catholic Bishops and students violated this Article. The arbitrary detention that Mr. Aleke Banda suffered is likewise a violation of Article 6"., 105/93 Alhassan Abubakar/Ghana; 39/90 Annette Pagnoulle (on behalf of Abdoulaye Mazou)/Cameroon- detention beyond the expiry of sentence, without judgement to extend it is a violation of Article 6.

1. the lawful detention of a person after conviction by a competent court

2. the lawful arrest or detention of a person for non-compliance with the lawful order of a court or in order to secure the fulfillment of any obligation prescribed by law.

3. the lawful arrest or detention of a person effected for the purpose of bringing him before the competent legal authority on reasonable suspicion of having committed an offence or fleeing after having done so;

4. the detention of a minor by lawful order for the purpose of educational supervision or his lawful detention for the purpose of bringing him before the competent legal authority;

5. the lawful detention of persons for the prevention of the spreading of infectious diseases, of persons of unsound mind, alcoholics or drug addicts or vagrants;

6. the lawful arrest or detention of a person to prevent his effecting an unauthorised entry into the country or of a person against whom action is being taken with a view to deportation or extradition.

An examination of the relevant provisions of the 1999 Constitution of Nigeria and the 1992 Constitution of Ghana will show that they contain similar provisions as those of the European Convention.[154]

Since the African Commission is not limited in this regard it stands to benefit and be influenced by both the provisions of the relevant conventions and constitutions as well as the appropriate judicial practice.[155]

---

[154] 1999, Constitution of Nigeria, S.35(1), 1992, Constitution of the Republic of Ghana, s.14(1). See 149/95, 149/96 Sir Dawda K. Jawara/Gambia, where the Commission held that the Economic Crimes (Special Offences) Decree of 25 November 1994, which was deemed to have come into force in July 1994, was a serious violation of the right.

[155] See *infra.*

Even though this aspect of the subject is to be discussed later, an insight into the Commission's position will be useful at this stage. In 224/98 Media Rights/Nigeria. The Commission, considering some aspects of fair hearing under Article 7 of the African Charter and the Commission's Resolution on the Right to Recourse Procedure and Fair Trial maintained that neither contains any express provision for the right to public trial. That not withstanding the Commission is empowered by Article 60 and 61 of the African Charter to draw inspiration from international conventions on human and peoples rights and to take into consideration as subsidiary measures other general or special international conventions, customs generally accepted as law, general principles of law recognized by African States as well as legal precedents and doctrines. Invoking these provisions the Commission called in aid of interpretation, General Comment 13 of the UN Human Rights Committee on the right to fair trial, which shall be discussed in the next subsection.

The provisions of Articles 60 and 61 are thus sufficiently elastic to support the kind of borrowing across jurisdictional lines that the Bangalore Principles envisage.[156]

The European Convention on Human Rights (Article 5(2); the UN Covenant on Civil and Political Rights, (Article 9) and the American Convention (Article 7) affirm rights which, by general state practice, are regarded as attaching to persons who have either been detained or arrested. Some of these rights such as the right to have his cause heard and which embrace the right to be tried within a reasonable time are to be found in Article 7 of the African Charter which deals with the right to fair hearing.

The kernel of these provisions to be found in other international conventions can be summarized as follows: That every one who is arrested should be informed promptly in a language which he/she understands of

---

[156] See *infra*. See in particular Article 7(1)(a).

reasons for his/her arrest and of any charge against him/her; that a detained or arrested person should be brought promptly before a judge or other officer authorized by law to exercise judicial power and shall be entitled to trial within a reasonable time or to release which may be conditioned by guarantees to appear for trial; that detained or arrested person shall be entitled to take proceedings by which the lawfulness of this detention or arrest shall be decided speedily by a court and his/her release ordered if the detention or the arrest is not lawful, that every one who has been a victim of arrest or detention in contravention of the law shall have an enforceable right to compensation.

5.6 Right to Fair Hearing

Article 7 of the African Charter which deals with fair hearing seems rather narrow in its formulation. Yet as an important guarantee of the right to enforce rights and duties, care should have been taken to ensure that it embraces the critical elements of fair hearing which have formed part of general state practice and where circumstances require more.

Article 7 provides that: Every individual shall have the rights to have his cause heard a right which comprises:

1. the right to an appeal to competent national organs against acts violating his fundamental rights as recognized and guaranteed by conventions, laws, regulations, and customs in force;

2. the right to be presumed innocent until proved guilty by a competent court or tribunal;

3. the right to defence, including the right to be defended by counsel of his choice;

4. the right to be tried within a reasonable time by an impartial court or tribunal.

The Commission, seized the opportunity of the Media Rights Agenda/Nigeria (224/98) to elaborate on this very important right indicating as well how far it is prepared to go to extend the amplitude of its competence to reach out for 'sources of inspiration' as guaranteed under the Charter. For this reason we set out the facts of the case as well as the finding on merits because we believe it may have significance for the Commission and Courts attitude to the substance of the rights guaranteed despite the economy of words employed to render them (i.e provision of the Charter) and the apparent, but not really open ended 'claw back clauses' that qualify many of the rights.

A Summary of Facts of the Case:

1. The communication, which was sent through e-mail, is dated 25 May 1998 and was received at the Secretariat on 26 May 1998.

2. The complaint is filed by Media Rights Agenda, a Nigerian Human Rights NGO based in Lagos, on behalf of Niran Malaolu, Editor of an independent Nigerian daily newspaper, "The Diet".

3. The author complains that Mr. Niran Malaolu was arrested together with three other staff of the newspaper by armed soldiers at the editorial offices of the "Diet" Newspaper in Lagos on 28 December 1997.

4. Neither Niran Malaolu nor his three colleagues were informed of the reasons for their arrest or shown a warrant of arrest.

5. The three colleagues who were arrested along with Malaolu were later released.

6. Niran Malaolu continued to be held without charges until 14 February 1998 when he was arraigned before a Special Military Tribunal for his alleged involvement in a coup. Throughout the period of his incarceration, Niran Malaolu was not allowed access to his lawyer, doctor or family members.

7. On 28 April 1998, after a secret trial, Niran Malaolu was found guilty by the tribunal of the charge of concealment of treason and sentenced to life imprisonment.

8. The complainant further alleges that Niran Malaolu's alleged involvement in the coup is connected with news stories published by his newspaper on the coup plot involving the then Chief of General Staff, Lt. General Oladipo Diya, as well as other military officers and civilians who have also been convicted by the tribunal and given sentences ranging from prison terms to death by firing squad.

9. One of such stories was an article entitled "The Military Rumbles Again", which was published in the "Sunday Diet" of 28 December 1997, based upon the announcement by the military government of the alleged coup plot it claims to have uncovered.

10. Further, the complainant alleges that Niran Malaolu was denied the right to be defended by lawyers of his choice, and, instead, assigned a military lawyer by the tribunal in contravention of the right to fair hearing.

11. The Special Military Tribunal that tried Niran Malaolu was neither competent, independent nor impartial in that members of the tribunal were hand-picked by the Head of State, General Sani Abacha, and the Provisional Ruling Council (PRC) against whom the alleged offence was committed. Besides, the President of the Tribunal, Major-General Victor Malu is also a member of the PRC, which is empowered by the Treason and Other Offences (Special Military Tribunal) Decree No.1 of 1986, to confirm the death sentences passed by the tribunal. These are alleged to be in violation of the rules of natural justice and, in particular, Article 7(1) (b) of the Charter.

12. The arraignment and trial of Niran Malaolu, a civilian before the Special Military Tribunal using special procedures is a breach of Principle 5 of the United Nations Principles on the Independence of the Judiciary and Article 7 of the Charter.

13. The complainant alleges further that under the provisions of the Treason and Other Offences (Special Military Tribunal) Decree No.1 of 1986, which established the tribunal that tried and convicted the accused, the right of appeal to a higher judicial authority is completely extinguished and those convicted may only appeal to the PRC, the composition and interests of which are indicated in paragraph (k) above.

14. The Author also contends that the trial of Niran Malaolu in camera was a violation of recognized international human rights standards, to wit: the right to a fair and public hearing.

15. Finally, that the arrest, detention, arraignment, trial, conviction and sentence of Malaolu was in breach of the norms of fair trial guaranteed in the Charter.

Complaint

The Author alleges that the following Articles of the African Charter on Human and Peoples Rights have been violated: Articles 6, 7, 9 and 26. For the above reasons, and also for the fact that, as alleged, there were no avenues for exhausting local remedies, the Commission declared the communication admissible.

Merits

1. The complainant alleges that the arrest and subsequent detention of Malaolu was arbitrary as he was neither shown any warrant of arrest nor informed of the offences for which he was arrested. Further, that Malaolu was arrested by armed soldiers from the Directorate of Military Intelligence at his office, on 28 December 1997, and detained incommunicado at a military fa-

cility in Lagos until he was moved to Jos, where his trial took place.

2. This, it is contended, is in contravention of Article 6 of the African Charter on Human and Peoples' Rights. The said article provides *inter alia:* Every individual shall have the right to liberty and to the security of his person. No one may be deprived of his freedom except for the reasons and conditions previously laid down by law. In particular, no one may be arbitrarily arrested and detained.

3. Further to this, the complainant alleges that until 14 February 1998 (that is, about two months after his arrest) when he was arraigned before a Special Military Tribunal for his alleged involvement in a coup, Mr. Malaolu was neither informed of the reasons of his arrest nor of any charges against him.

4. In its Resolution on the Right to Recourse Procedure and Fair Trial, the Commission had, in expounding on the guarantees of the right to fair trial under the Charter observed thus: the right to fair trial includes, among other things, the following: Persons who are arrested shall be informed at the time of arrest, in a language which they understand of the reason for their arrest and shall be informed promptly of any charges against them;

5. The failure and/or negligence of the security agents who arrested the convicted person to comply with these requirements is therefore a violation of the right to fair trial as guaranteed under Article 7 of the Charter.

6. The complainant alleges a violation of Article 7(1) (a) of the African Charter on Human and Peoples' Rights which states: Every individual shall have the right to have his case heard. This comprises; The right to an appeal to complement national organs against acts violating his fundamental rights as recog-

nized and guaranteed by conventions, laws, regulations and customs in force;

7. The complainant contends that the decision of the tribunal that tried and convicted Malaolu is not subject to appeal, but to confirmation by the Provisional Ruling Council, the composition of which is clearly partisan. Non-compliance of the competent authorities of Nigeria to this requirement is in breach of the provision of Article 7(1)(a) of the Charter.

8. The complainant alleges a violation of 7(1)(b) of the Charter which provides that: Every individual shall have ... the right to be presumed innocent until proven guilty by a competent court or tribunal; The complainant alleges in this respect that prior to the setting up of the tribunal, the military Government of Nigeria organized intense pre-trial publicity to persuade members of the public that a coup plot had occurred and that those arrested in connection with it were guilty of treason. In this regard, it alleges further, any possible claim to national security in excluding members of the public and the press from the actual trial by the tribunal cannot be justified, and therefore in breach of the right to fair trial, particularly, the right to presumption of innocence.

9. The government has not contested the veracity of the complainant's submissions. In this circumstance, the Commission is obliged to accept this as the facts of the case and therefore finds the Government of Nigeria in violation of Article 7(1) (b) of the Charter.

10. The complainant alleges that the exclusion of members of the public and the press from the actual trial by the tribunal was not justified, and therefore in breach of the right to fair trial.

11. The government argues that the right to fair hearing in public was subject to the proviso that the court or tribunal might ex-

clude from the proceedings persons other than the parties thereto in the interest of defence, public safety, public order, etc.

12. Neither the African Charter nor the Commission's Resolution on the Right to Recourse Procedure and Fair Trial contain any express provision for the right to public trial. That notwithstanding, the Commission is empowered by Articles 60 and 61 of the Charter to draw inspiration from international law on human and peoples' rights and to take into consideration as subsidiary measures other general or special international conventions, customs generally accepted as law, general principles of law recognized by African states as well as legal precedents and doctrine. Invoking these provisions, the Commission calls in aid General Comment 13 of the UN Human Rights Committee on the right to fair trial Paragraph 6 of the said Comment states:The publicity of hearings is an important safeguard in the interest of the individual and of society at large. At the same time Article 14, paragraph 1, acknowledges that courts have the power to exclude all or part of the public for reasons spelt out in that paragraph. It should be noted that, apart from such exceptional circumstances, the Committee considers that a hearing must be open to the public in general, including members of the press, and must not, for instance, be limited only to a particular category of persons...; The exceptional circumstances under the International Covenant on Civil and Political Rights (which the above Committee monitors), are for reasons of morals, public order or national security in a democratic society, or when the interest of the private lives of the parties so requires, or to the extent strictly necessary in the opinion of the court in special circumstances where publicity would prejudice the interests of justice. The Commission notes that these cir-

cumstances are exhaustive, as indicated by the use of the phrase "apart from such exceptional circumstances".

13. The government has only presented an omnibus statement in its defence to the effect that the right to fair hearing in public was subject to the proviso that the court or tribunal might exclude from the proceedings persons other than the parties thereto in the interest of defence, public safety, public order, etc. It has not specifically indicated which of these circumstances prompted it to exclude the public from such trial. The Commission therefore considers the argument not sufficient enough to avail the Government of Nigeria such defence.

14. Considering the fact that as alleged by the complainant, prior to the setting up of the tribunal, the government had organized intense pre-trial publicity to persuade members of the public of occurrence of a coup and the involvement of those arrested in connection with it, the Commission is constrained to find the exclusion of the same public in the actual trial unjustified and in violation of the victim's right to fair trial guaranteed under Article 7 of the Charter.

15. It is alleged that prior to his arraignment, precisely, for the 49 days he was detained, Mr. Malaolu was not allowed access to his lawyer, neither was he given the opportunity to be represented and defended by a lawyer of his own choice at the trial. Rather, he was assigned a military lawyer by the tribunal. The complainant submits that by refusing Mr. Malaolu access to his lawyer, the Government of Nigeria was in contravention of Article 7(1)(c) of the Charter which provides:Every individual shall have the right to defence, including the right to be defended by counsel of his choice.

16. In its resolution on the Right to Recourse and Fair Trial, the Commission in re-enforcing this guarantee observed in para-

graph 2(e)(i) thus: In the determination of charges against individuals, the individual shall be entitled in particular to; communicate in confidence with counsel of their choice; The denial of this right therefore is a violation of these basic guarantees.

17. The complainant alleged that the Special Military Tribunal which tried the convicted person was neither competent, independent nor impartial because members of the tribunal were selected by the Head of State, General Sani Abacha, and the Provisional Ruling Council (PRC), against whom the alleged offence was committed. Some members of the Tribunal are also serving army officers. For instance, the President of the Tribunal, Major-General Victor Malu is also a member of the Provisional Ruling Council, which is empowered by the Treason and Other Offences (Special Military Tribunal) Decree No. 1 of 1986, to confirm the sentences passed by the Tribunal. This is a breach of the right to a fair trial as stipulated in Article 7(1)(d) of the Charter, which states: Every individual shall have ... the right to be tried... by an impartial court or tribunal.

18. The government has not refuted this specific claim. It only states that the Treason and Other Offences (Special Military Tribunal) Act, Cap 444 of the Laws of the Federation of Nigeria, 1990 under which Malaolu was tried arose from the ashes of the Treason and Other Offences (Special Military Tribunal) Decree No. 1 of 1986 enacted by the then military government headed by General Ibrahim Babangida (Rtd.). Further, it asserts that its submission would not address the merits or demerits of the trial.

19. The Commission is not taking an issue with the history and origin of the laws nor the intention why they were promulgated. What is of concern here to the Commission is whether the said trial conforms to the fair hearing standards under the Charter.

The Commission is of the opinion that to answer this question, it must necessarily consider the merits or demerits of the trial, an issue the government does not want to be involved in.

20. Consequently, the Commission finds the selection of serving military officers, with little or no knowledge of law as members of the tribunal in contravention of Principle 10 of the Basic Principles on he Independence of Judges. The said principles states: Persons selected for judicial office shall be individuals of integrity and ability with appropriate training or qualifications in law.

21. In the same vein, the Commission considers the arraignment, trial and conviction of Malaolu, a civilian, by a Special Military Tribunal, presided over by serving military officers, who are still subject to military commands, without more, prejudicial to the basic principles of fair hearing guaranteed by Article 7 of the Charter.

22. It is fitting, in this regard, to cite the Commission's general position on the issue of trials of civilians by military tribunals. In its Resolution on the Right to Fair Trial and Legal Assistance in Africa, the Commission had, while adopting the Dakar Declaration and Recommendations noted thus: In may African countries military courts and special tribunals exist alongside regular judicial institutions. The purpose of military courts is to determine offences of a pure military nature committed by military personnel. While exercising this function, military courts are required to respect fair trial standards. They should not, in any circumstances whatsoever, have jurisdiction over civilians. Similarly, special tribunals should not try offences that fall within the jurisdiction of regular courts.

23. The Commission considers the said trial, which has not been refuted by the respondent state, save to the extent that it was

done under a law validly enacted by the competent authority at the time, in contravention of the right to fair trial guaranteed under Article 7 of the Charter. The Commission also finds the setting up of the said tribunal for the trial of treason and other related offences as impinging on the independence of the judiciary, in as much as such offences are being recognized in Nigeria as falling within the jurisdiction of the regular courts.

24. The Commission also finds the trial in contravention of the basic principles of fair hearing contained in Principle 5 of the United Nations Basic Principles on the Independence of the Judiciary (The UN Basic Principles) and Article 7(1) (d) of the African Charter. Principle 5 of the UN Basic Principles states: Everyone shall have the right to be tried by the ordinary courts or tribunals using established procedures. Tribunals that do not use the duly established legal procedures of the legal process shall not be created to displace the jurisdiction belonging to the ordinary courts or judicial tribunals.

25. Furthermore, in its General Comment on a similar provision of Article 14 of the International Covenant on Civil and Political Rights, the Human Rights Committee observed: The Provisions of Article 14 apply to all courts and tribunals within the scope of that article whether ordinary or specialized. The Committee notes the existence, in many countries of military or special courts which try civilians. This could present serious problems as far as the equitable, impartial and independent administration of justice is concerned... While the Covenant does not prohibit such categories of court, nevertheless the conditions which it lays down clearly indicate that trying of civilians by such courts should be very exceptional and take place under conditions which genuinely afford the full guarantees stipulated

in Article 14. (See also its Comment on the Report of Egypt –
UN Doc. CCPR/79/Add.. 3, paragraph a of August 1993)

26. It could not be said that the trial and conviction of Malaolu by a
special military tribunal presided over by a serving military officer, who is also a member of the PRC, a body empowered to
confirm the sentence, took place under conditions which genuinely afforded the full guarantees of fair hearing as provided for
in Article 7 of the Charter. This is also in contravention of Article 26 of the Charter which states: States parties to the Charter
shall have the duty to guarantee the independence of the courts
and shall allow the establishment and improvement of appropriate national institutions entrusted with the promotion and
protection of the rights and freedoms guaranteed by the present
Charter".

The rule against retroactive penal legislation is to be found in Article
7(2). Retroactivity is proscribed both with respect to offences for which
a person may be found guilty as well as penalties to be imposed. In
addition to the rights guaranteed under Article 7 of the African Charter,
the UN Covenant on Civil and Political Rights [Article 14 (3)] which is
more comprehensive and more in tune with general state practice, apart
from requiring that trial shall be in public stipulates that in the determination of any criminal charge against him, every one shall be entitled to
the following minimum guarantees, in full equality;

1. To be informed promptly and in detail in a language which
   he understands of the nature and cause of the charge
   against him

2. To have adequate time and facilities for the preparation of
   his defence and to communicate with counsel of his own
   choosing.

3. To be tried without undue delay;

4.   To be tried in his presence and to defend himself in person or through legal assistance of his own choosing, to be informed, if he does not have legal assistance of this right; and to have legal assistance assigned to him, in any case where the interest of justice so require, and without payment by him in any such case if he does not have sufficient means to pay for it;

5.   To examine or have examined the witnesses against him and to obtain the attendance and examination of witnesses on his behalf under the same conditions as witnesses against him

6.   To have free assistance of an interpreter if he cannot understand or speak the language used in court;

7.   Not to be compelled to testify against himself or to confess guilt;

Another provision of the Covenant relevant to the rights to fair hearing is the right to compensation by a person whose conviction has resulted in a miscarriage of justice as well as the affirmation of the rule against double jeopardy [Article 14 (6) and (7)].

Article 14(5) of the Covenant guarantees the right of everyone convicted of a crime to have his conviction reviewed by a higher tribunal according to law. For the trial of juvenile persons, the procedure adopted "shall be such as will take account of their age and the possibility of promoting their rehabilitation" [Article 14(4)].

The UN Committee has taken the following positions:[157] that all the guarantees apply not only where normal courts exercise jurisdiction, but also where special courts, like military courts or tribunal, have jurisdiction; that there have been violations of Article 14(1) where a trial took place in *camera* or in the absence of the accused or else where judgment

---

[157] See Lallah *op cit,* pp. 17-18.

was not made public: *Altesor Vs. Uruguay (10/77), Cuba Vs. Uruguay (70/80)*; that the right to a review of a conviction or sentence as stipulated in Article 14(5) does not leave the existence of the right to review to be regulated by domestic law, but rather the modalities of the review: *Salgar de Montego Vs. Colombia (70/80);* that there were violations where, as a consequence of the conditions for his detention the accused did not have access to legal assistance or did not have adequate time or facilities to prepare his defence [Article 14(3) (b)]: *Wight vs Madagascar(115.82);* and that the right under Article 14(3) (c) the right to be tried without undue delay – should be applied in conjunction with the right of reviewal by a higher tribunal under Article 14(5); *Pinkney Vs Canada (27/78).* In Pinkney's case, the Committee found that the appellant's right of appeal had been prejudiced because the transcripts of the lower court's proceedings had taken two and half years to be produced.[158]

The Australian case of *Jogo V. Judges of the District Court of New South Wales and others,*[159] further elaborates this point. Here the court of appeal citing Article 14(3) of the Covenant as "a (more) relevant guide to the statement of the common law on the right to speedy trials stated that the right to speedy trials was an attribute of the indisputable right to a fair trial and required a consideration of wide range of factors". This implies, of course, that each case will be decided on its own facts and merit. And in Jogo's case the court held that the delay in prosecuting the accused was extremely long and largely unexplained, there was insufficient prejudice to the accused in (the) case and the trial should proceed. The Court of Appeal in effect upheld the District Court's judgment,

---

[158] *Ibid.*

[159] (Appeal No. 259 of 1987) 10, May 1988 cited in Judicial Colloquium in Bangalore, *op.cit.*, Annex IX, p.221.

refusing the application of the Accused for a permanent stay of criminal proceedings".[160]

Bhagwati, J. citing with approval, the dynamic interpretation placed on Article 21(the right to speedy trial of the Indian Constitution) in the case of *Maneka Ghandi V. Union of India,*[161] brought some deeper insight into the legal significance of the right to speedy trial; speedy trial is of the essence of criminal justice and there can be no doubt that delay in trial by itself constitutes denial of justice, everyone arrested or detained shall be entitled to a trial within a reasonable time or to release pending trial. No procedure which does not ensure a reasonably quick trial can be regarded as "reasonable 'fair' or 'just', the state has a constitutional obligation to devise a procedure which would ensure speedy trial for the accused, and the Supreme Court has also the obligation as the guardian of fundamental rights of the people, to enforce fundamental rights of the accused by issuing the necessary directions to the state which may include positive action: *Hussainara Khartoon v. Home Secretary, State of Bihar (1979) air, 1369 s.c.*[162]

These instances from other jurisdictions, offer the African Commission, given its understanding of its mandate under Article 60 and 61 of the African Charter, the material with which to creatively build the jurisprudence that will guide the interpretation of the Charter rights and duties. Now that the African Court is in place, it is expected that it will give its imprimatur to this expansive approach to the mandate of interpreting them.

---

[160] *Ibid.*
[161] *Ibid* 224.
[162] *Ibid.*

5.7 Freedom of Conscience, the Profession and Religion

Article 8 of the African Charter guarantees the freedom of conscience, the profession and the free practice of religion. The enjoyment of these freedoms is only subject to constraints imposed by law and order.

Freedom of conscience may be defined in general terms as freedom to assert deeply held moral, ethical or religious beliefs the denial of which gives persons who hold such beliefs no rest or peace. (*Welsh v. United States* 398 US 344 (1970). The case involved conscientious objectors to being part of the instrument of war. It was the decision of the court interpreting the draft law, that it barred exemption based on essentially political, sociological or philosophical views or merely personal moral code.[163]

In a case involving the Jehovah's Witnesses of Zaire the Commission held that their persecution, including arbitrary arrests, appropriation of church property and exclusion from access to education violated the right to the freedom of conscience (56/91, Les Temoins de Jehovah/Zaire).

Freedom of religion, which is narrower than freedom of conscience, can be defined as the right of everyone to profess and practice the religion of his choice and to respect the right of others to do the same and in accordance with the law. Attempting to explain the meaning of Religion Abraham stated:

> "Each individual does, of course, posses the basic right, now one is universally guaranteed and protected under our constitution to believe what he chooses to worship, whom he pleases and how he pleases, always provided that he does not impermissibly

---

[163] H. Chand Fundamental Human Rights in Nigeria, Jos, Unico Press, 1980, p.33.

interfere with the rights of others. Hence… those who believe in nothing, those who believe but doubt, those who believe without questioning, those who worship the Judae-Christian God in innumerably different ways, those who adhere to Mohammed's creed, those who worship themselves, those who worship a cow or other animals, those who worship several Gods – to mention a few of the remarkable variety of expressions of belief that obtain.[164]

As with many other rights guaranteed by the African Charter and elsewhere, the freedom of religion is not absolute. In the words of the Charter, "no one may, subject to law and order, be submitted to measures of constraint restricting the exercise of these freedom(s)". The Commission had to decide on the issue of constraint in the case of allegation of religious persecution against the Sudan and it held that "…the unequal food distribution in prisons subjecting Christian prisoners to blackmail in order to obtain food – attacks on individual's on account of their religious persuasion [which] considerably restrict their ability to practice freely the religion to which they subscribe amounted to violation of Article 8 especially since the government provided no evidence or justification that would mitigate this conclusion".[165]

Thus the law may not permit the practices of religion where the ideas it propagates present a clear and present danger to the public peace and order. In *Cantwell v. Connecticut*[166] even though the court on the facts of the case held that there was no danger to public peace, it also held

---

[164] cited in H. Chand *op. cit,* pp. 32-33.

[165] See also 48/90 Amnesty International/Sudan, 50/91 Lawyers Committee for Human Rights/Sudan, 89/93 Association of Members of Episcopal Conference of East Africa/Sudan.

[166] 310 U.S. 296 (1940).

that had there been such a threat, public peace will take priority over the freedom of religion. In *Mc Gowan V. Maryland.*[167] The court distinguished between religious belief and religious act. While one would believe whatever one pleases ones religious acts are to be regulated by law in the interest of society and other dominant interests. Accordingly the Supreme Court rejected the argument by Jews, who observed Saturdays as the religious days that they suffered in their business as they had to close their shops on Saturdays because of their religion and on Sundays because of Sunday closing law.

In the Nigerian case of *Ojiegbe and or v. Ubani and or*[168] the appellants main bone of contention and ground of appeal was that the date fixed for election (Saturday) violated their freedom of religion as members of the Seventh Day Adventists since the ethics of their religion forbade them to do anything or any manner of work on a Saturday. The appellant avowed that they have abstained from voting on that day for fear of being excommunicated. Their earlier request to the Governor General to change the date to Friday had been rejected. The appellant's application contending that holding the election on Saturday infringed on their freedom of religion since they were restrained from voting for fear of being excommunicated failed.

It would appear from Ojiegbe's case that there was a conflict between the right, not duty, to vote and the freedom of religion. Perhaps if the conflict was between the duty to vote and the freedom of religion the court might have come to a different decision!

Several cases decided by the US courts give some insight into possible limitations to the freedoms guaranteed under Article 8 of the African Charter. On the facts of the case it was found that, a member of the Seventh Day Adventist, who had worked five days a week, and who

---

[167] 366 U.S. (1961).
[168] (1961) All N.L.R. 277.

having lost her job because the employer adopted a six day working week which would have involved working on Saturdays, contrary to her religious belief, did not have her right violated and could not claim unemployment benefit, because she left her job without a just cause, *Shebert v. Verner.*[169]

In *Torcaso v. Watkins*[170], the Supreme Court held that the state law requiring an applicant for appointment as a notary public to take an oath declaring his belief in the existence of God as part of his oath of office was violative of the freedom of religion.

Freedom of religion may also be violated by the adoption of state religion, by obliging pupils to follow a course of religious instructions in schools (whether public or private). But it may not be violated where children are required to salute the national flag despite their religious belief (Jehovah's Witness) to the contrary.

Many African countries have problems complying with the imperative of the freedom of religion. In some of them access to public office may even be influenced by the religion of the dominant social group. Statements by fundamentalists have been known to create tension and even civil strife. Yet few of those who refuse to see that others have the same right to believe in what they like and practice where they want insist that they alone possess this right. This is contrary to the clear guarantee against discrimination and of equality of all before the law and equal protection of the law.

S.10 of the 1999 Republican Constitution of Nigeria which prohibits the adoption by the federation or a state, of a religion, is supplemented by S.38 which guarantees the right to freedom of thought, conscience and religion. It would seem that conflicts might arise for African states

---

[169] 374 U.S. 398 (1963).

[170] 367 U.S. 488, See also H. Chand *op. cit.*, p.34.

which have adopted state religions with respect to their obligations under the African Charter, since even if other believers are allowed to practice their religion, the incidental preference given to the state religion might contradict the non-discrimination provision of the African Charter.[171]

5.8 Freedom of Expression

Article 9 of the African Charter simply provides:

1. Every individual shall have the right to receive information.
2. Every individual shall have the right to express and disseminate his opinions within the law;

The freedom of expression is a pillar of any free society. It includes where no express provision is made for it, press freedom. Its operative components are the freedom:

1. to hold opinions
2. to receive ideas and information
3. and to impart ideas and information

The freedom to hold ideas can only be manifested when it is communicated either orally through the media or other forms. It is, therefore, inseparable from the freedom of expression as such.[172]

The manner in which the freedom of expression is formulated, in both national constitutions and international human rights conventions, invariably admits of qualifications which imply that the exercise has corollary responsibilities and duties. thus in the words of Article 10(2)

---

[171] See *infra* for reservations.

[172] Osita C. Eze "Constitutional Protection and Legal Limits in Conflict Reporting" vol.1 (1992) I, PCC LJ, p.1.

of the European Convention on Human Rights, which encapsulates these qualifications:

> "The exercise of these freedoms, since it carries with it duties and responsibilities, may be subject to such formalities, conditions, restrictions or penalties as are prescribed by law and are necessary in a democratic society in the interests of national security, territorial integrity or public safety, for the prevention of disorder or crime, for the protection of health or morals, for the protection of the reputation or rights of others, for the disclosure of information received in confidence or for maintaining the authority and impartiality of the judiciary"[173]

The formulation represents the essence of possible limitations to the freedom of expression as adopted in many national constitutions, as well as in international human rights instruments. Furthermore it is generally accepted that the exercise of these freedoms should be without interference by public authority and regardless of frontiers.

The impact of the universalisation of the freedom of expression and judicial attitude to it will be discussed subsequently.[174]

National

Even though the law on the freedom of expression varies in many countries of the sub-region, there seems to be similarity between countries of members of the commonwealth in the West African sub-region on the one hand and those of the Francophone experience on the other hand. The former tend to embody justiceable human rights in their constitutions while the latter generally adopt the French practice of merely referring to adherence to the Declaration of Right of Man and Citizen

---

[173] For the text of the Convention see *Judicial Colloquium in Bangalore, op. cit,* Annex IV.

[174] See *infra.*

1789 and Universal Declaration of Human Rights in their preambles. It may be pointed out, however, that the Constitution of Senegal of 1960 revised in 1963 and amended in 1976 in its Article 8 guarantees everyone the right to freedom of expression and opinion, "subject to limitations imposed by laws and regulations".[175]

The Criminal Code imposes heavy penalties on the infringement of press laws such as by the publication, dissemination or reproduction or any such attempt by any means of "inaccurate reports".[176]

Article 49 of Act 79-44 of 1979 requires journalists to handle information objectively and impartially. Articles 50 proscribes "defamation, accusation made without established proof, falsification of documents, distortion of facts, deliberate inaccuracies and the use of any kind of deception in order to extort information or undermine anyone's good faith".[177] As will be demonstrated later, even when the constitution admits of limitation "by law" it is not all laws that are held to comply with the intendment of the constitution otherwise the very freedom guaranteed may be rendered illusory.

While the Constitution to Togo guarantees 'the rights and freedoms of the human person, the family and local communities as well as political, philosophic and religious freedoms'[178] there is no express mention of freedom of expression and opinion.

It may be argued, however, that to the extent that this rather general constitutional provision can be regarded as guaranteeing universally accepted human rights and freedoms the right to the freedom of expression is embraced by it.

---

[175] *Information, Freedom and Censorship World Report Article 19*, London, Library Association Publishing Ltd., 1991.
[176] *ibid* see article 255 of the Criminal Code.
[177] *ibid*
[178] *ibid*

The 1979 Constitution of Nigeria makes provisions for the freedom of expression without specific mention of the press even though press freedom is understood to be covered by it.

S.39 of the 1999 Constitution provides that:

1. Every person shall be entitled to freedom of expression including freedom to hold opinions and to receive and impart ideas and information without interference.

2. Without prejudice to the generality of subsection (1) of this section, every person shall be entitled to own, establish and operate any medium for the dissemination of information, ideas and opinions: Provided that no person, other than the Government of the Federation or of a State or any other person or body authorized by the President, shall own, establish or operate a television or wireless broadcasting station for any purpose whatsoever;

3. Nothing in this section shall invalidate any law that is reasonably justifiable in a democratic society:-For the purpose of preventing the disclosure of information received in confidence, maintaining the authority and independence of courts, or regulating telephony, wireless broadcasting, television or the exhibition of cinematograph films: or Imposing restrictions upon persons holding office under the Government of the Federation or of a State, members of the Armed Forces of the Federation or members of the Nigeria Police Force.

Further restrictions are imposed by laws, reasonably justifiable in a democratic society in the interest of defence, public safety, public order, public morality or public health or for the purpose of protecting the rights of others. (S.45(1) 1999 Constitution)[179]. It is for the courts to ensure that the laws made under these provisions do not go beyond the limits imposed by the constitution. In general both national (including Nigerian Courts) and international courts and tribunals have tended to adopt interpretations which are restrictive of limitations to human rights provisions.

Lester has pointed that "the European Court of Human Rights" has made it clear that, "in applying Article 10, it is faced not with a choice of conflicting principles (one of which is the freedom of expression), but with a principle of freedom of expression that is subject to a number of exceptions which must be narrowly construed" *(Sunday Times Case)[180]*. In the same vein the Supreme Court of India, per Pantanjali Sastri, J stated that:

> "Very narrow and stringent limits have been set to permissible legislative abridgement of the right of freedom of speech and expression, and this was doubtless due to the realization that freedom of speech and of the press lay at the foundation of all democratic organisations, for without free political discussion no public education, so essential for the proper functioning of the process of popular government is possible"[181]

---

[179] See Osita C. Eze "The Quest For Communication Freedom and Consequences For National Development" *Philosophy and Dimensions of National Communications Policy,* Vol. 1 eds. T Nnaemeka and E. Uvieghare, and Didi Uyo, Lagos, Centre for African Arts and Civilization 1989, pp. 361-371.

[180] Judgement of 26 April, 1979, Series A, No 30 2E NRA 245 at para 45 cited in Lester *Judicial Colloquium in Bangalore op. cit*, p. 37.

[181] A Lester "Freedom of Expression Relevant International Principles" *Judicial Colloquium in Bangalore, op cit.* p. 28.

The Nigerian courts have also adopted an expansive approach of constitutional interpretation in favour of protection of individual rights and liberties.[182]

International

The forerunner in the array of international instruments which specifically addressed the issue of freedom of expression is the Universal Declaration of Human Rights of 1948, which, even though not legally binding, attempted to give substance to the Charter provisions on respect for fundamental human rights and has influenced many national human rights provisions and international human rights instruments.

Article 19 of the Declaration stipulates that:

> "Everyone has the right to freedom of opinion and expression; this right includes freedom to hold opinions without interference and to seek, receive and impart information and ideas through any media regardless of frontiers"[183]

Article 19 of the International Covenant on Civil and Political Rights (1966)[184] following the general mode of Article 19 of the Universal Declaration but building on it and being more specific provides that:

1. Everyone shall have the right to hold opinions without interference;

2. Everyone shall have the right to freedom of expression; this right shall include freedom to seek, receive and impart

---

[182] See *Nafiu Rabiu Vs. The State* (1981) NCLR, 293 *Archbishop Okojie & Ors Vs. Attorney General of Lagos State* (1981) INCLR, 218 at 230; *Yesufu Garba & Ors Vs. The University of Maiduguri & Ors* (1986) INWLR, 550 at p.583; *Eyu Vs. The State* (1988) 2 NWLR, 602, at p.610.

[183] For text of the Universal Declaration see *Bangalore Colloquium, op. cit.* Annex 1; pp. 110-112.

[184] *ibid,* p. 112 *et sequ.*

information and ideas of all kinds, regardless of frontiers, either orally, in writing or print, in form of art, or through any other media of his choice;

3. The exercise of the rights provided for in paragraph 2 of this article carries with it special duties and responsibilities. It may therefore be subject to certain restrictions, but these shall only be such as are provided by law and are necessary; for respect of the rights or reputations of others; for the protection of national security or public order *(ordre public)* or of public health or morals.

Article 13 of the American Convention on Human Rights[185] seems more expansive than similar provisions in other international instruments and stipulates that:

1. Everyone has the right to freedom of thought and expression. This right includes freedom to seek, receive and impart information and ideas of all kinds, regardless of frontiers, either orally, in writing in print, in the form of art, or through any other medium of one's choice.

2. The exercise of the right provided in the foregoing paragraph shall not be subject to prior censorship but shall be subject to subsequent imposition of liability which shall be expressly established by law and be necessary in order to ensure; respect for the rights and reputations of others; orthe protection of national security, public order, or public health or morals.

3. The right of expression may not be restricted by indirect methods or means, such as the abuse of government or private controls over newsprint, radio broadcasting frequen-

---

[185] American Convention on Human Rights (1969), *ibid* Annex V p. 169 *et sequ.*

cies or implements or equipment used in the dissemination of information, or by any other means tending to impede the communication and circulation of ideas and opinions.

4. Notwithstanding the provisions of paragraph 2 above, public entertainment may be subject by law to prior censorship, for the sole purpose of regulating access to them for the moral protection of childhood and adolescence.

5. Any propaganda for war and any advocacy of national, racial or religious hatred that constitutes incitement to lawless violence or any other similar illegal action against any person or group of persons on any grounds including those of race, colour, religion, language, or national origin shall be considered as offences punishable by law".

The provision of paragraph 3 is instructive, in the sense that it legislates against indirect methods and means of chilling the freedom of expression and finds support in national and international judicial decisions. It makes for greater clarity and legal certainty by indicating what may amount to indirect method or means of restricting the freedom of expression, without pretending that the list is exhaustive, thus allowing the court to progressively interpret what indirect methods and means may be.

In the case of *Indian Express Newspapers (Bombay) v Union of India (1986) A IR 515. SC.* The Supreme Court held that while taxes may be imposed on newsprint, the government should exercise caution as such a tax may become unconstitutional if it is unduly burdensome. *Olivier V. Buttigieg (1967)* A. C. 115 (PC)[186] was an appeal from the Court of Appeal of Malta. The editor of the 'Voice of Malta' the respondent in this case instituted a suit against the Archbishop of Malta

---

[186] *Ibid* p. 226.

who condemned the newspaper saying that no one, without committing a mortal sin could print, write, sell buy, distribute or read it. In 1962 the Chief Governmental medical officer issued a circular to all the establishment of services in the medical and health department prohibition employees to take the Voice of Malta. The Privy Council, per Lord Morris of Borth-y-Gest, upholding the decision of the Court of Appeal of Malta held that: the respondent's right to freedom of expression guaranteed under S.14 of the Malta Constitution had been violated; that in particular the respondent was hindered in this right to impart information, and that when considering fundamental rights and freedoms of the individual a court "should be cautious before accepting the view that some particular disregard of them is of minimal account". In its judgment, the Privy Council cited with approval the supportive statement in the U.S. case of *Thomas v Collins* (1944)[187] that… "it is from petty tyrannies that large ones take root and grow".

Article 9 of the African Charter on Human and Peoples' Rights, as already indicated, is less forthright than the corresponding provisions of the American Convention when it provides that:

1. Every individual shall have the right to receive information

2. Every individual shall have the right to express and disseminate his opinion within the law.

The provision of the African Charter relating to freedom of expression deserves some comments. Firstly by employing the word 'shall' it made it abundantly clear that the right is strictly obligatory. Secondly by insisting that the freedom be exercised within the law it implies that most if not all restrictions, such as those in Article 19 of the International Covenant on Civil and Political Rights may be admissible.

---

[187] Ibid.

Thirdly as we had argued elsewhere by not specifically requiring that such restrictions should be necessary or justifiable in a democratic society, it may create opportunities for States Parties to the Charter to impose even more unqualified restrictions. This notwithstanding the African Commission on Human and Peoples' Rights charged with the promotion and protection of human and peoples' rights, in construing the Charter provision, since there exists some ambiguity in the formulation of the restrictions which may be imposed by national legislation on the freedom of expression, has done so with due regard to the aims and objectives of the Charter, namely to guarantee and protect rights enshrined in the Charter and the jurisprudence and case law of other jurisdictions on the freedom of expression and in the context of values of democracy which the Charter guarantees.

On a number of occasions, the Commission in determining the significance of 'within the laws' in the context of Article 9 has found that it cannot be interpreted as allowing the use of domestic law to set aside an international obligation thus affirming the supremacy of international human rights law, in addition since Article 9 does not itself expressly specify of any limitation, any limitation to it has to be found in Article 27(2) based on collective security, morality and common interest. And such a limitation may not erode a right such that the right itself becomes illusory [140/94, 141/94, 145/95 Constitutional Rights Project, Civil Liberties Organisation and Media Rights/Agenda/Nigeria. In 61/91, Amnesty International, Mauritania the Commission found that there was no violation of Article 9(2) because the alleged acts of distribution of a manifesto which provided statistics on racial discrimination and calling for dialogue with government took place before the coming into force of the African Charter.

In order instances the Commission held that: the proscription of certain newspapers, the Guardian, Punch and Concord, by a decree of 1994, locking up their offices, and harassment of journalists violated Article 9 and could lead other newspapers not so affected to engage in self-censorship, which was equally violative of Article 9, 140/94,141,94,145,95;[188] arrest and detention of journalists for articles published and questions asked deprived the journalists of the right to the freedom of expression and to disseminate information and the public the right to receive information [147/95, 149/96 Sir Dauda Jawara/Gambia (paragraph 65), arrest of a journalist for alleged coup plot [224/98 Media Rights Agenda/Nigeria] blanket restriction on the right in the name of public security a violation of Article 9(2), [48/90, 50/91, 52/93, Amnesty International, Comite Loosli Bachelard, Lawyers Committees for Human rights, Association of Members of Episcopal Conference of East Africa/Sudan], and that where the exercise of the rights violates the law (including the rights of another) the due process of seeking judicial remedy rather than arrest and detention must be followed. What was not done in the present case [232/99 John D. Ouko /Kenya].

Despite the variety of formulations of the freedom of expression in national constitutions and international instruments they share certain things in common:

1. Unlike other rights, the enjoyment of which national constitutions reserve to citizens (right to privacy and freedom of movement) freedom of expression is guaranteed to everyone; in many if not most constitutions.

2. The right is exercisable without interference and across national frontiers.

3. The restrictions must not be such as to render the exercise of the right illusory (by prior censorship or other measures such as excessive pricing of materials and facilities needed to effectively carry out the work of journalists);

---

[188] See *supra.*

4. The freedom encompasses a bundle of rights which include the right to freedom to hold opinion, to seek and receive information, to impart ideas and information as well as the right of individuals and the community at large to be informed.

An examination of a few decided cases from different jurisdictions and international tribunals will serve to confirm the universalisation of some of these constituent elements.

The celebrated judgment in the *Handyside Case,* even when the corresponding provision of the European Convention on Human Rights, the subject of judicial interpretation, may not be on all fours with other national (including Nigeria's) provision on the freedom of expression, represents what has been universally accepted as the meaning of the freedom of expression. The European Court in the instant case declared that.

"Freedom of expression constitutes one of the essential foundations of (democratic society), one of the basic conditions for its progress and for the development of every man... It is applicable not only to information or ideas that are favourably received or regarded as inoffensive or as a matter of indifference but also to those that offend shock or disturb the state or any sector of the population. Such are the demands of pluralism, tolerance and broad mindedness without which there is no democratic society".[189]

Implicit in this determination is that freedom of expression is better enjoyed in a democratic society, and not under a dictatorship, that indi-

---

[189] A Lester, *"Freedom of Expression Relevant International Principles"* Judicial Colloquium in Bangalore op. cit, p.28.

viduals or society have an interest, indeed a right to receive information imparted to them.

On the questions of the right to receive ideas and information, the constitutional court of Austria provides a useful insight. The kernel of this is that the freedom to receive ideas and information in strictly legal terminology does not oblige the government to give access to official information to anybody. It does, however, proscribe the government from restricting a person from receiving ideas and information available to the public. Thus where there is a riot and journalists have taken notes and or filmed it, their destruction will be violative of the constitutional right of freedom of expression.[190] In its judgment in *Leander v. Sweden*[191] where the applicant had sought and been refused access to information held on a police register on the basis of which he had been denied security clearance for employment, the European Court unanimously held that there was no violation of Article 10 in the circumstances and that:

> "…the right to freedom to receive information basically prohibits a government from restricting a person from receiving information that others wish or may be willing to impart to him. …Article 10 does not … confer on the individual a right of access to a register containing information on his personal position, nor does it embody an obligation on the government to impart such information on the individual."

Whether the same attitude will be taken in war situations is not clear as under the guise of national security in a period of emergency and for

---

[190] Judgement of the Constitutional Court of Austria of 16 March 1987 – 8154/86 (1987) See also Osita C. Eze, "Dissent in a Democratic Polity options in a Presidential System" in *Democracy and the Rule of Law,* Lagos, Federal Ministry of Justice, 1992.

[191] 26 March 1987, Series A No 116 9 EHRR, 433; See also Lester *op. cit,* p.33.

military considerations, journalists may be unjustifiably excluded or prevented from gathering information.

But with increasing calls for transparence in government activities inter alia, revelations of abuse of rights of prisoners of war in Iraq and Guantanamo Bayin Cuba, there may be no place to hide.

5.9.   Freedom of Association and Assembly

Articles 10 and 11 of the African Charter guarantee the right of association and assembly respectively. It can be said that typically the African Charter, practices an economy of words not found in other international conventions. Article 10 of the African Charter provides that: "every individual shall have the right to free association provided that he abides by the law.[192] The contents of the law are not specified. It is understood that the freedom of association includes the right to join political parties, trade unions, social organisations, clan or family organisations or age grade groups. And no one may be compelled to join an association. This is, however, subject to solidarity rights for which provision is made in Article 29(4) of the African Charter.[193]

The Commission has held interpreting Article 10 that: prosecution for being a student leader (232/99, John D Ouko/Kenya, harassment of human rights NGOs to undermine their capacity to work as organised groups to achieve their objective of respect for human rights (225/98 Huri Laws/Nigeria); imprisonment of some presumed supporters of the Ba'ah Socialist Party for belonging to a criminal association but not blacks for putting up a manifesto on racial discrimination because the 'unauthorised' meeting for which they were charged took place before

---

[192] The right to free association is subject only to the obligation of solidarity provided for in Article 29 i.e. duty provisions relating to the family, community and the State.

[193] See *infra.*

the Charter came into force. (54/91, 61/91, 98/95, 196/97, 210/98/,Mauritania cit), harassment by security officer for his political belief which manifested itself in the agitation for validation of the annulled June 12 election allegedly won by Chief M.K.O. Abiola (205/97, Kazeem Aminu/Nigeria); and finally the general prohibition placed on the right of association in all places, without special permission, being disproportionate to the measures required to maintain public order, security and safety (168/90, 80/90, 52/91 cit).

Article 22(1) of the International Covenant on Civil and Political Rights guarantees the freedom of association with the specific mention of the right to join trade unions. Article 22(2) of the Covenant specifies the nature and types of restrictions that can be imposed on this right. It stipulates that the restrictions that may be placed on the exercise of that right are those prescribed by law and which are necessary in a democratic society[194] i) in the interest of national security, ii) public safety, iii) public order (*ordre public*), iv) the protection of public health or morals, v) or the protection of the rights and freedoms of others.

Lawful restrictions may, however, be imposed on members of the armed forces and the police in their exercise of this right. It seems that this reservation is intended to give states wider discretion in limiting the exercise of the right in so far as it relates to members of the armed forces and the police.

The freedom to join trade unions is normally understood to include the right to strike. The history of trade union movements and indeed of popular organizations such as the trade union movements, academic staff unions has invariably been subverted by many if not most African governments. The approach has been to co-opt the leadership of the trade unions by whatever means or to disband them thereby making them illegal to function. The right to strike is often circumscribed in

---

[194] See *infra.*

such a manner that to all intents and purposes the right does not exist. This is so in the so called democracies and even more so in military dictatorships. Twice in a decade the Nigerian military governments have dissolved the Nigeria Labour Congress[195] and appointed administrators, banned National Association of Nigerian Students (NANS) and the Academic Staff Union of Universities (ASUU).

An example of government's interference with the right of association is to be found in Communication 101/93 Civil Liberties Organization in (respect of the Nigerian Bar Association,/Nigeria). Government by the Legal Practitioners Decree, which ousted the jurisdiction of the courts, abolished the governing body of the Nigerian Bar Association replacing it with the Body of Benchers made up of mostly government nominees. The Commission in finding that it violated Article 10 held:

"Freedom of association is enunciated as an individual right and is first and foremost a duty for the state to abstain from interfering with the free formation of associations. There must always be a general capacity for citizens to join without state interference in associations in order to attain various ends. In regulating the use of this right, the competent authority should not enact provisions which would limit the exercise of the freedom. The competent authorities should not override constitutional provisions or undermine fundamental rights guaranteed by the constitution and international human rights standards".

In the determination the Commission cited with approval the Resolution on the Right to Freedom of Association, adopted at its 11th Ordinary Session. The Resolution states that "the regulation of the exercise of the right to freedom of association should be consistent with states' obligation under the African Charter on Human and Peoples' Rights". This

---

[195] The elected Central Labour Organisation to which trade unions are affiliated.

principle applies to all rights guaranteed under the Charter (142/95, 149/96, Sir Dawda K. Jawara/Gambia para. 68).

Similar practices exist in other African countries.[196] Even though, the governments claim commitment to the enthronement of democracy every effort is made to stifle organisations that represent the building blocks for democracy and a catalyst for its attainment. Ironically, because of the repression of these organisations or in spite of it there has been a tendency for the growth and spread of democratic forces mostly in the form of non-governmental organisations NGOs - and the deepening of resistance to mindless dictatorships.

Even in cases where the government pretends not to interfere in the exercise of the right to join and freely organize trade unions it has done so by 'organising' the elections to the offices of trade union movements. It is therefore, not surprising, that the Covenant on Civil and Political Rights did provide in its Article 22(3) That: "Nothing in this Article shall authorize states parties to the International Labour Organization Convention of 1948 Concerning Freedom of Association and Protection of the Right to Organize to take legislative measures which would prejudice, or apply the law in such a manner as to prejudice the guarantees provided for in that convention".

The 1948 ILO Convention referred to in Article 22(3) provides that states parties shall guarantee:

1. that workers and employers, without distinction whatsoever, shall have the right to establish and, subject only to the rules of the organisation concerned, to join organisations of their own choosing without previous authorizations;

---

2. that workers and employers organisations shall have the right to draw up their constitutions and rules, to elect their representatives, in full freedom, to organize their administration and activities and to formulate their programmes;

3. that public authorities shall refrain from any interference which would restrict the right or impede the lawful exercise, thereof, and

4. that workers' and employers' organisations shall not be liable to be dissolved or suspended by administrative authority.[197]

In the light of the above undertakings by states, acts such as the dissolution of the NLC executive and two or so affiliated unions, the appointment of administrators charged *inter alia* with conducting elections would seem to amount to violations.

Article 11 of the African Charter guarantees the right to assemble freely subject only to necessary restrictions provided for by law in particular those enacted in the interest of national security, safety, health, ethics and rights and freedoms of others. In Dawda K Jawara's case discussed above, the Commission also held that the banning of political parties was in violation of Article 11(147/95, 149/96). It however found that, where the petitioners, concerning the manifesto case were accused of holding an unauthorised meeting before the entry into force of the African Charter there was no violation (59/91, 61/91, 98/93, 164/97, 210/98 cit).

Article 21 of the Covenant on Civil and Political Rights which guarantees the right of assembly is similar to Article 11 of the African Char-

---

[197] The United Nations and Human Rights, New York, 1984, pp. 87-88; See also ILO Convention 87; Human Rights Watch Africa-Nigeria "The Dawn of a New Age" Vol. 6 No. 8 Oct. 1994, Nigeria ratified Convention 87 in 1960.

ter. There are, however, two points that need to be mentioned. Firstly while the African Charter guarantees the right to assemble freely, the Covenant guarantees the right of peaceful assembly. It can be assumed that the difference in formulation is more apparent than real for an unpeaceful assembly is not only likely to confront the maintenance of law and order but is also most likely to interfere with right of others – the right of peoples to national peace to which individuals can lay claim as members of groups [Article 23(1)].

The freedom of assembly has in many instances been violated by requirements for prior permit, blanket ban on assemblies, etc. which tend to go beyond the limitation permissible under the African Charter and many African Constitutions with similar provisions.

5.10   Freedom of Movement

Article 12 of the African Charter makes provision for the freedom of movement and residence of every individual within the borders of a state provided he abides by the law. [Article 12(1)]. This provision is capable of being applied differently to citizens (nationals) and non nationals. A national is assumed to be lawfully within his country (state) and while he is there is free to exercise within the state rights guaranteed. A non-national that is an alien, who is lawfully in the country may exercise the right subject to greater restrictions than a national for instance in security zones. An alien who is not lawfully in the country can in general be expelled from that state.

In 97/93 John K. Modise/Botswana, the Commission held that the deportation of Modise a citizen from Botswana violated his right under Article 12. Again in the Mauritanian case, the Commission held that forcing the black Mauritanians to go abroad after confiscating their property and land violates Article 12(1), 54/91, 61/91, 98/93.

Article 12(2) of the African Charter guarantees the right of every individual to leave any country including his own, and to return to his country. The right may only be subject to restrictions, provided for by law for the protection of national security, law and order, public health or morality. While the right of exit, subject to limitations imposed by law, applies to both aliens and nationals the right of entry is available, subject to any contrary international obligation by the state in question, to only nationals. The latter appears less restrictive than Article 12(4) of the International Convention Civil and Political Rights (ICCPR) which provides that "No one shall be arbitrarily deprived of the right to enter his own country".

The Commission has held that there was a violation of Article 12(2) where: a person was forced to flee his country of nationality for fear of persecution by government or its agencies (32/99 John D. Ouko/Kenya and 215/98 Rights International/Nigeria), where citizens were arrested at the airport on their return to the country, in circumstances not falling within the limitations by law for the protection of national security, law and order, public health and morality – envisaged under Article 12(2) [225/98 Huri-Laws/Nigeria; the Secretary General of a political party 'Bloc Socialiste Burkinabe' was prevented from leaving the country following the publication by the said party of a statement on the situation in the country; 204/97 Movement Burkinabe des Droits de l'Homme et des Peuples/Burkina Faso.

Provision is made in the African Charter to prevent the arbitrary expulsion of aliens legally in a territory of a state. Such a person may only be expelled by virtue of a decision taken in accordance with the law. Article 12(5) of the Charter proscribes the mass expulsion of non-nationals in order to stem the tide of mass expulsions of non-nationals for political or economic reasons or as a consequence xenophobia which unsure and unstable civilian or military regimes effect in order to secure short term interests[198]. 'Mass expulsion' is defined as that which is aimed at national, racial, ethnic or religious groups" (Article 12(5)).

In communication 71/92 Recontre Africaine pour la Defense des Droits de l'Homme/Zambia, the Commission held with respect to the expulsion of West Africans from Zambia, after interpreting Article 2 of the Charter on non-discrimination as imposing 'an obligation on the contracting states to secure the rights protected in the Charter to all persons within their jurisdiction, nationals or non-nationals' that it

> "will not dispute that the Zambian state has the right to bring legal action against all persons illegally residing in Zambia, and to deport them if the result of such legal action justify it. However the mass expulsion of the individuals in question here, including their arbitrary detention and deprivation of the right to have their cause heard, constitutes a flagrant violation of the Charter".

With due respect if all the rights are equal for all, nationals and non-nationals alike, why should the issue of deportation arise at all in the case of aliens. Isn't the crux of the matter that Article 12 proscribes mass expulsion because, inter alia, due process is highly unlikely in such circumstances when what is guaranteed is the right of the individual. But it must be conceded that some rights such as the right to have ones cause heard is nationality neutral.

The Commission also came to the conclusion that the expulsion of certain West Africans from Angola violated Article 12(4) and (5) [159/96 Union Inter Africaine des Droits del'Homme and others/Angola.

It seems from a reading of the Zambian case that, in the case of mass expulsion, the right of access to courts or appropriate tribunals, is available to non nationals even when they are illegally in the country. Article

---

[198] Nigeria and Ghana had in the past carried out such mass expulsions.

12(4) expressly reserves the right to non-national(s) legally admitted into the country.

Article 12(3) is concerned with asylum seekers and refugees.

It provides that:

"Every individual shall have the right, when persecuted, to seek and obtain asylum in other countries in accordance with the law of those countries and international conventions".

A reading of the provision will reveal, particularly when the right to seek asylum read together with domestic legislations and conventions on refugees, that while may exist, the right to obtain asylum will stand or fall depending on the relevant laws and conventions.[199]

As is the general pattern the relevant provisions of the American Convention on Human Rights is more elaborate than the corresponding provision of the African Charter. Article 22(5) is unequivocal in stating that "no one can be expelled from the territory of the state of which he is a national or be deprived of the right to enter it". Article 22(7) is similar to the provisions on asylum in the African Charter except that unlike the latter it specifies that the asylum regime is applicable where the seeker is being pursued for political or related common crimes. Apparently in a case where a person is being pursued for political and related grave crimes he would not qualify for asylum.

Art. 22(8) reaffirms the well established principle of *non-refoulement* which prohibits an alien from being deported or returned to a country, regardless of whether or not it is his country of origin, if in that country his right to life or personal freedom is in danger of being

---

[199] See *infra.*

violated because of his race, nationality, religion, social status, or political opinions.[200]

An examination of Article 12 of the African Charter in conjunction with the relevant national laws and conventions will show that the right to seek asylum and the principle of *non-refoulement* are part of conventions and laws on refugees.[201] It is a moot point whether generalized and consistent state practice, over time, has transformed them into part of customary international law or at least elevated them to the status of general principles of law recognized by civilized nations.

For the purpose of this section of the book, apart from Article 12 of the African Charter three conventions are relevant: the UN Convention Relating to the Status of Refugees, 1951,[202] the UN Protocol Relating to the Status of Refugees, of 31st January 1967[203] as well as the OAU Convention Governing Specific Aspects of Refuge problems in Africa of September 1969.[204]

Before going into the substance of the laws governing asylum and refugee status it is necessary to indicate that Africa has probably the largest number of refugees numbering millions. The reason why people flee from their country of nationality or country of residence to seek refuge in other countries vary from internal political, social and economic disorder, including repression by unconscionable dictatorships, or just

---

[200] See Article 33 of the 1951 UN Convention, Article 3(1) of the UN Declaration on Territorial Asylum (1951), see generally I.Diallo *Les Refugees en Afrique: Cadre Regional et International de Reglement,* Vienna, Wilhelm Broumatter 1974, Osita C. Eze, Human Rights in Africa *op. cit,* pp. 177-178.

[201] Ibid.

[202] *Collection of international Conventions, Agreements and other Texts Concerning Refugees* (UN HRC, 1971) p. 28.

[203] *ibid,* pp. 53-59.

[204] For the text of the African Convention, see Osita C. Eze, *Human Rights in Africa op. cit* appendixes.

sheer incapacity or unwillingness to manage public affairs and public resources with transparency, accountability and a good measure of fairness or justice that places the common good before the public officials private good, to civil wars and ecological disasters.

The recent debacles in Rwanda with hundreds of thousands, dead and its over one million refugees seeking asylum in Zaire and elsewhere not to mention the large number of displaced persons, or intractable conflicts in Congo Democratic Republic (formerly Zaire), Chad, Sudan and Somalia as well as the continuous instability in the Mano River are indications that forces which lead to forced migration, particularly given the instability of many African countries and the high potential for internal conflicts, economic downturn, inequitable socio-economic systems, corruption, exacerbated by orthodox SAP and its new forms, and the increasing tension between the fight for democracy and the desire of self seeking kleptomanic rulership to stall it, are not likely to decline in the near future. More recently Ivory Coast, Ethiopia/Somalia and Kenya have become new centres of conflict. It is therefore in the interest of all and sundry that a stable legal regime exits, for millions of Africans who are likely to graduate to the status of refugees now and in the future.

The word 'asylum' is often used interchangeably with the word 'refugee'. The former seems however wider in scope. Starke states that:

"The conception of asylum in international law involves two elements:

1. Shelter which is more than mere temporary refuge and

2. A degree of active protection on part of the authorities in control of the territory of asylum"[205]

---

[205] J. S. Starke, *Introduction to International Law*, Ninth Edition, (London Butteworths 1984), p. 345.

When asylum is granted by a state on its territory it is referred to as territorial asylum. If granted for and in respect of legations, consular premises, international headquarters, warships and merchants vessels to refugees from the authorities of the territorial state it is extra territorial.[206]

Since the conventions mentioned appear to deal primarily with territorial asylum, a word or two on diplomatic asylum will be in order. Article 22 of the Vienna Convention on Diplomatic Relations provides for the inviolability of the premises of a mission. The agents of the receiving state may only enter such premises with the consent of the head of mission.[207]

Furthermore the receiving state is under a special duty to take all appropriate steps to protect the premises of the mission against any intrusion or damage and to prevent any disturbance of the premises or the peace of the mission or impairment of its dignity.[208] The inviolability of the premises of a mission has created opportunities for the grant of asylum within it-diplomatic asylum. The practice of granting diplomatic asylum was well known in Latin America even though it was founded on conventions concluded by Latin American states rather than general or regional customary international law.[209] Permissible basis for the grant of diplomatic asylum are not settled.

A persuasive position seems to have been adopted by Ronning who maintains that:

---

[206] *ibid* pp. 345-349.

[207] Article 22(1). For the text of the Convention, see Harris *op. cit.,* p. 265 *et sequ.*

[208] Article 22(2).

[209] Asylum Case (Columbia Vs Peru) ICJ Reports, 1950, p.266.

"The only generalization which seems at all acceptable is that the practice of states in this regard is not based on any generally recognized right of asylum so far as general international law is concerned. Instead it is de facto result of the fact that international law accords to the various accredited diplomatic officers certain well recognized immunities from local jurisdiction, such as immunity of their official residence and offices from invasion by local authorities. Humanitarian, political or other motives may lead to the original grant of asylum but once the refugee is inside the legation the territorial state is faced with an insoluble dilemma. Assuming the state of refuge will not surrender the refugee, the territorial state can apprehend him only by violating the immunity of the diplomatic premises or possibly by breaking diplomatic relations. The fact is that such extreme measures are considered too high a price to pay for apprehension of the refugee".[210]

A state which has sufficient reason to believe that the grant of diplomatic immunity is such as to threaten its essential security' might take the[211] risk and act in breach of the diplomatic immunity.

There is yet another distinction between territorial and extra-territorial asylum "the differences between the principles applying to the two kinds of asylum" as Starke points out "Flow from the fact that the power to grant territorial asylum is an incident of territorial sovereignty itself, whereas the granting of extra territorial asylum is rather a derogation from the sovereignty of the territorial state in so far as the state is

---

[210] Harris *op. cit* p. 274.

[211] U.S. Diplomatic and Consular Staff in Tehran, (U.S. Vs Iran) ICJ Reports 1983, p. 3.

required to acquiesce in fugitives from its authorities enjoying protection from apprehension.[212]

What then is the meaning of the term refugee under the UN law and OAU Convention?

The term refugee is not defined by customary international law. The meaning of the word would thus have to be gathered from several of the international agreements dealing with refugees. A more comprehensive definition is to be found in the Statute of the Office of the United Nations High Commissioner for Refugees (the UNHCR Statute), adopted by the UN General Assembly on 14 December 1950.[213] The UN Convention of 1951 has adopted a similar definition. In both instruments certain categories of refugees are specified as being entitled to the protection and facilities provided therein.

Under the UN Convention the term refugee is defined to include any person who has been considered a refugee under the arrangements of 12 May 1926 and 30 June 1928 or under the Convention of 28 October 1933 and 10 February 1938, the protocol of 14 September 1939 or the Constitution of the International Refugee Organization' (UN Convention, Article 1 A(1) the UNHCR Statute, [Article 6A(i)].

It is clear from the wording of this provision that for a person to qualify as a refugee he must have to be recognized as such under the relevant conventions or instruments. While restrictive and liberal interpretations are possible, it would seem in view of the humanitarian aspect of refugee protection that a more liberal interpretation would be preferred. This is more so if one takes into account the Recommendation of the Final Act of 28 July 1951, in which the Conference of Plenipotentiaries expressed the hope "that the convention relating to the status of

---

[212] Starke, *op cit,* p.345, See also *Asylum Case supra.*

[213] See fn. 75 *supra.*

Refugees will have value as an example exceeding its contractual scope and that all nations will be guided by it in granting so far as possible to persons in their territory as refugees and who would not be covered by the terms of the convention, the treatment for which it provides"[214] This line of reasoning is also supported by the fact that the United Nations General Assembly has by various resolutions authorised the High Commissioner for Refugees to use his good offices for the benefit of refugees who did not come within the competence of the United Nations, that is, those refugees who do not come within the conventional meaning of the term. The manner of interpretation will, in any case, ultimately depend on the authority with the competence to determine refugee status.[215]

A reservation was made, however, in relation to those refugees who had not been considered as qualifying for the purposes of the International Refugee Organisation. In such cases the negative decision of the IRO 'shall not prevent the status of refugee being accorded to persons who fulfill the conditions of paragraph 2 of this section' (UN Convention, Article 1 A(1); Statute of UNHCR, Article 6 A (ii)).

Paragraph 2 of Article 1(A) of the UN Convention in effect gives a general definition of refugees, and this definition is substantially adopted in the OAU Convention on Refugees.[216] As will become evident from what follows, the provisions of this paragraph as formulated in the UN Convention were intended to apply only to those who became refugees as a result of events occurring before 1 January 1951. This time limitation has, however, been eliminated in the definition of refugees as embodied in the Protocol Relating to the Status of Refugees of 31 January 1967, which came into force on 4 October 1967.

---

[214] UN. Doc, A/CONF.2/108/3.

[215] A/1167 (XVI) 26 Nov. 1967; A/Res/ 1388 (XIV), 20 Nov. 1959; A/Res/1499 (XV) 5 Dec. 1960; A/Res 1671 (XVI) and A/Res 1673 (XVI), 18 Dec 1961.

[216] Osita C. Eze, *Human Rights in Africa, op.cit* p.291, fn 25.

Article 1 A(2) of the UN Convention defines 'refugee' for the purposes of the Convention as a person who (as a result of events occurring before 1 January 1951 and)[217] owing to well-founded fear of being persecuted for reasons of race, religion, nationality or political opinion is outside the country of his nationality and is unable or, owing to such fear, is unwilling to avail himself of the protection of that country, or who not having a nationality and being outside the country of his former habitual residence as a result of such events is unwilling to return to it (UN Convention, Article 1 A(2); Statute of UNHCR, Article 6A (ii OAU Convention, Article 1(1)[218]

As with the interpretation of the term 'refugee' under the Article 1(A)(2) of the UN Convention, practice has varied from liberal to restrictive interpretation. It has been pointed out in connection with the UN Convention that "a liberal attitude has been adopted in requiring from a person the proof of his refugeehood although this is done with caution. Where there is a difference between a person's first statement to the authorities of a country of refuge and the statement made later at the time when his claim to refugee status is adjudicated the general rule has been to let his first statement prevail although great caution is applied in doing so".[219]

The rationale for this approach is not very clear; although it may be that a refugee is likely to tell the truth at the point of first interrogation while the lapse of time may encourage lies being told at the time when his refugee status falls to be determined.

---

[217] *See supra.*

[218] A person does not qualify as a refugee under the Statue of the UNCHR if his flight is for reasons of personal convenience. See Chapter 1 Article 6A(ii) while there is no similar provision in both the 1951 Convention, the 1967, UN Protocol and the OAU Convention, such a person would not qualify as a refugee under any of these instruments.

[219] S.P. Sinha, *Asylum in International Law*, The Hegue, Nijhoff, 1971, p.100.

Some comments on the operative clauses of the definition are called for. The aspect of the UN Convention which limits the operational scope in time and space has already been discussed, and needs no further comment.

The second requirement for satisfying the conditions for refugee-hood is that the person is outside the country of his nationality or the country of former habitual residence. A strict interpretation of this requirement would mean that the 'refugee should in fact be physically outside his country of nationality of former habitual residence. But the provision had been interpreted to mean that he has to leave or remains outside.[220]

According to this interpretation, he could either be an escapee or refugee *sur-place*. While the interpretation which implies that 'he has to leave' or 'shall leave' may appear anticipatory, refugee status can only fall to be considered when the refugee is actually outside. It is only then that the fulfillment of those conditions can be taken into account in determining a person's refugee status. Besides, as already indicated international protection of refugees only comes into play where a person seeking refuge has moved from one country to another. A refugee *sur-place* is one who while already outside his country of nationality or habitual residence seeks refuge in another country.

Thirdly, his being outside the country of nationality or of former habitual residence must be due to well-founded fear of being persecuted. Subjective and objective tests have been applied to determine whether the fear of persecution is well-founded or not. A subjective test will try to ascertain the actual state of mind of the person seeking refuge, while the objective test is often formulated in terms of whether a reasonable man would have had well-founded fear of persecution in the circum-

---

[220] *Ibid.*

stances.[221] While it might be possible to envisage how a reasonable man would behave in given circumstances, it is not difficult to understand that a person who would normally qualify as a reasonable man might behave unreasonably under similar circumstances. In some cases, both the subjective and objective tests are applied. In many cases, however, even where it is claimed that the subjective test has been applied, evidence may show that the objective test has also been applied, simply because it is very difficult, in most cases to discover the actual state of a person's mind. With respect to the mass movement of refugees prevalent in Africa, particularly as a result of armed conflicts, there is an obvious difficulty in applying the subjective test since this is relevant only to individual determination of refugee status. It has also been pointed out that the requirement that 'fear' must be well-founded is often jettisoned since it is now frequently the case of anyone outside his country of nationality or residence and who claims to be a refugee is regarded *prima facie* as one.[222]

Fourthly, persecution must be for reason of race, religion, nationality or membership of a particular social group or political opinion. In the case of a stateless person, persecution may well be on the ground of lack of nationality. This requirement clearly embraces grounds other than purely political ones. It may prove difficult to establish what amounts to persecution for reasons of political opinion. The holding of political ideas opposed to those of the government could certainly lead to fear of persecution and warrant the grant of refugee status. An unsuccessful attempt to overthrow an existing regime could also lead to a justifiable fear of persecution for political reasons. This could be the position in the case of an unsuccessful attempt to stage a coup d'etat. A problem arises, however, where fear of persecution arises as a consequence of an act or

---

[221] Sinha, *op. cit,* p.102.

[222] M. Rubin, "Africa and Refugees", *African Affairs* Vol. 73, 1974, p.293.

conducts which is both political and criminal. Is it the motive for the act that determines its character?

A person normally flees from his country of nationality or of habitual residence because he can no longer rely on that state to protect him. The conditions leading to fear of persecution might result directly from the conduct of the state itself or its agencies, or they might result from the fact that the state is either unwilling or unable to protect him. Thus, as has been the case in some African countries, the state will be responsible where through one of its organs or agencies it helps in collaboration with a given sector of the population in decimating members of particular tribal or ethnic groups.

Fifthly, the person claiming refugee status is unable or, owing to well-founded fear of persecution, is unwilling to avail himself of the protection of the country of his nationality. Where he does not have a nationality, he is unable, or owing to his fear, is unwilling to return to the country of his former habitual residence. It is thus the inability or unwillingness of the person, rather than the conduct of the state as such that determines whether this requirement for refugee status is satisfied. But the inability to avail himself of the protection of his country of nationality or unwillingness to return to his country of former habitual residence, as the case may be, must be objectively tested in the light of the overall conduct of the state in question.

The OAU Convention contains an additional provision which is probably intended to cater for the peculiarities of Africa. Paragraph 2, Article 1 provides that 'the term "refugee" shall also apply to every person who, owing to external aggression, occupation, foreign domination or events seriously disturbing public order in either part or the whole of his country of origin or nationality is compelled to leave his place of habitual residence in order to seek refuge in another place outside his country of origin or nationality'.

This aspect of the OAU Convention definition of refugees requires some comments. The first element of the definition is that a person seeking refugee status must be compelled to leave his place of habitual residence. This requirement is more flexible than that of the UN Convention, which stipulates that the person should be outside his country of nationality or of habitual residence. A proper interpretation of the provision of the OAU Convention would, it is submitted, imply that the person 'has to leave, shall leave,' a meaning which can be ascribed to the UN Convention only be a liberal interpretation of its relevant provision. It is also submitted that a person may also qualify where he is compelled to leave his country of nationality, since the place of habitual residence might not always correspond with the country of nationality, and in any case 'country of habitual residence' can also apply to persons without any nationality. It may be that this formulation was adopted with refugees from colonial territories in mind, although there is no reason why it should not embrace refuges from independent African states.

The second requirement is that the person be compelled to leave because of external aggression, occupation, foreign domination or events seriously disturbing public order in either part or the whole of his country of origin or nationality. On the face of it, external aggression would become relevant where foreign countries invade or occupy an independent African state, and foreign domination may also occur in relation to African states, while events seriously disturbing the public order in the country of origin or nationality might be as a result of external aggression, occupation or foreign domination, serious internal upheavals as well as of the coups d'etat which have beset Africa since the early 1960s even though the democratization process since the 90s seems to have rendered them less attractive.

If this provision were interpreted, however, in the light of the acceptance of the principle of self-determination, it would have a wider application. The recognition of the principle of self-determination as applicable to dependent territories before the liquidation of colonialism imported to them some international personality necessary to assert that right. The colony could, therefore not be regarded as part of the metropolitan territory, and consequently, the relation between the metropolis and the colony were not regarded as falling within the domestic jurisdiction of the administering power.[223] This interpretation in effect implied that the phrases 'foreign aggression', 'occupation' or 'foreign domination' could qualify acts of the administering power perpetrated against a colony. It is probable that the drafters of this convention had this interpretation in mind. With the end of colonialism, this requirement seems to be irrelevant. .Be that as it may, the requirement that a person seeking refugee status must have been compelled to leave his place of habitual residence in order to seek refuge in another place poses a problem where it is thought to include liberation movements within the meaning of Article 1(2) of the OAU Convention. The main objective of liberation movements is not just to seek refuge, but to seek a base from which to seize power from the colonial or occupying power. Does this objective override the need to seek refuge, or is the desire to seek refuge for no matter what purpose sufficient? Could it also be that since the right to liberate is recognized, the grant of refugee status can only enhance it?

Whatever the problems of interpretation may be, it is submitted that Article 1(2) of the OAU Convention must have been intended to cover all manner of refugees, whether they be those from independent or dependent African States, and in the case of the latter, whether they are engaged in a liberation war or not. They must, however, satisfy the con-

---

[223] Hannah Bokor Szego, *New States and International Law*, Budapest, Akademika Kiado, 1970, p.36.

ditions laid down therein before they can qualify as refugees entitled to the protection which the Convention provides.[224]

Prior to the overthrow of Apartheid and the enthronement of an elected multiracial government, in South Africa, there was an obstacle to the termination of the refugee status of those fleeing from the colonial and racist regimes. There was the requirement by some African governments that such persons be approved by one of the recognized liberation movements. The problem was further compounded where a government recognized one of the competing liberation movements and the person seeking asylum did not belong to the one recognized. Such a situation could have led not only to the internment of refuge-seekers, but also the infringement of their political rights as envisaged in the several refugee conventions.

In addition to provisions which deal with the termination of refugee status, both the UN and OAU Conventions specify circumstances under which the respective provisions would not apply. They shall not apply to any person with respect to whom there are serious reasons for considering that:

1. he has committed a crime against peace, a war crime, or a crime against humanity as defined in the international instruments drawn up to make provisions in respect of such crimes;

2. he has committed a serious non-political crime outside the country of refuge prior to his admission to that country as a refugee;

3. he has been guilty of acts contrary to the purposes and principles of the United Nations with respect to both the UN and the

---

[224] P. Weis, "The Convention of the Organisation of African Unity Governing the Specific Aspects of Refugee Problems in Africa", *Human Rights Journal*, 1970 Vol. III, pp.450-451.

OAU Conventions and of Acts contrary to purposes and principles of the Organisation of African Unity with respect to the OAU Convention. (UN Convention Article 1 F(a) – (c); OAU Convention, Article 1(5)(a) – (d). The OAU Convention, thus, narrows down the definition of refugees by making termination dependent on non-conformity with the purposes and principles of the OAU Charter.[225] Unlike in the UN Convention, it is expressly stated in the OAU Convention that it is the country of asylum which can determine whether any of the above-mentioned acts has been committed.[226] It is submitted that the non express provision for this in the UN Convention does not make it different from similar provisions of the OAU Convention since, under the UN Convention, it is the country of asylum that can determine refugee status.[227] There is, thus, a danger that extraneous considerations may influence decision on refugee status.

The UN Convention also states that the convention shall not apply to those who are receiving from organs or agencies of the United Nations other than the United Nations High Commissioner for Refugees, protection or assistance. Where, however such protection or assistance has seized, for any reason, without the position of such persons being definitely settled in accordance with the relevant resolution adopted by the General Assembly, these persons shall *ipso facto* be entitled to the benefit of the convention (Article 1D).

The UN Convention does not apply to a person who is recognized by the competent authorities of the country in which he has taken refuge as having rights and obligations which are attached to the possession of

---

[225] O.A.U. Charter Article III.

[226] *Ibid* Article 1(5).

[227] *Ibid* Article 1(6). But the UNHCR determines refugee status in relation to those under his/her charge.

nationality of that country (Article 1E). Formal acquisition of the nationality of the country in question is therefore not necessary. It is sufficient if the person who was originally admitted as a refugee acquires rights and obligations akin to those of nationals in the country of residence.

It is clear from our discussion of the UN instruments that the conventional meaning of the term 'refugee' is rather restrictive; it could exclude those who might otherwise 'qualify' as refugees, and is inadequate in the African context. For instance, the UN definition would not embrace those commonly referred to as *de facto* refugees or refugee without official status or non-statutory refugees; all of which means the same thing. They include *inter alia* those whose application or refugee status has been rejected and are unable or unwilling for reasons of race, religion, nationality or membership of a particular social group or political opinion to return to their country of origin as well as stateless persons not recognized as refugees, but who for the same reason would also be unable and unwilling to return to their country of origin.[228] It has also been pointed out the UN Convention, by laying too much emphasis on nationality as a criterion for qualification particularly in view of relatively free movement across African boundaries and by not being sufficiently wide to embrace refugees from erstwhile colonial and dependent territories, and those from countries hitherto under other forms of alien rule did not meet African requirements.

Article 1(2) of the OAU Convention, already alluded to, is a welcome development in that it is broad enough to include those refugees that have arisen in Africa who might not have been envisaged by the drafters of the UN Convention, who were more concerned with European refugees. It is a moot point whether refugee seekers from countries

---

[228] See P. Weis "Convention Refugees and De Facto Refugees in *African Refugees and the Law*, ed by G. Melander et al, 1978, pp. 12-18.

afflicted by ecological disasters as occurred in Sahel would qualify for protection. An expansive interpretation of the OAU Convention, since it is a humanitarian convention, might well provide justification for willing state authorities to assimilate such persons to the status of refugees under the convention.

The OAU Convention recognizes, inter alia, the right of a refugee not to be repatriated to a country where his life of freedom will be threatened on account of race, religion, nationality or membership of a particular social or political group. The OAU Convention falls short of according refugees certain socio-economic and cultural rights envisaged under the UN regime, although it is expected that parties to the former should also ratify the latter and that the OAU Convention is a supplement to the UN Convention. The Bureau for the placement and education of African refugees with professional qualifications or university degrees have been able to find employment in some African countries for a few highly qualified refugees.[229]

Parties to the OAU Convention reserve the right to grant or refuse to grant asylum. In the absence of a regional organ for the determination of refugee status, individual states decide on who qualifies for refugee status, either alone or with the solicited assistance of the United Nations High Commission for Refugees. Determination by one state is not necessarily opposable to other states. African states should, however, accept the rights of other states to grant asylum or refugee status to their political opponents, particularly since general international law and the OAU Convention on refugees make provisions to ensure that they do not pose threats to their regimes. The OAU Convention regards refugee status as temporary and envisages that refugees will ultimately settle in their own

---

[229] See Osita C. Eze, *Human Rights in Africa, op. cit* p.164.

countries or in the countries of refuge or other countries willing to accept them.[230]

With several million refugees, Africa has the largest number of refugees. She is likely to grapple with the problem of refugees for some time to come. The Convention is, therefore, a welcome development in the field of protection of human rights, and should be liberally interpreted and applied by members of OAU/AU.[231]

Conflicts in Africa have also resulted in millions of displaced persons. These must be distinguished from refugees as they are normally found within the territories of states of which they are nationals or habitually resident. But because they are more vulnerable, there is greater obligation on the state to ensure that the rights guaranteed under the Charter are not undermined.

Since refugee status imports rights for refugees, it is important to examine how these are actualized. The O.A.U. (AU) has competent organs charged with the responsibility for refugee matters:

- The Refugee Commission charged with the responsibility of examining issues relative to refugees and making recommendations to the OAU Council of Ministers (now Executive Council of the African Union) on measures for relocating them and providing necessary assistance. In this, it is assisted by the Committee for the Coordination of Assistance to Refugees and the Division of Refugees, Displaced Persons and Humanitarian Affairs.
- Committee for Coordination of Assistance to Refugees – This is a consultative organ composed of representatives of the OAU/AU, the United Nations, Intergovernmental Organizations

---

[230] *Ibid.*
[231] *Ibid.*

and NGOs. The Committee is charged with matters and programme that are of benefit to refugees, and

* The Division for Refugees, Displaced Persons and Humanitarian Affairs (formerly known as the Bureau for the Placement and Education of Refugees) has *inter alia* the following functions:

1. monitor the refugee situation in Africa,

2. keep member states of the OAU/AU and the international community informed of the causes and consequences of movement of refugees in Africa,

3. give assistance and protection, in collaboration with the Bureau of the High Commission for Refugees, to refugees who are not informed about their rights and intercede on their behalf before their host governments,

4. assist them to get better educated by giving them financial assistance as well as acquire skills that will enable them make a living,

5. in collaboration with the High Commission for Refugees, ensure settlement of qualified refugees by seeking employment for them in member states.[232]

Regional organizations, such as CEDEAO, ECOWAS, IGAO, SADC and CEEA, have at the instance of the OAU/AU established mechanism for the prevention, management and resolution of conflicts, which provide one of the main sources of African Refugees.[233]

---

[232] Mubiala Mutoy, La mise en oeuvre du droits des réfugiés et des personnes déplacées en Afrique: Problématique et perspectives (updated), forthcoming, pp. 82 *et sequ.*

[233] Mubiala *ibid.* It is important to note that the AU and its project, the new Partnership for Africa's Development(NEAPAD) provide for, good governance, corporate governance, conflict prevention, management and resolution all of which are intended to ensure peace and stem the tide of refugee flows.

The implementation and 'supervision' of the OAU refugee convention is sought to be achieved, by provisions made in Conventions adopted by the OAU. Violation of refugee rights in Article 12 of the African Charter on Human and Peoples Rights, as well as those of Women (Article 11(2) Protocol to the African Charter on Human and People's Rights on Rights of Women in Africa), and the Child. [234] (Article 23...) are subject to the mechanisms under the respective conventions.

Furthermore, African Refugees Economic Communities (RECs) such as SADC, CEDEAO, as has the OAU, have entered into agreement with the United Nations High Commission for Refugees for the purpose of implementing both the UN and OAU/AU refugee regimes.[235]

Finally, the OAU/AU collaborates with national institutions on refugees for the implementation of the Convention and other associated matters.

5.11 The Right to Participate in Government and of Equal Access to Public Service and Public Property

Article 13(1) of the African Charter guarantees the democratic right of every citizen to participate freely in the government of his country either directly or through freely chosen representatives in accordance with the provision of the law. It may be maintained that such law is

---

[234] Protocol to the African Charter on Human and People's Rights on the Rights of women in Africa (2003).

[235] Cooperation Agreement between the Office of the United Nations High Commission for Refugees and the Organisation of African United, 9, April, 2001, Memorandum of Understanding between the Southern African Development Community and the United Nations High Commission for Refugees, 25, July, 1996; Protocol d'Accord entre communate economique des Etats de l'Afrique de O'Ouest, ci-apres denommee "HCR" d'autre party, 19 November 2001; Memorandum of Understanding between the African Commission on Human and Peoples Rights and the United Nations High Commissioner for Refugees (unrelated) for Text: Mubiala, *op. cit.*

concerned only with the manner of freely exercising this right and not with the substance. Yet there are other related rights without which this right cannot be effectively exercised, such as the right to hold opinion, freedom to receive and impart information, of association and movement and the right to education, all of which are guaranteed under the Charter.

In communication 44/90 Peoples Democratic Organisation for Independence and Socialism/Gambia, the new government accepted that the allegations of deficiencies in the electoral register that might violate Article 13 'are valid and logical' and was in the process of reviewing the electoral register. This communication is instructive in the sense that it is indicative of the possibility of election 'rigging' even at the voter registration stage.

In other cases the Commission held that the attempt to take away the citizenship of Mr. Kenneth Kaunda one time President of Zambia, and prevent certain category of Zambians from contesting for the post of president or demoting a Botswanan citizen by birth to a citizen by registration, the latter depriving him of the right to participate in politics or have access to public office violated Article 13 [211/98 Legal Resource Foundation/Zambia; 97/93 John Modise/Botswana]. Equally violative of Article 13 was the banning of former Ministers and Members of Parliament of the former regime from participating in politics and government [147/94, 149/96 Sir Dawda Jawara/Gambia].

Participation in the political process is supplemented by participation in the enjoyment of the public services of their country to which the right of access of every citizen is guaranteed [Article 13(2)], and public properties and services to which the right of access of every individual is guaranteed in strict equality before the law, [Article 13(3)]. It is not quite clear why the right of access to public services is extended to every individual in Article 13(3) for if the intention is to guarantee the right of access to every person, in strict equality before the law, then Article 13(2) is superfluous. Participation in government whether directly or indirectly is better secured in a democratic system which entrenches the principle of the Rule of law.

What then is Democracy and what do we understand by the Rule of law? There is hardly any contention that the Rule of law is a constituent element of democracy for it is opposed to the Rule by Man or Rule by Law the latter two of which may serve anti-democratic ends. The existence or non-existence of the Rule of law has, therefore, serious legal and political implications for human and peoples' rights as well as constitutional and orderly succession of government.

Because of the relevance and contemporary nature of the issue of democracy and encouraged by the successful conduct of elections in South Africa[236] that appeared to have insurmountable problems, that has laid the foundation for a multiracial democracy and because some of the countries which have been very vocal in urging it have proved to be tragic disappointments, I intend to examine the concept of democracy and Rule of law which is its component much more closely. Secondly, it is important to understand the minimum contents of democracy if the test often applied to limitations to rights of what is necessary in a democratic society is to be understood.

---

[236] Ghana has had two successful elections, December 2000 and December 2004. The passing away of President Eyadema of Togo and the installation of his son by the Military as President, with a necessary amendment to the Constitution has apparently been rejected by the AU. A subsequent election followed the constitution.

Meaning of Democracy

The often quoted definition of democracy[237] as government of the people by the people and for the people begs the question in so far as African states are concerned in as much as, for the most part, it is used to describe systems of government in which a tiny minority wields actual political power while the majority neither has access to knowledge nor the capacity to generate the same and are invariably confined, without adequate knowledge of issues at stake and therefore subject to pervasive manipulations, to the ritual of voting at periodic elections. Whether democracy is defined as "a political system one of the characteristics which is the quality of being completely or almost completely responsive to all of its citizens[238] or as comprising "consent, political equality, majority rule and popular consultation"[239] we run into difficulties. With respect to the former responsiveness may depend on the benevolence of the ruling elites or be motivated by the enlightened interest for self survival. The latter is preferable because it addresses such issues as popular participation and peoples' sovereignty. Both, however, ignore the 'centrality of political culture' which has its foundation in the nature of socio-economic system in place, the social relations that arise in the process of production, who gets what and in particular the role of state in its interactions with political and economic forces.

---

[237] For a discusson of the meaning of Democracy and the rule of law with particular reference to Nigeria see Osita C.Eze "The Future of Democracy and Rule of Law in Nigeria; From Analysis of form to Explosion of Substance" Alumni lecture, Enugu State University of Science and Technology, April 1993.

[238] Robert A. dahl, *Polyarchy; Participation and Opposition*, New Haven/ London, Yale University Press, 1971, p.1.

[239] Dennis G. Sulivan, Robert T Nakamura and Richard F. Winters, How America is Ruled, New York, John Wiley & Sons, 1980 cited in Richard A. Joseph, *Democracy and Prebendal Politics in Nigeria, The Rise and Fall of the Second Republic,* Ibadan Spectrum Books Ltd. 1991. p.16.

At another level there is great controversy as to what kinds of systems of government and institutional arrangements will better serve the ends of democracy

As a special category, democracy which is generally put forward as falling primarily within the sphere of political rights, even when it is evident that it will have little or no meaning for the majority unless they also enjoy economic, social, civil and cultural rights, which is more easily attainable if they also control the process and institutions that produce goods and services, presents, therefore, special problem of interpretation.

In other words it can be maintained that for democracy to thrive, there must be both economic, social democracy and political democracy. Without one there cannot be true democracy. Furthermore to be sustainable, since it is a journey, it must be sensitive to the catalytic cultural factor in the environment for it does not grow in a vacuum. All are agreed that it should present a choice as to both the system of government and those who govern. Beyond that there is hardly any agreement as to whether the objectives of democracy can be achieved under a one party state or whether this is possible only under a multiparty system, whether representation without participation will meet the ends of democracy and whether 'capitalist democracy' or 'socialist democracy' is to be preferred. In effect what do we really mean by democracy. [240]

For Kolakowski who derides all kinds of spurious and fraudulent usages of it (democracy) 'socialist democracy', 'peoples democracy' 'Islamic democracy') the concept as usually understood includes three components.

---

[240] Osita C. Eze, "Dissent in a Democratic Policy; Options in a Presidential System" In: Democracy and the Rule of Law, Lagos, Federal Ministry of Justice, 1992.

First we think, of a set of institutions aimed at assuring that the power and influence of political elites correspond to the amount of popular support they enjoy.

Second we have in mind the independence of the legal system from the executive power, the law acts as an autonomous mediating device between individual or corporate interests and the state, and is not an instrument of the ruling elites.

Third, we think of enforceable barriers built into the legal system that guarantee both the equality of all citizens before the law and basic personal rights, which (though the list is notoriously contestable) include freedom of movement, freedom of speech, freedom of association, religious freedom and freedom to acquire property"[241].

According to him these three components are not necessarily linked, they may exist separately both conceptually and as a matter of historical experience.[242] These criteria divorced from the socio-political and economic environment in which they usually operate serve as mere abstractions without due regard to reality. The first criterion is mute on whether merely representative or participatory democracy as well is envisaged, the second assumes, contrary to our position, that the legal system can be autonomous in a class society without emphasizing that the apparent relative autonomy relates primarily to intra ruling class conflicts and is allowed to exist to the extent necessary to safeguard the system and give it an appearance of impartiality and legitimacy, while the third assumes that the law by itself can ensure equality of all, even when its socio-economic foundations create conditions of inequality.

For us democracy should have the following components:

---

[241] L Kolakowski, "Uncertainties of a Democratic Age" Journal of Democracy, Winter, 1990, p. 47 *et sequ,* G. H. Fairbanks.
[242] L Kolakowski, *loc cit.*

1. Capacity to choose, direct and control those who govern and to terminate their mandate, even if periodically;

2. The right not just to be represented but to participate in decision making and implementation at various levels of government and ultimately to shape the national political economy;

3. The enthronement of a just and equitable socio-economic system and mobilization process that raises the level of social and political consciousness of citizenry and provides them with the material and psychological basis for meaningful participation in the political process; and;

4. The establishment of institutions, legal and administrative superstructure that guarantee the egalitarian foundations of a true democracy[243]

Despite views expressed to the contrary and the present crisis of socialism capitalism has clearly undergone a crisis and has been undergoing one as is evident with the global economic downturn that won't go away and increasing global tension and insecurity occasioned by the drive for resources and profit. What are the lessons learnt for ordering a more rational human social order?

Typically capitalist democracies guarantee the liberal freedoms including the right to vote and be voted for as well as the freedom of expression and even the right to participate in government within the framework of multiparty system. It emphasizes political freedom but does not promote social and economic justice[244]. Control and ownership of the means of production and polity by a minority marginalizes the

---

[243] Osita C. Eze "Dissent in a Democratic Polity" *op. cit.*

[244] See infra for progress made in the revised European Social Charter, 1996 (ETS No. 163). For text of the Revised European Social Charter, see Human Rights in International Law, Collected Texts-2nd Edition, Council of Europe Publishing, 2004, pp. 291-318.

majority and makes it impossible for the majority to fully participate in the political process despite the formal guarantee of political rights.[245]

In socialist societies, on the other hand, the workers, peasants and the masses are expected to control the economy and government. In such societies government is expected to own and operate business in the interest of the people. Such systems also guarantee civil, political, socio-economic and cultural rights, even if in practice there have been limitations to political rights and liberal freedom in favour of socio-economic rights and grassroots participation in government has tended to be derailed by autocratic and highly centralized bureaucracies and parties.[246] It is important to distinguish between the theory of socialism and actual practice for it is the shortcomings in the latter that have led to the present crisis of socialism. Typically socialist societies tend to work within the framework of single parties. And it should not be forgotten that pre-colonial African governments did not have space for opposition 'groups' as communities whether hierarchical or not had rulers who governed their subjects or people who governed themselves. Opposition was from within.

Socialism does not proscribe a multi-party system even though where several parties exist they are invariably on the left.

While both capitalist democracy and socialist democracy, in theory proffer popular democracy, the practice for the most part has tended to produce different results. The former is eminently opposed to peoples' empowerment. What has been termed 'alternative development' or the 'third way' is nothing but a variation of capitalist or socialist democracy

---

[245] Political Education Manual, Abuja, Directorate For Social Mobilization, p. 8-9.

[246] Md. Raham, "The Roles and Significance of Participatory Organisations of the Rural Poor, Alternative Strategies of Rural Development: Theory and Experience – an Overview", *Third World Legal Studies*, 1982, p. 13.

with emphasis on the ingredients of the latter. Capitalism is rejected because its emphasis on profit has tended to promote socio-economic inequality.

Orthodox Marxist-Leninism is equally rejected because the Marxist vanguard party with a high level of social consciousness and which is apparently equipped to liberate (dealienate) the masses has derailed from its set objectives by[247]

1. Allowing elite monopoly of power and its consequent domination of the masses through polarized distribution of social power over knowledge and the process of its production.

2. Not making sufficient progress in realizing the objectives of dealienation of the masses and self-reliant participatory development even given the potency of orthodox theory guided by radical action.

3. As a result of (1) and (2) above encouraging the elite totalitarianism.

In a sense of the *African Charter for Popular Participation in Development* (1990) (E/ECA/CM.16/VI) postulates both political and economic democracy. The participants at the conference held in Arusha, Tanzania in 1990, believed "strongly that popular participation is in essence, the empowerment of the people to effectively involve themselves in creating the structures and in designing policies and programmes that serve the interests of all, as well as to effectively contribute to the development process and share equitably in its benefits. Therefore there must be an opening of political process to accommodate freedom of opinions, tolerate differences, accept consensus on issues as

---

[247] Paul and Dias "Generating and Sharing Knowledge of Law for People Centred Development, *"Third World Legal Studies*, 1987, pp. 17-18; Osita C. Eze, "Law and Rural Development" in Imo State University, Okigwe (IMSU) 1990.

well as ensure effective participation of the people and their organisation and associations (preamble para ii).

Emphasis was placed on the basic fact that the role of the people and their popular organisations is central to the realization of popular participation. They have to be fully involved, committed and indeed seize the initiative. In this regards, the Charter points out, "it is essential that they establish independent peoples' organisations at various levels that are genuinely grass-root, voluntary, democratically administered and self reliant" (para 13). The constituent elements of popular participation enumerated above correspond by and large with our definitions of democracy with emphasis on peoples empowerment and sovereignty.

Most of Africa, particularly after the collapse of the Soviet Union, is in transition from military to civilian rule to democracy. Each country has to make its own journey and in this process it will make its own encounters and responses, always bearing in mind that even when the end of the journey might be manifested in different ways there are certain minimum constituent elements which are by no means agreed. In the process some might make progress and even consolidate, while there may be stagnation and even reversals in some and yet all are to be judged by the standard of what is either 'necessary' or justifiable in a democratic society.

Some may argue, and we share this view, that there is a right to democracy, given not only the guaranteed right to participate in government, but also the cognate rights and freedoms of opinion, expression, association, movement, etc. as well as the foundation economic, social and cultural rights, the latter which might be contested by some.

Having gone through this debate, we need to gather the essential elements that are normally required in a democratic setting as a tool and the aid in interpreting rights as understood, in particular by courts of law and other similar tribunals charged with adjudicating disputes. Taking the freedom of expression as his point of departure Seighart argues that:

The questions which then fall to be considered are the needs or objectives of a democratic society in relation to the right or freedom concerned; without a notion of such needs, the limitations essential to support them cannot be evaluated. For example, freedom of expression is based on the need of a democratic society to promote the individual self-fulfillment of its members, the attainment of truth, participation in decision-making, and the striking of a balance between stability and change. The aim is to have a pluralistic balance between the wishes of the individual and the utilitarian 'greater good of the majority'. But democratic societies approach this problem from the standpoint of the importance of the individual, and the undesirability of restricting his or her freedom. However, in striking the balance, certain controls on the individual freedom of expression may, in appropriate circumstances, be acceptable in order to respect the sensibilities of others. In this context, freedom of expression is commonly subject in a democratic society to laws importing restrictions considered necessary to prevent seditious, libelous, blasphemous, or obscene publications. Indeed, the legal codes of all the Member States contain legislation restricting in one way or another the right to freedom of expression, in the context of indecent, obscene, or pornographic objects and literature. This can be regarded as a clear indication of the need for such legislation in a democratic socie-ty.[248]

In the classical formulation of the principle in the *Silver Case (Silver V. United Kingdom*, Judgment of 23 March, 1983, Ser.A., No. 6 (1983) 5 EH RR 347 Para 97. It was stated:

---

[248] *Op. cit.*

1. the adjective necessary is not synonymous with indispensable neither has it the flexibility of such expressions as 'admissible', 'ordinary', 'reasonable' or 'desirable';

2. the contracting parties enjoy a certain but not unlimited margin of appreciation in the matter of imposition of restrictions, but it is for the Court to give the final ruling on whether they are compatible with the convention

3. the phrase 'necessary' in a democratic society means that, to be compatible with the convention, the interference must, inter alia correspond to a 'pressing social need and be proportionate to the 'legitimate aim pursued;'

4. those paragraphs of Articles of the convention which provide for an exception to a right guaranteed are to be narrowly construed. (Cf. the Handyside v. United Kingdom (Judgment of 2 December 1976, Ser. A, No. 24, (1979-80) IEH RR, 737 para 26 of the judgment where it was indicated that the Court, in determining whether a state was acting within the powers, is obliged to pay utmost attention to the principles characterizing 'a democratic society.')[249] In the above the requirement that a limitation must be based on "a pressing social need and be proportionate to the legitimate aim pursued would seem to be appropriate to any form of democratic society.

The Rule of Law

In a narrow sense the Rule of Law requires that every person organ or agency of government is subject to the Law and must act in accordance with its rules and principles. While the primacy of the Rule of Law

---

[249] Osita C. Eze, "Non Discrimination and its Application to Matters of Racism and Racial Discrimination, Intolerance and Discrimination Based on Religion and Xenophobia" in Judicial Excellence: Essays in Honour of Hon. Justice Anthony I. Iguh J.S.C., C.O.N., eds, J.O. Irukwu (SAN) and I.A. Umezulike (OFR) (Judge) Enugu, Snaap Press Ltd. 2004 pp. 99-100.

is guaranteed in most modern legal systems this does not tell us anything about the nature and essence of the laws that must be obeyed, they may be fascist, authoritarian or democratic. Yet the Rule of law assumes, in a democratic setting, that the laws should be just and serve the ends of social justice.

The African Charter does not specifically use the expression 'Rule of Law'. But by insisting on equality of all before the law and equal protection of all by the law as well as by requiring that all concerned, states parties, individuals and peoples are subject to it enthrones the principle of the Rule of Law. Furthermore, by regaining that independent national tribunals/courts decide on issues of violations of rights guaranteed it gives institutional backing to them. Ultimately the African Commission and Court will serve as the guarantors of these rights at the international level[250].

In our context, the 1999 constitution of Nigeria entrenches the supremacy of the Rule of Law by stipulating in the very first section that the Constitution is supreme and its provisions shall have binding force on all authorities and persons throughout the Federal Republic of Nigeria.[251] By the same token all laws validly made pursuant to the constitution are binding on all authorities and persons within the Federation or the State as the case may be[252]. Seen in this context, any take over of government otherwise than as provided in the constitution, [Article 1(2)] is a negation of the primacy of the Rule of Law. The justification for *ex post facto* legitimization of the new order is founded on the argument that a military coup, which is a revolution in law, has the capacity to

---

[250] See infra: and Articles 1, 7 and 26 of the African Charter.

[251] 1999 Constitution, s.1(1). See also Kanda v. The Governor of Kaduna State (1985) 6 N.C.L.R. (Part 35) p. 381.

[252] 1999 Constitution, s.1(3).

establish a new legal order.[253] And it may be maintained that the first legislative act which invariably legitimizes the new order and sets in motion the practice of retroactive legislation and ouster of courts jurisdiction not only leads to 'instability' in the judicial process but also derogates from the Rule of Law as we understand it. In particular the ouster clauses by purporting to preclude judicial competence even where the provisions of the relevant decrees have not been adhered to by the authorities fall short of the standards required by the principle of the Rule of Law.[254] Such derogations are sometimes justified on the ground that military rule, because of its character, is not expected to conform fully with the imperatives of democracy and the Rule of Law.

His Lordship, Hon. Justice A. Aniagolu, JSC (retired) put the matter in a proper perspective when in *Dr. O.G.S. Sofekan v. Chief N.O. Akinyemi & Others*, he declared:

It is essential in a constitutional democracy such as we have in this country, that for the protection of the rights of the citizens, for the guarantee of the rule of law which includes according fair trial to the citizen under procedural regularity, and for checking arbitrary use of power by the Executive or its agencies, the power and jurisdiction of the courts under the Constitution must not only be kept intact and unfettered but also must not be nibbled at. To permit any interference with or usurpation of, the authority of the courts, as afore stated is to strike at the bulwark which the Constitution gives and guarantees to the citizen, of fairness to him against arbitrariness and oppression.

---

[253] A. Ojo *"Constitutional law and military law in Nigeria"*, Ibadan, Evans Brothers (Nigerian Publishers) Ltd 1987, p.94 *E.O. Lakanmi and Kikelomo Ola v. The Attorney-General* (Western State) UILR Vol. 1.

[254] C Okpaluba, *Judicial Approach to Constitutional Interpretation in Nigeria, op. cit* p.95 *et sequ.*

Indeed, so important is this preservation of, and non-interference with, the jurisdiction of the courts

That our present constitution (Decree No. 25 of 1978) has specifically provided (s.4(8) that neither the National Assembly nor a House of Assembly shall 'enact any law that ousts or purports to oust the jurisdiction of court of law or a judicial tribunal established by law[255].

Seen from the perspective of world currents and in particular of the liberal school of jurisprudence, which insists that the Rule of Law includes the right to free elections (with laws enacted by duly elected representatives of the people affording equal protection to all, and that the Rule of Law *can only be fully realized* under a system of government established by the will of the people) the shortcomings of a military government and in fact dictatorships in this regard are more readily understood.[256]

The Rule of law, therefore goes beyond the obligation to obey the laws by all and "should be employed not only to safeguard and advance civil and political rights of the individual in a society, but also to establish social, economic, educational and cultural conditions under which his legitimate aspirations and dignity may be realized".

Thus conceived the Rule of Law is not merely restrictive and inhibiting but purposeful and dynamic for the spectrum of human rights listed constitute critical elements of democracy and the Rule of law.

---

[255] Cited in C, Okpaluba, op. cit. p. 90. See also S. Livingstone "The Rule of Law, Human Rights and Democracy: *in Managing the protection of Human Rights op. cit.* p. 14.

[256] Osita C. Eze "Theoretical Perspectives and Problematic" In Society and the Rule of Law, Osita C. Eze ed, op cit, pp 17-20' The Rule of Law and Human Rights: Principles and Definitions Geneva, International Commission of Jurists, 1966, pp. 2-3.

It is true that the African Charter does not as is the case with the European and American Conventions, explicitly mention democracy but as already indicated by guaranteeing the right of people to participate in government and the related rights of association etc. it guarantees the right to participatory democracy. By definition democracy can not thrive without the Rule of Law-broadly defined.

6

SOCIO-ECONOMIC
AND CULTURAL RIGHTS

6.1 Introduction

Socio-Economic and Cultural rights are sometimes referred to as 'second generation rights' because they developed much later than civil and political rights. The genesis of these rights could be traced to the papal Encyclical Rerum Novarum of Pope Leo XIII of 1891[257] and the Marxist critique of 19th century capitalism.[258]

The Encyclical Rerum Novarum and the socialist or Marxist ideology share a number of things in common. They represented responses to increasing impoverishment of the working class that resulted from nascent capitalism. They also represented historical landmarks that decisively contributed to the evolution of socio-economic rights, that later became known as "second generation rights" as opposed to civil and political rights that are categorized as "first generation rights". Despite these similarities Rerum Novarum could be aptly described as an "anti-social Manifesto". The Divinely guided society of men seemed in every sense opposed to the socialist materialist conception of history and there was a contradiction between the predilection of the former for

---

[257] London Catholic Truth Society, 1960.

[258] Milton Viorst The Great Documents of Western Civilization, London, Chilton Books Company, 1965 pp. 241-248, Osita C. Eze Human Rights in African, op cit p. 5.

private ownership of property and the insistence of the latter on the dominance of public ownership of the means of production.[259]

6.2 Some National and other Experiences

Apart from the right to property (private) and association (trade unions) found in constitutions of countries of liberal persuasion the other economic, social and cultural rights found their way first in constitutions of socialist countries and countries of socialist orientation. Most constitutions of countries of liberal persuasion either do not include them or when included they are regarded as non-justiceable i.e. that they are not capable of creating the basis for legal action. The Directive Principles of State Policy, in chapter (IX of Ghana's 1992 has gone a step further than the Nigerian equivalent in making provision for ensuring the implementation of these directive principles. Even though under the 1979 Republican Constitution of Nigeria, parliament had the competence to establish institutions to ensure compliance nothing was done.[260] The same has been the case since the coming into force of the 1999 constitution which contains the same provision.[261] The provision has been implemented piecemeal by for example the legislation on education for children and the project law on the rights of women.[262]

Article 34(1) of the 1992 constitution of Ghana provides:

"The Directive principles of state policy contained in this chapter shall guide all citizens, parliament, the President, the judiciary, the Council of State, the cabinet 'political parties and other bod-

---

[259] Osita C. Eze "Human Rights, Peace and Rerum Novarum of Leo XIII" in Catholic Social Teachings En-Route in Africa, Obiora F. Ike Ed, Enugu, CIDJAP, 1991, p.1.

[260] Second Schedule, para 57(a).

[261] Second Schedule, para 60(a).

[262] This is caused by the provision for Universal Basic Education (UBE).

ies and persons in applying or interpreting this constitution or any other law and in taking and implementing any policy decisions, for the establishment of a just and free society".

Article 34(2), is concerned with the realization of the objectives of the directive principles and requires the president to report to parliament, at least once a year "all steps taken to ensure the realization of basic human rights, a healthy economy, the right to work, the right to good health care and the right to education."

It is not expressly stated that the directive principles contained in the 1992 constitution of Ghana are non-justiceable as is the case with the 1979 and 1999 constitutions of Nigeria) a factor which in appropriate circumstances may offer opportunities for judicial activism in the case of Ghana.

Economic, social and cultural rights are contained in the 1948 Universal Declaration of Human Rights – which is not a legally binding instrument. It is contested whether the International Covenant on Economic Social and Cultural Rights did create immediate obligations for the parties as Article 2(1) stipulates that:

"Each State Party to the present Covenant undertakes to take steps individually and through international assistance and co-operation, especially economic and technical, to the maximum of its available resources, with a view to achieving progressively the full realization of the rights recognized in the present covenant by all appropriate means, including particularly the adoption of legislative measures"

Movchan argues that "the vague reference to the maximum of its available resources" which can be interpreted differently and also the reference to "achieving progressively the full realization of the rights" makes it possible to delay indefinitely the implementation of the provision of the Covenant on Economic, Social and Cultural Rights[263]. Movchan further argues, and we agree with him that "the absence of clearly formulated obligations imposed on States to implement these human rights means that ratification by States of the Covenant on Economic, Social and Cultural rights may turn out to be a vague promise which either will be fulfilled by some unspecified date or will not be fulfilled at all.[264] A careful reading of this position does not really deny the absence of a legal obligation but laments its lack of clarity and the degree of appreciation it offers to states.

The practice within the European Community might have influenced the adoption by the UN of two separate covenants civil and political rights and economic social and cultural Rights borne out of the 1948 Universal Declaration, since the former in 1950 adopted the European Convention on Human Rights[265] which encompasses civil and political rights and in 1960 the European Social Charter[266] which covers economic, social and cultural rights. While the 1950 convention guarantees to individuals the rights contained therein and creates obligations for the parties to ensure their enjoyment (Article1), the latter obliges the states parties "to accept as the aim of their policy, to be pursued by all appropriate means, both national and international in character, the attainment of conditions in which the following rights may be effectively realized (part 1). Under Article 20 (1) (a) of the European Social Charter, each of the contracting parties undertakes to consider part 1 of the charter as a declaration of the aims which it will pursue by all appropriate means.

---

[263] A Movchan, Human Rights and International Relations, Moscow Progress Publishers, 1982, p.132.

[264] *Ibid.*

[265] For the text of the European Convention for the protection of Human Rights and Freedoms (Rome 4. xi 1950) as amended, see Judicial colloquium in Bangalore op. cit pp. 127-143.

[266] For the text of the European Social Charter, see ibid., pp. 145-168.

Each of the contracting states also undertakes to consider itself bound by at least five of the following Articles of part 11: Articles 1 (right to work), 5 (right to organize), 6 (right to bargain collectively), 12, (right to social security), 13, (the right to social and medical assistance), 16, (The right of the family to social, legal and economic protection), and 19 (the right of migrant workers and their families to protection and assistance).[267] Under the Revised European Social Charter Article 7 (the right of children and young persons to protection) is included and parties undertake to be bound by a least 6 of the Articles.[268]

Apart from efforts at reinforcing some of the rights new rights are added to the Revised Social Charter. Some of these are: the right to protection in cases of termination of employment (Article 24); the right to dignity at work (Article 26); the right of workers with family responsibilities to equal opportunities and equal treatment (Article 27); the right to protection against poverty and social exclusion (Article 30); and the right to housing (Article 31).

The Revised Charter has also introduced a non-discrimination clause, not found in the European Social Charter. The European Convention on Humans in its Article 14 makes provision for this which we have discussed earlier. Part V Article E of the Revised Charter provides.

> The enjoyment of rights set forth in this Charter shall be secured without discrimination on any ground such as race, colour, sex, language, religion, political or other opinion, national extraction or social origin, health, association with a national minority, birth or other status.

There has since been further consolidation of ECOSOC rights within the European system with the revision of the European Social Charter in

---

[267] See Article 20(1) under which parties may undertake to be bound by additional Articles in Part II. (b).

[268] Part III, Article A(b).

1996[269] and the Additional Protocol[270] to the European Charter providing for a System of collective complaints. Apart from the right of association and the right to organize which, in any event are guaranteed under the European Convention on Human Rights and are therefore, justiceable thereunder the rights recognized in the Social Charter do not appear justiceable. There is an obligatory reporting system by States Parties under the Social Charter which is retained under the Revised Charter (Part IV Article C)[271] on the rights which they have undertaken to be bound by which reports are to be made at two yearly intervals to the secretary general of the Council of Europe are examined by committee of experts (article 25) which shall have also before it any comments forwarded to the Secretary General.

Article 23(2) of the Social Charter requires the Contracting Parties to forward to the Secretary-General of the Council of Europe reports received from national organisations if so requested by them. The reports of the contracting parties and the conclusions of the committee of experts are submitted for examination to a sub-committee of the Governmental Social Committee of the Council of Europe. The sub-committee shall present to the Committee of Ministers a report containing its conclusions and append the report of the Committee of experts. [Article 27(1) and (3)]

---

[269] Council of Europe ETS, no. 163, European Social Charter (revised) Strasbourg. 3v. 1996.

[270] Additional protocol to the European Social Charter; ETS, May 5, 1988, (not in force as at 8/2/02).

[271] Part IV Article C provides: The implementation of the legal obligations contained in this Charter shall be submitted to the same supervision as the European Social Charter. The sections of the supervisory system cited in the text are as in the European Social Charter See Protocol Amending the European Social Charter 1991 (ETS No.142) which has introduced some amendments.

The Secretary-General of the Council of Europe transmits to the Consultative Assembly the conclusions of the Committee of Experts. The Consultative Assembly then communicates its views on these conclusions to the apex body, the Committee of Ministers (article 28).

By a majority of two-thirds of members entitled to sit on the Committee, the Committee of Ministers may, on the basis of the report of the sub-committee, and after consultation with the Consultative Assembly, make to each Contracting Party any necessary recommendations [Article 29].

The preamble to the revised European Social Charter recognizes the indivisibility of all categories of rights (1st and 2nd generations). It recognizes the developmental aspect of Social rights by agreeing to secure them in order to improve the Standard of living and Social well-being of their population. The revision had as its objective the updating and adaptation of the substantive contents of the Charter in order to take account particularly of the fundamental social changes, which have occurred since the Charter was adopted. The Revised Charter is to progressively take the place of European Social Charter. The rights guaranteed by the Charter have been amended by the rights guaranteed by the Additional Protocol of 1998 and added new rights.

Similar undertakings exist with respect to part 1 of the Charter (considered as a declaration of aims) and part II as regards to the obligation of parties for certain provisions. Under the Revised Charter as already indicated there is a minimum of six out of nine articles of part II, as opposed to a minimum of five under the Charter. The Revised Social Charter includes in addition the right to equal opportunities and equal treatment in matters of employment and occupation without discrimination on grounds of sex (article 20).

Article I, part IV provides for implementation of Articles 1- 31, of the Revised Charter without prejudice to the methods of implementation foreseen in these Articles, by

- laws and regulations,
- agreements between employers or employers organisations and workers organisations,
- a combination of these two methods,
- other appropriate means[272].

The system of collective complaints introduced under the Additional Protocol to the European Social Charter provides for a system of collective enforcement of the social rights guaranteed by the Charter (preamble). Under the Protocol Contracting Parties undertook to accept the right of some organisations to submit complaints alleging unsatisfactory application of the Charter.

1. International organisations of employers and trade unions referred to in paragraph 2 of Article 27 of the Charter – these "not more than two international trade union organisations as it [sub-committee of the Governmental Social Committee] may designate to be represented as observers in a consultative capacity in its meetings. Moreover it may consult no more than two representatives of international non-governmental organisations having consultative status

---

[272] Article I(2) provides that: Compliance with undertakings deriving from the provisions of paragraphs 1, 2, 3, 4, 5, and 7 of Article 2 (right to just conditions of work); paragraphs 4, 6 and 7 of Article 7 (the right of children and young persons to protection); paragraphs 1, 2, 3 and of Article 10 (the right to vocational training); and Article 21 (the right to information and consultation), and 22 (the right to take part in the determination and improvement of the working conditions and working environment); of the Revised Charter shall be regarded as effective if the provisions are applied in accordance with paragraph one of this article, to the great majority of the workers concerned.

with the Council of Europe, in respect of questions with which the organisations are particularly qualified to deal, such as social welfare, and the economic and social protection of the family. It is probable that the right of the Governmental Committee to 'designate' may have been reduced.

2.   Other international organisations which have consultative status with the Council of Europe and have been put on a list established for this purpose by the Governmental Committee.

3.   Representative national organisations of employers and trade unions within the jurisdiction of the Contracting Party against which they have lodged a complaint.

A State has the option to declare that it recognizes the right of any other representative national non-governmental organisations within its jurisdiction, which has particular competence in the matters governed by the Charter. Such declaration may be made for a specified period [Articles 2(1) and (2)].

The complaints which pass through the Committee of Independent experts and to the Committee of Ministers ends up with a recommendation to the Contracting Party concerned and is adopted by a two thirds majority of Ministers voting (Articles 8 and 9).

It is thus clear that despite the substantial progress made in the interactive conception of rights, their reformulation in some cases and the adoption of new rights as basic as protection against poverty that neither the supervisory system nor the system of collective complaints provides for binding decisions in the manner of the European Court.

The provisions of Additional Protocol to the European Social Charter providing for a system of collective complaints shall apply to undertakings given in the Charter for states which have ratified the protocol. [Part IV Article D(1)].

Article C Part IV of the Revised Protocol as already indicated covers the competence of the existing machinery to supervise the implementation of the undertakings under the Revised Charter [Part IV Article C].

6.3 The Position of the African Charter

In view of the dichotomy created between the civil and political rights and economic, social and cultural rights in the international human rights conventions examined, it is quite clear, as we shall demonstrate later, that the African Charter has gone a step further by not only including civil, political, economic, social and cultural rights in one instrument but also by, since they all create rights whose enforcement are ensured, placing them on the same legal pedestal. The issue of their actualization is a different matter.

Article 14 of the African Charter guarantees the right to property which may only be encroached upon in the interest of public need or in the general interest of the community and in accordance with the provisions of appropriate law. The right to property may thus be limited and from the wordings of the provision it can be deduced that room is left for dominance or subordination of private property depending on the outlook of a particular government. And it may appear with respect to compensation that the unsettled Eurocentric law on nationalization might not be applicable.[273]

Under the Charter every individual is guaranteed the right to work under equitable and satisfactory conditions and to equal pay for equal

---

[273] Osita C. Eze "The Crisis of International Law and Regulation of Private Foreign Investments; The Quest for a New Legal Order" Nigeria Journal of International Studies vols. 5-7 1981-83, p. 26 et seq.

work (Article 15): in 39/90 Annette Paguoulle (on behalf of Abdoulaye Mazou)/Cameroon the Commission found that by not reinstating Mazou in his former position, after the Amnesty law, the government had violated Article 15 of the African Charter because it had prevented Mr. Mazou to work in his capacity of a magistrate even though others who had been condemned under similar conditions had been reinstated. In another communication relating to the expulsion of some West Africans from Angola the Commission affirmed the right to work (159/96). In its words this type of deportation calls into question a whole series of rights recognized and guaranteed in the Charter, such are the right to property (article 14), the right to work (article 15), the right to education (article 17) and results in the violation by the state of its obligation under Article 18(1) "that the family shall be the natural unit and basis of society, it shall be protected by the state which shall take care of its physical and moral health".

As constructed the right envisaged under Article 15 could be interpreted as the right not to work per se but the right, when one is employed to work under equitable and satisfactory conditions and for equal pay for equal work. There is good judgment, however, in the expansive interpretation which the Commission has given to it..

The right to enjoy the best attainable state of physical and mental health is guaranteed to every individual just as the states parties have the obligation to take the necessary measures to protect the health of their people and to ensure that they receive medical attention when they are sick. (Article 16(1)& (2)). Communication 139/96 already affirms the right to health as a legal right. The Commission has held that the responsibility of the state is even more in the event of detention to the extent that detention centres are its exclusive preserve, hence the physical integrity and welfare of detainees is the responsibility of the competent public authorities [210/98].

Article 17 guarantees to every individual the right to education as well as to freely take part in the cultural life of his community. In communication 10/93 discussed above the Commission held that the circumstances under which universities and secondary schools were closed for two years in Zaire violated Article 17. It is gratifying that the Commission has taken the first but cautious steps not only to affirm the obligatory character of ECOSOC rights but in interpreting them. developments elsewhere, on how the interpretation of ECOSOC rights could be approached would in our view be of use to the Commission.

In communication 225/98 Huri-Laws/Nigeria, the Commission held that the search of Civil Liberty Organization's office, without warrant and seizure of its property in circumstances not justified either by public need or community interest as required by the Charter violated Article 14. Also the Commission held that a Decree which permitted a newspapers premises to be sealed up and for publications to be seized could not be said to be "appropriate" or in the interest of the public or the community in general. In elaborating on the elements of the right to property it stated "the right to property necessarily includes the right to have access to one's property [146/94, 141/94, 145/95 Constitutional Rights Project, Civil Liberties Organisation, Media Rights Agenda/Nigeria]. The confiscation of Modise's belongings and property by the Botswanan government[274] the loss of their property as a result of the brutality meted to some West Africans citizens who were then expelled, from Angola[275] as well as the confiscation of the land and property of blacks in Mauritania before they were forced out of the country[276] were all held to be in violation of Article 14.

---

[274] 97/93.

[275] 159/96.

[276] 54/91, 61/91, 98/93, 164/97, 96/97, 210/98.

It was, however, in 25/89, 47/90, 56/91, 100/93 Free Legal Assistance Group and ors/Zaire that the Commission attempted a broad elaboration of the nature of the obligation in this regard. It stated that "the failure of the Government to provide basic services such as safe drinking water and electricity and the shortage of medicine as alleged in communication 100/93 constitutes a violation of Article 16.[277]

The manner in which ECOSOC rights were formulated, particularly in the Universal Declaration of Human Rights (1948) and the International Convention on Economic Social and Cultural Rights (ICESCR) (1966) as to the 'progressive' nature of their attainment which depends as well on 'available resources' raises issues as to whether they are justiceable or not. In particular, the fact that there were two conventions, one for civil and political rights within the EU of having one convention for civil and political rights and the social charter for ECOSOC rights tended to reinforce this dichotomy.

Only in the African Charter on Human and Peoples Rights have ECOSOC rights, including people's rights which have ECOSOC contents, been elevated to the status of justiceable rights as evident from the language employed and the interpretation which the Commission has placed on them.

6.4 Nature of Legal Rights and Obligations

It is now accepted that despite the manner of its formulation ECOSOC rights under ICESCR, and similar formulations in other UN instruments, create immediate obligations from which progress based on available resources can be measured. A fortiori, in the case of the African Charter, where obligation is imposed the formula for establishing various levels of the responsibility, particularly given the implications of

---

[277] See also Eze and Eze Onyekwere, Study of Right to Health in Nigeria, Shelter Rights Initiative 2001.

resource constraint, and the practice of the Commission to rely on established international standards, will aid interpretation. The baseline obligations according to the Maastricht[278] guidelines are:

Obligation to respect

The obligation requires States to refrain from interfering with the enjoyment of economic, social and cultural rights. Thus, the right to housing is violated if the state engages in arbitrary forced eviction.

Obligation to protect

The obligation to protect requires states to prevent violation of such rights by third parties viz, failure to ensure that private employers comply with basic labour standards may amount to a violation of the right to work and the right to just and favourable conditions of work.

Obligation to fulfill

Obligation to fulfill requires the state to take appropriate legislative, administrative, budgetary, judicial and other measures towards the full realization of such rights. Thus, failure to provide essential primary health care to those in need may amount to a violation.

It is particularly at the level of obligations to fulfill calling on state to invest resources that problem mostly arises. But practice of international bodies has to a large extent shown the way. It is important to note that at each level of responsibility, the state has a margin of discretion in selecting the means of implementation. But state conduct can increasingly be measured by the standard norms and jurisprudence (universal minimum standards) developed by international treaty, monitoring bodies, as well as domestic courts (such as the evolving jurisprudence in South Africa and elsewhere). These standards have contributed in establishing the

---

[278] For the text of the Maastricht Guidelines, see Osita C. Eze and Eze Onyekpere, *op. cit*, pp.121-131.

scope, nature and limitation of ECOSOC rights.[279] The Maastricht Guidelines are in order when it is stated that".

The fact that the full realization of most economic, social and cultural rights can only be achieved progressively, which in fact also applies to most civil and political rights, does not alter the nature of the legal obligation of states which requires that certain steps be taken immediately and others as soon as possible. Therefore, the burden is on the state to demonstrate that it is making measurable progress towards the realization of the rights in question. The state cannot use the "progressive realization provisions in Article 2 of the Covenant as a pretext for non compliance. Nor, can the state justify derogations or limitations of rights recognized in the Covenant because of different social, religious and cultural backgrounds (para 8).

Minimum Core Obligations

Violation Occur Inter Alia

When a state fails to satisfy 'minimum core obligations' to ensure satisfaction of, at the very least, minimum essential levels of each of the rights. Thus, for example, a state party in which any significant number of individuals is deprived of essential foodstuffs, of essential primary health care, of basic shelter and housing or of the most basic forms of education is, prima facie, violating the covenant. Such minimum core obligations apply irrespective of the availability of resources of the country concerned or any other factors or difficulties. (para 9)

Violations through Acts of Omission

Violations of economic, social and cultural rights can also occur through the omission or failure of States to take necessary measures stemming from legal obligations. Examples of such violations include:

---

[279] *Ibid.*

1. the failure to take appropriate steps as required under the covenant;

2. the failure to reform or repeal legislation which is manifestly inconsistent with an obligation of the Covenant;

3. the failure to enforce legislation or put into effect policies designed to implement provisions of the covenant;

4. the failure to regulate activities of individuals or groups so as to prevent them from violating economic, social and cultural rights'

5. the failure to utilize the maximum of available resources towards the full realization of the covenant;

6. the failure to monitor the realization of economic, social and cultural rights, including the development and application of criteria and indicators for accessing compliance;

7. the failure to remove promptly obstacles which it is under a duty to remove to permit the immediate fulfillment of a right guaranteed by the Covenant;

8. the failure to implement without delay a right which it is required by the Covenant to provide immediately;

9. the failure to meet a generally accepted international minimum standard of achievement, which is within its powers to meet;

10. the failure of a state to take into account its international legal obligations in the field of economic, social and cultural rights when entering into bilateral or multilateral agreements with other states, international organisations or multinational corporations (paragraph 14).

Violations through Acts of Commission

Violations of economic, social and cultural rights can occur through the direct action of States or other entities insufficiently regulated by states. Examples of such violations include:

1. the formal removal or suspension of legislation necessary for the continued enjoyment of an economic, social and cultural rights that is currently enjoyed;

2. the active denial of such rights to particular individuals or groups, whether through legislated or enforced discrimination;

3. the active support for measures adopted by third parties which are inconsistent with economic, social and cultural rights;

4. the adoption of legislation or policies which are manifestly incompatible with pre-existing legal obligations relating to these rights, unless it is done with the purpose and effect of increasing equality and improving the realization of economic, social and cultural rights for the most vulnerable groups;

5. the adoption of any deliberately retrogressive measures that reduces the extent to which any such rights if guaranteed;

6. the calculated obstruction of, or halt to, the progressive realization of a right protected by the Covenant, unless the State is (para.14)

7. the reduction of diversion of specific public expenditure, when such reduction or diversion results in the non-enjoyment of such rights and is not accompanied by adequate measures to ensure minimum subsistence rights for everyone [Paragraph 14].

Of great significance is the place of the determination of the Committee on Economic, Social and Cultural Rights on the legal status and violations of ECOSOC rights. The Committee in determining whether a state has or has not met its obligations would be making a judgment as to whether there has occurred a violation or not and it has therefore the inherent authority to do so. It is in this light that the two statements, one general and the other more specific, on ECOSOC rights by the Committee become very cogent.

The first which relates to justiceability states:

"On the basis of the extensive experience gained by the Committee, as well as by the body that preceded it, over a period of more than a decade of examining States Parties' reports the Committee is of the view that a minimum core obligation to ensure the satisfaction of, at the very least, minimum essential levels of each of the rights is incumbent upon every state party. Thus, for example, a State party in which any significant number of individuals is deprived of essential foodstuffs of essential primary health care, of basic shelter and housing, or of the most basic forms of education is, prima facie, failing to discharge its obligations under the Covenant. If the Covenant were not to be read to establish such a minimum core obligation, it would be largely deprived of its raison d'etre ... In order for a state party to be able to attribute its failure to meet at least its minimum core obligations to a lack of available resources it must demonstrate that every effort has been made to use all resources that are at its disposition in an effort to satisfy, as a matter of priority, those minimum obligations".[280]

The second re-echoes and expands the position of the Committee on the nature and components of obligation and reads:

---

[280] See Committee on Economic, Social and Cultural Rights General Comment No. 3 (Fifth December 1990) UN Doc E 1991/23 Annex III paragraph 10. Emphasis mine.

"It is important in this regard to distinguish between justiceability (which refers to those matters which are appropriately resolved by the courts) and norms which are self executing (capable of being applied by courts without further elaboration). While the general approach of each legal system needs to be taken into account, there is no Covenant right which could not in the great majority of systems be considered to possess at least some significant justiceable dimensions. It is sometimes suggested that matters involving the allocation of resources should be left to the political authorities rather than the courts. While the respective competence of the various branches of government must be respected, it is appropriate to acknowledge that courts are generally already involved in a considerable range of matters which have important resource implications. The adoption of a rigid classification of ESC rights which puts them, by definition beyond the reach of the courts will thus be arbitrary and incompatible with the principle that the two sets of human rights are indivisible and interdependent. It would also drastically curtail the capacity of the courts to protect the rights of the most vulnerable and disadvantaged groups in society[281].

6.5 The Jurisprudence of the African Commission the African Charter on Human and Peoples Rights

Even though as indicated in my Article – Significance of ECOSOC Rights for Development, the language of ECOSOC Rights enumerated therein, create instant, legal obligations and rights, given the level of socio-economic development, and understanding that 'the minimum core obligations' would have to be interpreted in context, the principles of interpretation elaborated for ICESCR, will apply pro tanto.

The African Commission has in a number of cases, already discussed as well as those referred to below, 'ruled' that there had been violations

---

[281] *Ibid.*

of ECOSOC Rights, but it has not been forthright in either elaborating the underlying jurisprudence or in providing for remedies. {See in particular 30/90 Annette Pagnoulle (On behalf of Abdoulaye Mazou) Cameroon (Art 15-work), Communications 25/89, 47/90, 56/91, 100/93 Free Legal Assistance Group, Lawyers Group for Human Rights, Union Interafricaine des Droits de l'Homme, Les Temoins de Jahouah/Zaire, Art. 16 – health), and, (Art. 17 education), 159/96. Union Interafricanine des Droits de l'Homme, Recontre Africaine des Droits de l'Homme, Organisation Nationale des Droit de'Homme Senegal and Association Malienne des Droits de'Homme vs. Angola (Art. 18 – family) 11th Annual Report"}.

If we have gone some length in examining the Maastricht guidelines as well as the jurisprudence of the Human Rights Committee, it is for two reasons:

Firstly, we wish to assist in generalizing the basis for advocacy that will promote both the guarantee of and enforcement of ECOSOC rights in the constitutions of African countries as the growing trend found in the constitutions of Ghana, Uganda and South Africa since this creates an effective rear for the African Charter.

Secondly, also by making it generally accessible, particularly to human rights lawyers and NGOs we hope that by adopting them creatively they will reinforce the Commission and now the Court in their movement towards finding a proper jurisprudence for ECOSOC rights guaranteed in the African Charter. This is particularly so since as we shall see the African Court has a clearer mandate to interpret and apply other human rights conventions to which members are parties.

The possibility of actualizing socio-economic and cultural rights entrenched in the African Charter must be considered in the light of SAP (The Structural Adjustment Programme) and its new ranging from NEEDS to the regime under the WTO as well as the attitude of Western donor countries to the protection of economic, social and cultural rights which has markedly improved since the spate of revisions of the European Social Charter. Orthodox SAP emphasizes growth to the detriment of basic needs – increase in the price of food, cost of shelter and because the state retreats to the background in terms of provision of social services, health care and education become unaffordable to the majority who are the most vulnerable. The deregulation of the labour market in order to allow for optimal play of market forces weakens workers organisation, leads to reduced earning power and retrenchment of workers.[282] In the circumstances, even where the will exists to ensure the protection of economic and social rights, the IMF/World Bank inspired "Liberalization and deregulation peal" portends negative results. And there is no guarantee that growth, which is its central concern, is readily achievable.

Professor Adebayo Adedeji, the then Under-Secretary General and Executive Secretary of the Economic Commission for Africa, (ECA) who was a key figure in formulating the African Alternative to SAP, (AA-SAP), (SAP with a human face) put his finger on it when he stated:

> "Africa needs fundamental change and transformations not just adjustment. The change and transformation required are not just narrow economic and mechanical ones. They are broader and fundamental changes that will bring about, over time, the new Africa of our vision where there is development and economic justice, not just growth, where there is democracy and accountability not despotism, authoritarianism and kleptocracy; and where the governed and their governments are moving hand-in-hand in the promotion of the Common good, and where it is the

---

[282] Amos Wako, "Social Dimensions of Structural Adjustment Programmes: A Human Rights Issue" in Africa; A new Lease on Life" op. cit, p. 237, Peter Peek, "Workers Organisations and Structural Adjustment", ibid., pp. 241 –243, Osita C. Eze "Technological Transformation of Nigeria" Paper presented as A MAMSER workshop (1992) (forthcoming).

will of the people rather, than the wishes of one person or a group of persons, however powerful, that prevails.[283]

The Catholic notion of "The Common Good[284] also evinces the principles of solidarity and social justice. "The common good stands in opposition to the good of rulers or of a ruling (or any other) class. It implies that every individual, no matter how high or low, has a duty to share in promoting the welfare of the community as well as right to benefit from that welfare. "Common" implies 'all-inclusive': the common good cannot exclude or exempt any section of the population. If any section of the population is in fact excluded from participation in the life of the community, even at a minimal level, then that is a contradiction to the concept of the common good and calls for rectification" (paragraph 70).

On the market,

"Catholic Social Teaching recognizes the fundamental and positive value of business, the market, private property and free human creativity in the economic sector. But sometimes market forces cannot deliver what the common good demands and other remedies have to be sought. The real 'poor' in a relatively prosperous Western society are those without sufficient means to take part in the life of the community. This means they cannot participate in the formation of public policies that might protect them from the community, and they are denied the rights of member-

---

[283] "African Charter for popular Participation in Development" cit, p. 37.

[284] The Common Good and the Catholic Social Teaching: A statement by the Catholic Bishops Conference of England and Wales; 1997; See also VATICAN COUNCIL II, the Concillar and Post Concillar Documents, General Editor, Austin Flannery, O.p, 1988, Revised Edition, Dublin, Dominican Publications, 1998, p. 968.

ship. Their choices are circumscribed; they have little personal freedom". (paragraph 74).

More directly with respect to conflicts, it is maintained that

"The church's social teaching can be summed up as the obligation of every individual to contribute to the good of the society, in the interests of justice and in pursuit of the 'option for the poor'. This is the context most likely to foster human fulfillment for everyone, where each individual can enjoy the benefit of living in an orderly, prosperous and healthy society. A society with insufficient regard for the common good would be unpleasant and dangerous to live in, as well as unjust to those it excluded" (paragraph 73).

The demands of social justice and the need to enthrone principle of common good are even more urgent in developing countries which are more prone to conflicts. It is even more urgent in that the social and economic system tends to exclude the majority and understandably the greatest security (physical and psychological) threat to this ever growing mass of the poor is confronted by the need to escape from poverty.

As for the attitude of Western donor countries that actually control the World Market, there appears to have been some shift from the position they held just after the crisis of Socialism and the Gulf War. At the time they tended to emphasize as conditionality for the grant of loans the enthronement of democracy and respect for civil and political rights. The view of the then American Ambassador to Nigeria Mr. Brian Brown sums up this position:

"We realize that there is a school of thought stressing the primacy of economic, social and cultural rights over political and civil liberties. In many countries, this has been used as a rationale to suppress free expression and other civil liberties. While the U.S.

Government recognizes the importance of these aspirations, experience has sadly taught us that where civil liberties are held subordinate to economic aspirations, a system is created where usually neither of these rights is delivered. Consequently, our human rights policy focuses on basic political freedoms and civil liberties".[285]

According to him the United States Government seeks to develop programmes to bolster democratic institutions and values such as openness in government, the free press, an independent judiciary, and the rule of law.[286] How civil and political rights are to be achieved if at least equal emphasis is not given to economic, social and cultural rights is apparently not a matter of serious concern:

The position of the Council of Europe in this matter is reflected in its Declaration on Human Rights Democracy and Development, made on 25 v. 93 in its paragraph 5:

"The Community and its Member States draw particular attention to the universality and indivisibility of human rights and the obligations of all states to respect them. They stress the important role of development assistance in promoting both economic, social and cultural rights as well as civil and political liberties by means of representative democratic government based on respect for human rights.[287] Ordinarily we would not quarrel with this

---

[285] "Ambassadors' Colloquium": Human rights and Democracy Reform as Conditions for Development Aid", Lagos, Human Right Africa, 1990, p.15.

[286] *Ibid.*

[287] Africa: A New Lease on Life, op cit; p.287; See Also D. Diuglaris, on European Community Policy which uses the performance of a Country relative to Civil, Political, economic, social and cultural rights as Criterion for economic cooperation "Ambassadors Colloquium, op. cit. p. 31. See also Osita C. Eze; "Africa, New World Order Human Rights and Democracy" 1992 Inaugural Lecture, Imo State University (now Abia State University) UTURU'.

'new' position but lurking behind its apparent neutrality is the insistence on the dominance of market forces and privatization. Does this not infringe our right to self-determination and could it not amount to the imposition of certain alien values and interference in our internal affairs, particularly since under SAP, officers of the IMF/World Bank are invariably breathing down the necks of our central bankers and other government officials.Despite the danger emanating from the practice of IMF/World Bank and donor countries, the EU position is that: "while the European Community is certainly active in encouraging the development of Democracy and Human Rights in non-member countries, it is recognized that the Prime movers in this direction are, and must be, the peoples of these nations themselves. The European Community is strictly respectful of the sovereignty of the independent nations, and considers it a basic principle of international relations".[288]

To all intents and purposes the World Trade Organisation, WTO, institutionalizes the process to manage the key elements of SAP which by hind sight aided the foundation for and fast-tracked globalization. The poverty eradication programme of the World Bank, by whatever name called[289], that is at best peripheral to the issue of socio-economic transformation like SAP before it, is more of a diversion and unless situated in the context of overall agenda for economic development is likely to continue to impede the maximal actualization of ECOSOC rights. What is more it has become increasingly recognized that the WTO agreements, enthrone social injustice through a mechanism of

---

[288] Perkins J., Confessions of an Economic Hit Man, New York, PLUME, Pengium Group, 2006, pp 273-274.

[289] It has mutated from NAPEP to NEEDS.

unequal exchange that has led inter alia to the de-industrialization and therefore under development of developing countries.[290]

Doha addressed the inequity of WTO as is exemplified in the statement by the Nigerian Minister of Commerce:

"The Fourth Session of the WTO Ministerial Conference is taking place at a time when the greatest challenge confronting the WTO is the need to reassure all that the multilateral trading system intends to and can operate equitably and fairly to promote prosperity for the generality of the world's population. The 4th Ministerial WTO Conference is also timely as it affords the WTO yet another opportunity to convince the forces of protesters against globalization that have become a normal sight at economic gatherings since Seattle two years ago of its good intentions. It is my delegation belief that the WTO must be seen to be fair to all, since no system, however, rule-based can command the respect of all unless it is also regarded as equitable fair and just. I would therefore urge you, as I did in Seattle, to give this issue the urgent attention that it deserves so that we can both individually and collectively ensure the system works for all".

The WTO Conference in Cancun Mexico in 2003 has drawn the line between those who feel left behind in the process of globalization and others. Since Cancun, the WTO has been on the retreat. I had argued

---

[290] Luke Adione-Egom Globalization at the Crossroads Capitalism or Communalism; Lagos, Global Market Associates, 2002, Osita C. Eze "solving the intellectual Property rights Deadlock," paper presented at a Discussion panel of a Conference Organized by the Foundation for Democracy in Africa, International Conference Centre, Abuja, 25-28 Feb, 2002.

that central[291] to this debacle therefore was the issue of distributive justice-fairness and equity and it is based on the assumption that:

1. the market as it works currently, particularly with the increasing economic disability of many if not most developing countries, is neither equitable nor fair and does not contain an automatic mechanism to adjust in that direction

2. the WTO agreements declaration that benefits of economic development will follow membership is not self-executing.

3. the basis of membership, with all its implications needs to be reviewed to address more concretely the developmental problems of developing countries and,

4. the structure of the world system of unequal exchange has in part contributed to this stage of globalization, and enriched the developed world at the expense of the developing areas and we by no means neglect the national causes of Africa's underdevelopment which need to be urgently addressed, and

5. if deep seated historically, rooted antagonisms are not to rock a future world and even undermine the whole globalization project those who have unduly benefited and continue to benefit have more than a moral duty to put back something from where they have reaped.

The underlying principle is that of enhanced free trade by the substantial reduction of tariffs and other barriers to trade and the elimination of discriminatory treatment in international trade relations. The WTO Agreement entrenched this principle which it affirms by the resolve of its members to develop an integrated , more viable and durable multilat-

---

[291] *Ibid.* See also generally Osita C. Eze, *Nigeria and the World Trade Organisation,* Lagos, Nigerian Institute of International Affairs, 2004, and in particular Chapter 2, 3 and 9.

eral trading system encompassing the General Agreement Tariffs and Trade, the results of past trade liberalization efforts, and all the results of "Uruguay Round of Multilateral Trade Negotiations". Accordingly, member states were determined to preserve the basic principles and to further the objectives underlying this multilateral trading system.

The push for market driven international trading system is based on certain basic assumptions, which may be contested. These assumptions are embedded in the recognition "that their relations in the field of trade and economic endeavour should be conducted with a view to raising standards of living, ensuring full employment and a large and steadily growing volume of real income and effective demand, and expanding the production of and trade in goods and services, while allowing for the optimal use of world resources in accordance with the objectives of sustainable development seeking both to protect and preserve the environment and to enhance the means of doing so in a manner consistent with their respective needs and concerns at different levels of economic development.

Even though the principles make some concession to developing countries, it is couched, apart from some others not so substantive concessions, in the WTO Agreement, viz: TRIPS, in very permissive language for the member states recognize the "need for positive efforts designed to ensure that developing countries and especially the least developed among them, secure a share in the growth in international trade commensurate with the needs of their economic development.

Since the initiative is now to be left to the private sector and governments are to assume the back seat, it will be interesting to see how member states will mediate the dominant objective of profit that is the motive force for globalization. In the absence of a global government, with the primary responsibility for everybody's welfare and security, this remains the crux of the problem. And it is in this context, given the limited and dwindling resources of many developing countries that the difficulty of actualization of ECOSOC rights which the African Charter guarantees and the jurisprudence of the African Commission affirms is posed.

As a prelude to what follows it is important to state that the rights of both the first and second generations' tail into the third generation rights and that they are all mutually reinforcing. This is so because the 3rd generation rights contain elements of the first and second generation rights which to some extent provided their building blocks.

7

PEOPLES RIGHTS
(THIRD GENERATION RIGHTS)

7.1 General

The African Charter may also be said to be unique not just in the recognition of peoples' rights, for the right of minorities, and those of dependent peoples to independent statehood were already part of a general international law, but that of extending their scope and raising those of hitherto dubious character, such as the right to a general satisfactory environment and the right to economic, social and cultural development, to the level of legal rights. The third generation rights include:

- the right to equality of all peoples and freedom from domination;
- the right to economic, social and cultural development;
- the right to freedom;
- the right to separate identity;
- the right to dispose of their wealth and natural resources;
- the right to national and international peace and;
- the right to a general satisfactory environment

The right of self-determination and of all peoples to freely dispose of their wealth and natural resources, deriving as they do from the principle of sovereign equality of states and to a limited extent the right of peoples within the sovereign entity to share in the derivative right of auto determination, was already part of general international law. A close examination of socio-economic and cultural rights whether with respect to individuals or groups will show not only their inseparability, but also their self reinforcing character for whether they are attributable to individuals or groups, it is the individual who in the last resort stands to benefit.[292] Shepherd Jr. rightly points out "Peoples" rights are sometimes referred to as the "third generation" human rights. Some international lawyers use the term to express the difference with civil and political and the "economic and social" generations that followed it. These third generation rights are not meant to replace or even supersede the rights of the first two generations. They simply add another dimension. For

example, the right to development is not new, considering the various economic rights that are commonly accepted such as those that specify the second generation's rights as basic and human needs. What is new is the idea that certain groups of people in a disadvantaged context such as those in states below the poverty line have a special claim on the world community for assistance in achieving their development goals".[293]

The African Charter itself recognizes that while fundamental (individual) human rights stem form the attributes of human beings and that while their international protection is justified "it is above all the reality and respect of peoples' rights which effectively guarantee human rights".[294] To a certain degree these presumptions may be justified on the ground that given the level of socio-economic development of African countries in spite of the slow but emerging individualism consequent upon the imposition of capitalist doctrine and practice group

---

[292] Osita C. Eze, Human Rights in Africa, *op. cit.*

[293] G.W. Sherpard Jr. 'African Peoples Rights: The Third Generation in a Global Perspective" In Emerging Human Rights, Sherpard and Anikpo ed. *op. cit*, U. O. Umozurike, "Autochthony in the African Charter on Human and Peoples' Rights" *op. cit*, Quashigah, E.K Human Rights in Traditional and Modern Africa An Analytical and Comparative Study, Ph.D. Thesis, University of Nigeria, 1989, p. 358 et sequ.

[294] Preamble paragraph 6.

solidarity in terms of clans, villages, and even the extended family, as ultimate protectors of individual rights persist.

Furthermore, even in the more developed societies, as in the underdeveloped ones, rights can only make sense in the context of society whether national or international or in terms of categories of persons such as women, children, the old or other disadvantaged groups. The main difference between the two societies is that in the latter, groups peculiar to them do in addition have claims against the wider society.

In the last resort, whatever controversy surrounds the concept of 'people' it is arguable that any group with identifiable core attributes and interests, whether it be tribal, national or minority group should be entitled to exercise people(s)[295] rights within the states and by extension at the international level.

The rights of peoples are exercisable at the international level because the African Charter says so. And because they are actors at the level of international law having been endowed with international personality and are, therefore, capable of bearing rights and obligations under international law as well as possessing procedural capacity to enforce such rights. To deny this would imply that the guarantee of peoples' rights in the African Charter is of no consequence.

---

[295] There is growing literature on the concept of 'peoples' in the African Charter. See Fn 41; Prince E.K. Ouashighah, Human Rights In Traditional And Modern African; An Analytical and Comparative Study Ph.D. Thesis in law, University of Nigeria, Nsukka, Enugu Campus p. 352 et seq, G. Kiwanuka "The Meaning of 'people in the African Charter on Human and Peoples' Rights" Am JIL, Vol. 82, 1988; Onu, 'The Concept of Peoples Rights in the Banjul Charter' Paper presented at the international conference on Human Rights Education in Rural Environment, 1985, Faculty of Law University of Lagos, H. Green "Rights, to Development: Notes Towards An operational Approach" Third World Legal Studies, 1984; see also supra.

The manner in which the concept of peoples evolved in relation to the decolonization process by attaching the right of independent statehood, to colonized territories could also be interpreted as implying that independent African States continue to possess the character of 'peoples'. It is in this context that they could justifiably whether individually or collectively exercise group rights including the right to development on the basis of economic co-operation and integration signifying collective self-reliance as well as 'collective' self-determination.

7.2 The Right to Equality of All Peoples and Freedom From Domination

Article 19 provides that:

All peoples shall be equal they shall enjoy the same respect and shall have the same rights. Nothing shall justify the domination of a people by another.

In communication 54/91 Malawi African Association/Mauritania, the Commission held that the information made available to it did not allow it to establish with certainty that there had been a violation of Article 19 of the Charter along the lines alleged.

7.3 The Right of Self-Determination

It needs to be restated that the right of self-determination for dependent territories imports the right to independent statehood.[296] Article 1(1) common to the 1966 covenants provides in relation thereto that:

---

[296] UN Declaration on the Granting of Independence to Colonial Countries and Peoples (1960) adopted by resolution 1514 (xv); The United Nations and Human Rights, op. cit, p. 32.

"All peoples have the right to self-determination. By virtue of that right they freely determine their political status and freely pursue their economic, social and cultural development." The right derives from and is a manifestation of sovereignty, and underscores the right of states to take decisions and actions in these matters, without external interference. This in effect summarizes the external manifestation of the right to self-determination.

The African Charter building on similar provisions in the 1948 Universal Declaration of Human Rights and the two 1966 covenants has somewhat elaborated on the right to self-determination. Article 20 of the Charter provides that

"All peoples shall have right to existence. All peoples shall have an imprescriptibly and inalienable right to self-determination. They shall freely determine their political status and shall freely ensure their economic and social development according to the policy they have freely chosen."

As to this right the Commission held that a military coup even when peaceful, by denying the people the power to chose their leaders amounted to a violation. Article 19(1) [147/95 149/96]. With respect to the right of self-determination the Commission, affirmed our argument that[297], self-determination could be exercised as an aspect of internal democratization process. Thus in Communication 75/92 Congres de Peuple Katangais/Zaire where there was a request that the African Commission should recognize the Katangese Peoples Congress as a liberation movement entitled to support in the achievement of independence for Katanga, recognize the independence of Katanga and help secure the evacuation of Zaire from Katanga, the Commission held that in the absence of concrete evidence of violations of human rights to the point that the territorial integrity of Zaire should be called to

---

[297] Osita C. Eze Human Right in Africa... op cit.

question and in the absence of evidence that the people of Katanga are denied the right to participate in government as guaranteed by Article 13(1) of the African Charter, Katanga is obliged to exercise a variant of self-determination that is compatible with the sovereignty and territorial integrity of Zaire.

The import of this determination is of course that there are circumstances which may justify the calling into question the territorial integrity of a state that may possibly justify secession[298] and in any event, the principle of *uti possidetis* is addressed primarily to states that might wish to interfere in the current state of colonial boundaries and not to peoples.

The Article also guarantees to all peoples the right to the assistance of States Parties to the Charter in their liberation struggle against foreign domination, be it political, economic or cultural. This right, is submitted, attaches to both 'dependent' and sovereign African states as both can be subject to foreign domination in all its manifestations. As will become evident the right of self-determination already fore-shadowed the right to development which has been elevated to a conventional right under the African Charter.

The rights envisaged are civil, political, economic, social and cultural and the equality of treatment as well as non-discrimination, provisions apply *pro tanto* to all peoples' rights entrenched in the African Charter.

The application of this right to multinational states in African is incontestable. Together with the right to separate identity it could in certain extreme cases justify secession. Current experiences, such as the Eritrean secession, the fragmentation of the Soviet Union and other occurrences in Europe show that the resistance to secession has waned in the face of overwhelming reality. And even the injunction of the OAU Charter and the Constitutive Act of the AU against acts which undermine the territorial integrity of member states is addressed to states

---

[298] *Ibid.*

parties and not to groups within the state. It may be argued that States may be held responsible for such acts where foreseeable and they did nothing to stop it or where after the event, they fail to take measures against the perpetrators.

7.4 The Right of Peoples over their Natural Wealth and Resources

Like the right of self-determination, the right of peoples to freely dispose of their natural wealth and resources is not new.[299] It has antecedents in the conventions and resolutions adopted by the United Nations and the specialized agencies.[300] The African Charter affirms the principle of sovereignty over natural wealth and resources.[301]

Peoples have the right to freely dispose of their wealth and natural resources in their own exclusive interest and shall in no case be dispossessed of it. It is obviously for each people to determine what is in their best interest, and it may be maintained that free disposal on a mutually beneficial basis would not amount to deprivation. Provision is made in the case of expropriation of peoples' wealth and natural resources. In such a case the dispossessed peoples shall have the right to the lawful recovery of their property as well as to an adequate compensation. This interpretation provides the legal basis for reparation and recovery where independent states continue to be dispossessed or deprived of their natural wealth and resources under conditions of for-eign domination and exploitation. For rights have no meaning unless they continue to have validity and can be asserted against infringers. The

---

[299] Article 21 of the African Charter.

[300] See Osita C. Eze "Legal Aspects of Reparation Arguments for and Against in Property and Conveyancing Contemporary Law Journal (maiden issue), also United Nations and Decolonization in Southern Africa, Nigerian Journal of International Affairs, Vol. 3, Nos. 1-2, 1977.

[301] See supra.

question of who owes the obligation to make reparation has to be determined in specific cases.[302]

The freedom to dispose of wealth and natural resources is to be exercised without prejudice to the obligation of promoting international economic co-operation on the bases of mutual respect, equitable exchange and the principles of international law. Yet it is not stated what principles of international law become relevant. We have argued elsewhere that in view of the fact that there is disagreement in respect of certain rules of international economic law obligation should be limited to those expressly undertaken by states[303].

Until such time as definitive customary law rules governing international commercial transactions evolve, it would be precarious to adopt a formulation that could be interpreted to include customary international law, let alone general principles of law recognized by civilized nations, in so far as they purport to deal specifically with such transactions.[304] The fact that the World Trade Organisation (WTO) that now manages globalization that goes beyond merchandise trade and covers such issues, as investments and intellectual property law in some detail confirms the absence of general customary international law in this area.[305] The right to free disposal of their wealth and natural resources can be exercised individually or collectively (on the basis of solidarity or co-operation) by states with a view to strengthening African unity and solidarity. Obligation is also imposed on states parties to the African

---

[302] Osita C. Eze, "Legal Structure for the Resolution of International Problems in the Domain of private foreign investments; A Third World Perspective Now in the future" Georgia Journal of Internal and Comparative Law Vol. 9 1979.

[303] *Ibid.*

[304] See Supra see also O. Gye-Wado "Human Rights: The Right to Development And the African Challenges" in proceedings of the 7th General Assembly of the Social Council.

[305] Osita C. Eze, Nigeria and the World Trade Organisation, Lagos, Nigerian Institute of International Affairs, 2004. See also fn. 9 supra.

Charter to eliminate all forms of foreign economic exploitation, particularly that practiced by international monopolies (TNCs et al in the context of a global economic architecture nurtured and managed by the WTO, the IMF and the World Bank and the capital exporting countries) so as to enable their peoples to fully benefit from the advantages derivable from their natural wealth and resources. The objective is to create a united front and promote self-reliance not dependence.

7.5 Right to Development

The right to socio-economic and cultural development is one of the core rights protected under the African Charter. It represents an aspect of the right of self-determination and can be manifested in the right of peoples to freely dispose of their wealth and natural resources.[306] In a broader sense the right to development requires the establishment of a New International Economic Order, promotional of development. Article 22 of the African Charter provides that "All peoples shall have the right to their economic, social and cultural development in strict respect of their freedom and identity and in equal enjoyment of the common heritage of mankind" As conceived it would seem that the intendment of the Article is to emphasize that development should not be used as justification for the violation of the peoples freedom and the right to separate identity.[307] As part of the right to development, peoples have the right to share equal enjoyment of the common heritage of mankind. It would seem that the 1970 General Assembly Declaration of Principles Governing the Sea-Bed and The Ocean Floor, and the Subsoil thereof, beyond the limits of national jurisdiction (the Area) as well as the resources pf the Area, are the common heritage of mankind neither of which is capable of appropriation by any means by states or persons,

---

[306] See *supra.*

[307] See Gye Wado, *op. cit.*

natural or juridical nor capable of being subjected to the exercise of sovereignty or sovereign rights. Problems arose, however, as to the manner in which this agreed principle should be implemented. While it was agreed that the resources of the area should be exploited in such a way as to meet the needs of both developed and developing countries the former advocated exploitation by states or national undertakings subject to a system of licensing while the latter pressed for exploitation by an international body – The Authority.[308] In the end some of the industrialized countries opted out of this regime and adopted an additional instrument to reject a 'planned' exploitation of the 'common heritage'.

Since most Western countries reject the right to development as a legal right as such and the status of the common heritage of mankind is undermined by the rejection of the Western Countries of the regime for the management and exploitation of the Area, the issue arises as to the import of the right to development in the African Charter. There is no doubt that the African Charter is the only international convention that has elevated that right to the status of a legal right. Accordingly, African peoples have the right to development. African states have in addition the duty, separately or in co-operation with others, Africans and non-Africans alike to ensure the exercise of the right to development. But for non-African states, that duty is non-obligatory, except where its constituent elements, such as the sovereign equality of states, right of self-determination have become part of general international law, only for those who accept it.[309] From the point of view of the place of human rights in the context of African Economic co-operation the duty imposed on African states to cooperate in order to ensure the exercise of the right to development is in accord with the philosophy of collective self-

---

[308] See *infra*, see also Articles 62-66.
[309] The United Nations and Human Rights, op. cit. pp.93-95.

reliance in the Lagos Plan of Action (LPA) (1960) which has found concrete expression in the Treaty for African Economic Co-operation.

The question may then be asked who the subjects of the right of development are. Our interpretation of the relevant provision of the African Charter indicates that at the level of international (at least conventional) law states are the primary subjects of this right. In other words states are entitled to claim the right to development by insisting on NIEO and the 'foundation' rights of self-determination and the right over natural wealth and resources. Peoples other than states are entitled to the exercise of that right both at the national and international planes, for the rights of peoples have been recognized under international law and in particular under the African Charter where they can assert, under certain circumstances, their right before the African Commission and African Court on Human and People's Rights, and at the domestic level where the right is matched by a corresponding duty on the states to ensure its exercise. What has been said with respect to peoples' right to development applies with equal force to individuals. In effect, states, peoples, where they do not correspond to states and individuals are the subjects of the right to development. It would be absurd if states can claim the right to development and peoples and individuals who are the ultimate beneficiaries of the right are excluded from its enjoyment. If the right to development requires the establishment of NIEO, it also presumes the erection of a New National Economic Order. The Former can hardly exist without the latter.

It is in this context that the New Partnership for Africa's Development has to be understood for a proper contextual interpretation of NEPAD will indicate that far from the external partnership which appears to be emphasized that there are three other partnerships implicit in it. These are new partnerships at the

- Pan African level (AU and NEPAD)

- regional level – the regional economic communities RECs that are the building blocks of the AU, and
- national level – the foundation for all integration efforts.

At each of these three levels certain guiding rules are implanted – peace and security, popular participation, that should conduce to good governance, transparency and accountability and socio-economic development. Thus at each level, at least in some, there already exist parliaments and courts. And the ultimate objective is the supremacy of the Rule of Law. Understood in this manner NEPAD consists of four layers of partnership

- National
- Regional
- Pan African or Continental
- External

Without the first three partnerships, which require fundamental changes, the fourth is likely to be of limited utility.

In a report completed by the UN Commission on Human Rights in 1979 it:

- reiterated that the right to development was a human right and that equality of opportunity for development was as much a prerogative of nations as individuals within nations
- recognized that it was indispensable to establish a more equitable and just international economic order which would permit the achievement of balanced development levels in all countries.[310]

The very conduct of capital exporting countries particularly with respect to NIEO is an eloquent testimony to their aversion to the realiza-

---

[310] The United Nations and Human Rights, *op. cit*, pp. 93-95.

tion of the right to development and related economic, social and cultural right for underdeveloped countries.

7.6 The Right to National and International Peace and Security

It can be maintained that without peace, development will be an uphill task and without development human rights protection will remain precarious and peace illusive. Both have therefore a symbiotic relationship. The interdependence between peace, development and human rights is eloquently captured by the UN Charter in its 'purposes' provisions which insist on:

- the maintenance of international peace and security
- the development of friendly relations among nations based on respect for the principles of equal rights and self-determination of peoples and the taking of other appropriate measures to strengthen universal peace, and
- the achievement of international co-operation in solving international problems of an economic, social, cultural and humanitarian character and the promotion and encouragement of the respect for human rights and freedoms for all without distinctions as to race, sex, language and religion.

Parties to the UN Charter already reaffirmed, in the first paragraph of the preamble, their faith "in fundamental rights, in the dignity and worth of the human person, in the equal rights of men and women of nations large and small: and were determined to promote economic and social advancement of all peoples. For these ends they were determined:

"to practice tolerance and to live in peace with one another as good neighbours and to unite (their) strength to maintain international peace and security, and to ensure, by the acceptance of principles and the institutions of methods, that armed force shall not be used, save in the common interest, and to employ international machinery for the promotion of the economic and social achievements of all peoples"[311].

The reaffirmation of faith in human rights and in equal right of men and women and of nations large and small is seen as necessary for peace. In other respects the UN Charter recognizes the sovereign equality of states which is the basis of economic rights and duties of states, the right to development, and the right of self-determination for *inter alia* dependent territories. It established the Economic and Social Council which under the authority of the General Assembly is to promote;

- higher standards of living, full employment, and conditions of economic and social progress and development;
- solution of international, economic, social, health and related problems, and international cultural and educational co-operation, and;
- universal respect for, and observance of human rights and fundamental freedoms without distinction as to race, sex, language or religion" (Article 55).

It is clear from what has been elaborated above that the UN Charter recognizes the importance of socio-economic rights as important for the full enjoyment of human rights. These general provisions of the Charter were to be subsequently elaborated and further developed by the UN Commission on Human Rights. Three years after the adoption of the Charter the Commission elaborated the Universal Declaration of Human Rights adopted by Resolution 217A (III) of the UN General Assembly of December 10, 1948 "as a common standard of achievement for all peoples and all nations". Members of the United Nations are deemed to accept the purport of the Declaration which has to a great extent

---

[311] Preamble.

influenced many independence constitutions and the African Charter on Human and Peoples' Rights.

The Declaration as already indicated even though not legally binding, has given concrete expression to the provisions of the UN Charter by combining civil and political rights on the one hand with socio-economic and cultural rights on the other hand. The two Covenants 1966 the one on Civil and Political Rights and the other on Socio-Economic and Cultural Rights which by and large replicate the provisions of the 1948 Declaration have since come into force as treaties.

In formulating the provisions of the African Charter, cognizance was taken of the provisions of human rights, limited though they were, contained in the OAU Charter. States parties to the African Charter also re-affirmed:

"their adherence to the principles of human and peoples' rights and freedoms contained in the declarations, conventions and other instruments adopted by the Organisation of African Unity, "the Movement of Non-Aligned Countries", and the United Nations".[312] The African Charter apart from guaranteeing the right of all peoples to international peace and security also provides for the right of all people to national peace and security (Article 23). It thus emphasizes the link between national and international peace and security for both are essential for national development. It is accepted that the principles of solidarity and friendly relations affirmed by the Charter of the United Nations and reaffirmed by that of the Organisation of African Unity shall govern relation between states.

Article 23(2) with a view of strengthening peace, solidarity, and friendly relations, confirms adherence to some principle of general international law governing state responsibility. Firstly, it is provided that any person enjoying the right of asylum under the Charter shall not engage in subversive activities against his country of origin or any other

---

[312] Preamble paragraph 10.

state party to the Charter. Secondly, it proscribes the use of territories of states parties to the Charter as bases for terrorist activities. Understandably the specific mention of these activities, which are by no means exhaustive of the principles of state responsibility in international law, derive from Africa's concrete experiences and is intended to protect African States from external subversion while at the same time removing the hostility often attached to states granting asylum to political refugees by the states of their nationality or habitual residence from which they have been obliged to flee.

7.7 The Right to General Satisfactory Environment

The right of all people to a general satisfactory environment favourable to their development represents yet another of the third generation rights. It is realized that ecological deficits may compound problems of underdevelopment and that the preservation of sustainable environment is a right worthy of protection both for peoples and individuals alike. Indeed the right to environment has been embodied in some national constitutions and we have argued elsewhere that the right to environment is directly related to the right to life and health without which there can be no development. And that the loss of life deriving from environmental degradation may in appropriate cases amount to violation of the right to life.[313] The right to environment is indisputably linked to the survival of mankind and planet earth and qualifies for global concretization as human and people's rights. The African Charter has set the pace.[314]

---

[313] Osita C. Eze "Jurisdiction in National and Transboundary Oil Pollution"

[314] For crimes against environment as a crime against development. See Upendra Baxi "Crimes Against Development" in Human Rights Activism in Asia; Some Perspectives, Problems and Approaches, Asian Coalition of Human Rights Organisation (ACHRO) 1984, p. 62 et seq.

8

DUTIES UNDER THE AFRICAN CHARTER

8.1 Introduction

In general legal doctrine the existence of a right implies a corresponding duty to respect that right. General references are to be found in some of the international instruments on human and people's rights imposing specific obligations on either the state, peoples or individuals. Article 29(1) of the 1948 Universal Declaration provides that "every one has duties to the community in which alone the free and full development of his personality is possible". The International Covenants on Economic, Social and Cultural Rights and on Civil and Political Rights each in paragraph 5 of the preamble 'realised' not only the duties which the individual owes to other individuals and to the community to which he belongs but also his responsibility to strive for the promotion and observance of rights recognized in the respective instruments.[315]

---

[315] This section is culled mostly from Osita C. Eze "The place of Human Rights in the Context of African Economic Cooperation prepared for an "International Conference Organised by the Nigerian Institute of Advanced Legal Studies, Abuja, Jan. 29, 1992. See also American Declaration of the Rights and Duties of Man (1948); Article XXIX (Duties to Society); Article XXX (Duties towards children and parents); Article XXI, (Duty to receive instruction); Article XXXII (Duty to Vote); Article XXXIII (Duty to obey the Law); Article XXXIV (Duty to serve the community and the nation); Article XXXV (Duties with respect to social security and welfare); Article XXXVI (Duty to pay taxes) Article XXXVII (Duty to work); and Article XXXVII (Duty to refrain from political

8.2 General Provisions

The tone for duty provisions of the African Charter was already set in the preamble. Firstly the States Parties considered that the enjoyment of rights and freedoms also implied the performance of duties on the part of everyone. Secondly they were convinced of their duty to promote and protect human and peoples rights[316] and freedoms taking into account the importance traditionally attached to these rights and freedoms in Africa. They were also conscious of their obligation to dismantle all forms of discrimination particularly those based on race, ethnic group, colour, sex, language, religion or political opinion.

On a more substantial level the States Parties have obligation to recognize the rights, duties and freedoms enshrined in the Charter. They also undertook to adopt legislative or other measures to give effect to them (Article 1). This provision which has provided occasion for pronouncements by the Commission merely puts on a conventional basis, the principle, as we have shown elsewhere in this work, that, even where a state fails to domesticate a treaty and as a consequence is in breach thereof, this inadequacy in domestic law is not a defence.

The responsibility of a State Party in this regard is well stated by the Commission in communication 147/95, 149/96 Sir Dawda K Jawara/Gambia thus:

Article 1 gives the Charter the legally binding character always attributed to international treaties of this sort. Therefore, a violation of

---

activities in a foreign country). See also American Convention of Human Rights. 1969, which unlike the 1948 Declaration creates rights and duties: Article 1 (obligation of states to respect rights); Article 32 (responsibility of every person to his family, his community and mankind, in Article 32(2) it is stated that: "the rights of each person [is limited] by the rights of others, by the security of all, and by the just demands of the general welfare in a democratic society."

316 Other Conventions which make reference to peoples' rights are, UN Charter Article 1(2), 73, and 76 (b) and (c) and the two U.N. Covenants of 1966.

any provision of the Charter automatically means a violation of Article 1. If a State Party to the Charter fails to recognize the provisions of the same, there is no doubt that it is in violation of this Article. Its violation therefore goes to the root of the Charter.

The implication of this finding is clear. It is that whenever there is a finding of the violation of any provision of the Charter, there is also a violation of Article 1.

The issue of independence of courts and tribunals has been problematic particularly under military regimes that not only oust the jurisdiction of the courts but also establish tribunals which both in composition, procedures and power confront the basic principles of due process and procedural guarantees.

In Communication 48/90, 50/91, 52/91 and 89/93, the Sudanese government was found to be in violation of Article 26 'by providing for a court whose impartiality cannot be guaranteed'. National legislation at the time permitted the president, his deputies and senior military officers to appoint these courts to consist "three military officers or any other persons of integrity or competence" a factor which gave indication of lack of impartiality, in violation of Article 7(1)(d). It has also been held that the establishment of a section responsible for matters relating to state security within the Special Tribunal – presided over by a military officer – constituted a violation of Article 7(1)(d) of the Charter by virtue of their composition, what is reserved to the discretion of the executive organ – the Mauritanian state was reneging on its duty to guarantee the independence of the courts. (54/91, 61/91, 98/93, 164/97 196/97, 210/98).[317]

---

[317] See *infra.*

8.3 Specific provisions

But the African Charter has gone beyond this general postulate to emphasize the notion of duty in a manner not found in other international instruments on human rights. With respect to the state, it is provided that it shall protect the family as the natural unit and basis of society; assist it as the keeper of the morals and traditional values recognized by a community, ensure the elimination of every discrimination against women and also ensure the protection of the rights of the woman and the child as stipulated in international conventions and obliquely to ensure that special measures of protection are provided for the aged and disabled. (Article 18). In Communication 61/91 Amnesty International/Mauritania, the Commission held that holding people in solitary confinement, both before and during trial and during such detention which is, on top of it all, arbitrary... and depriving them of their right to a family life constitutes a violation of Article 18(1). So were several deportations of Mr. Modise a Botswan citizen from Botswana, thus depriving him of his family and his family support held to be in violation of Article 18(1) (97/93 J. K. Modise/Botswana). Equally in Communication 143/95 Constitutional Rights Project and Civil Liberties Organisation, holding detainees incommunicado thereby preventing them from communicating with their families was held a violation.

Other duties imposed on the state include those of promoting and ensuring awareness of and respect for the rights guaranteed in the Charter through teaching, education and publication, as well as that of guarantying the independence of Courts and Tribunals and allowing the establishment and improvement of appropriate institutions for the promotion and protection of human and peoples' rights (Article 25 and 26)[318].

---

[318] Human Rights in Africa, op.cit p.215.

Another duty imposed on states parties is the promotion and protection of morals and traditional values, recognized by the community. These obligations are additional to that imposed by Article 1 of the Charter.[319]

Individuals have also certain duties imposed upon them. Accordingly it is provided that he has duties towards the family and society and towards the international community. In exercising his rights and freedoms the individual, has the duty to respect the rights of others, collective security, morality and common interest. He has also the duty to respect and consider his fellow beings without discrimination, and to maintain relations aimed at promoting, safeguarding and reinforcing mutual respect and tolerance (Articles 27 and 28). Finally, every person has the duty to work for the cohesion of the family, to contribute to African unity, to serve the national community by placing one's physical and intellectual abilities at its service, not to compromise the security of the state, to preserve and strengthen national independence and the territorial integrity of the country and contribute to its defence (Article 29). As formulated in the African Charter the duty to preserve the harmonious development of the family includes the duty to respect (his) parents at all times and to feed and help them in case of need. It is to be noted that these 'duty' provisions capture the age old African tradition of respect of 'age' and parents, as well as, institutionalize the extended family system which provides both social and psychic security within the African family and society. Further argument supportive of the legal

---

[319] G.W. Cherpard Jr. "African Peoples 'Rights: The Third Generation in a Global Perspective" In Emerging Human Rights.. Sherpard and Anikpo ed. Op. cit, Development in the African (Banjul) Charter on Human and Peoples' Rights cited in Sherpard Anikpo op cit. See also infra; U.O. Umuzurike, "Autochtony in the African Charter on Human and Peoples' Rights" op cit Quashigah, Human Rights In Traditional And Modern African An Analytical and Comparative Study, Ph. D. Thesis UNN, 1989, p.358 op. seq.

nature of the obligations imposed on individuals is to be found in Chapter 9.

Even though no express provision on duties is made for peoples' it can be inferred that they have the obligation to respect the rights of other peoples such as the right to separate identity, of equality and freedom from domination. They also have the obligation to respect rights and freedoms of individuals.

I may be permitted to cite my reaction to the duty provisions of the African Charter as elaborated in 1984

> "what is remarkable is that the duty provisions enumerated above comprehend issues of basic concern for African - countries underdeveloped, lacking generalized social security, which is often provided by the family and invariably relying on self-help programmes, eager to minimize cultural domination and ever concerned with safeguarding national security and territorial integrity that should conduce to development."[320]

That assertion, remains with respect, valid now as it was when it was first made.The issue of the nature of the duty provisions and, therefore, their enforceability will be dealt with in the subsequent section. Suffice it to say that they raise problems which need to be clarified and resolved.

---

[320] Osita C. Eze, Human Rights in Africa *op. cit* p.215.

9

NATURE OF RIGHTS GUARANTEED, DUTIES IMPOSED AND RELATED MATTERS

9.1 Introduction

In considering the subject matter of this part four things become relevant namely:

- the legal nature of the rights and duties guaranteed or imposed, that is to say, whether they create the basis of enforceable' rights and duties or whether they do not;
- limitations to the rights and duties; and
- the issue of admissibility of reservations;
- under what circumstances derogations may be considered permissible.
- who or what may infringe the rights guaranteed under the African Charter;
- who are the beneficiaries of the rights guaranteed

9.2 The Legal Nature of Rights Guaranteed and Duties   Imposed

It is interesting to note that the language of the Charter with respect to the three generations rights and duties appears prescriptive. Thus the Charter in its Article 2 provides that every individual 'shall' be entitled to the enjoyment of the rights and freedoms recognized and guaranteed in the present Charter without distinction of any kind such as race, ethnic group, colour, sex, language, religion etc. (Articles 2-17). But Article 1 of the Charter, which legal significance has been the subject of the Commission's determination, has already set the tone for the legal nature of these provisions when it states:

The Member States of the Organisation of African Unity parties to the present Charter shall recognize the rights, duties and freedoms enshrined in this Chapter and shall undertake legislative or other measures to give effect to them.

While the words rights, duties and freedoms recognized in this *Chapter,* appears in the Charter, the Commission's determination in communication 147/95 and 145/96 (Sir Dawda K. Jawara/The Gambia) replaces the word 'chapter' with 'Charter'. If the matter had ended here, one would have considered this occurrence a *lapsus linguae.* But in the very next paragraph the Commission stated:

Article 1 gives the Charter the legally binding character always attributed to international treaties of this sort. *Therefore[321] a violation of any provision of the charter automatically means a violation of Article I.* If a State Party to the Charter fails to recognize the provision of the same, there is no doubt that it is in violation of this Article. The violation therefore goes to the root of the Charter.

Thus construed, it means that the duty provisions for individuals, creates obligations, which failure to recognized by the parties is violative of Article 1. And as indicated the language of these provisions is prescriptive[322].

The language of the Charter with respect to the peoples' rights also appears prescriptive. Thus Article 19 provides that: "All peoples shall be equal, they shall enjoy the same respect and shall have the same rights. Nothing shall justify the domination of a people by another. In the same

---

[321] Emphasis mine.

[322] See Chapter 8 Supra.

vein provisions are made for the right to self-determination (Article 20), to freely dispose of their natural wealth and resources (Article 21), to their economic, social and cultural development (Article 22), to international peace and security (Article 23) and to a general satisfactory environment (Article 24). So also are provisions on duties and obligations of individual and states. It should be noted, however, that the provisions on peoples' rights fall within Chapter 1 of the Charter and are therefore expressly made obligatory.

Certain problems arise with respect to the all encompassing scope of the African Charter. One might ask whether parties to Charter really intend that the socio-economic and cultural rights contained therein should be enforceable in law. If the right to development has been elevated to a legal right imposing an obligation on the parties to the African Charter are states non-parties obliged to honour it and can persons and peoples within states parties insist on its implementation and by whom or what. Against whom may African states parties to the African Charter have resource? Or can we insist that the right to development is synonymous with an amalgam of principles and rights already established under general international law: state sovereignty, right to self-determination, right to freely dispose of natural wealth and resources etc. And even if this argument were tenable, how, since communications for violations can only be made against states parties, which must be African States, can one bring a non-African violator state within the competence of the African Commission or Court? To the extent, however, that the right to development is synonymous with the rights and principles which have become part of general international law, every state has a right against any state which violates it and the mode of enforcement will depend on the choice between one of the several modes of peaceful resolution of conflicts -judicial, arbitration etc.

In general the duty provisions may also present problems of interpretation. For instance how does one interpret the provision that every individual shall have duties towards his family and society, the state and other legally recognized communities and international community? [Article 27(1)]. What are these duties? Does family include extended family and what exactly is the import of society in the Article? And who may ensure compliance with this duty the State or the individual, in either case the Statecentric character of the African Charter which identifies the State as the potential violator posses a problem. In spite of the implicit notion that an individual can be a violator, current practice thus far does not seem to promote it.

Even though the manner of drafting most of duty provisions may appear rather general it may turn out to be an advantage in the long run since it allows room for creative and dynamic interpretation that may prove to be more responsive to the needs of African peoples. Secondly as they stand they lay the legal foundation for the development of positive law at the national level.

In the last resort we have it on good authority that all generations' rights and duties are justiceable. The communications alleging their violations and the determinations of the Commission amply affirm the equally binding nature of the rights, freedoms duties enshrined in the African Charter[323]. What remains is for the passage of time to enable both the Commission and now the African Court on Human and Peoples Rights to extend, develop and deepen the jurisprudence of on which to better appreciate the essence of the relevant provisions.

9.3 Limitations

The manner in which some of the limitations to guaranteed rights have been drafted may also create problems of interpretation. The right

---

[323] See Supra; see also Article 1 of the African Charter.

to express and disseminate opinions is to be exercised 'within the law' [Article 9(2)]. Every individual shall have the right to free association provided he 'abides by the law' [Article 10(1)]. The exercise of the right to the freedom of movement and residence within the borders of a state is guaranteed provided that the person 'abides by the law'. A few other Articles contain more elaborate limitations. The exercise of the freedom of conscience etc., is subject to 'law and order' (Article 8).

The right to assemble freely with others is subject only to necessary restrictions provided by the law in particular to those enacted in the interest of national security, the safety, health, ethics and rights and freedoms of others' (Article 11). A similar limitation is imposed with respect to the right of the individual to leave any country and return to his own country [Article 12(2)].

We have indicated that unlike the European Convention and the American Convention, the African Charter does not specifically mention democracy, even though it is assumed as implicit in the right to participate in government and associated freedoms of expression, movement association etc. Equally implicit in the guarantee of the right of equality before the law and equal protection of the law, as well as other rights superintended over by independent and impartial courts and tribunals as the ultimate arbiter prior to the Charter machinery is the principle of the Rule of Law. (See Silver case above). The implication of this, as we have argued elsewhere,[324] is that even though there may appear to be 'claw back' clauses the limitations are not open ended. With respect it is submitted that whatever limitations are imposed must stand or fall depending on whether they conform to what is reasonable in a democratic society and the principle of the Rule of law. And this is supported not only by the American and European Conventions on Human Rights but also by the judicial practice of most countries (including

---

[324] Osita C. Eze The African Charter and the Enforcement of Rights and Duties, Ime Umanah Chair Lecture, op. cit.

African countries) whose constitutions have been influenced by the European Convention and UN law.

Again, even though the limitations in the African Charter do not refer to the 'law that is necessary', but to 'necessary restrictions' the decision of the Supreme Court of Papua, New Guinea seems persuasive even though it was based on the construction of relevant provisions of the constitution of Papua, New Guinea on the freedom of expression. The court held per Kapi, D.C.J.

> "The word 'necessary' implies that fundamental rights should not be regulated or restricted if there is another way of effectively protecting the public interest. In addition a law that is necessary does not necessarily mean that it is also reasonable in a democratic society - the test is an objective one and must be considered within the context of the subject matter or circumstances of each case."[325] *The State V. NTN Pty Ltd and MBN Ltd.,* Supreme Court of Papua New Guinea, 7, April, 1987 (No Sc. 323).[326]

The Inter-American Court of Human Rights in *Compulsory Membership of Journalists Association,* Advisory Opinion OC – 5/85 of 13 Nov. 1985, 8 EHRR, 165 para. 45) gave further insight into the significance of the requirement of necessity in fundamental human rights issues. Even though the analogous provision of the American Convention, on the freedom of thought and expression is not identical in language with the equivalent provision of the European Convention it took the position that European case law provided the clearest source of guidance in this area. Article 10(2) of the European Convention speaks of restrictions as "are necessary in a democratic society" while the American Convention in Article 13(2) is concerned with "restrictions that are necessary" in order to achieve one of the stated objectives. This

---

[325] *Ibid.*

[326] Judicial Colloquium in Bangalore, op. cit. p. 227.

difference notwithstanding the Inter-American Court of Human Rights in the instant case advising on the legality of the compulsory licensing of journalists held that for a restriction on free speech to be "necessary" under Article 13(2) the government must satisfy the test articulated by the European Court of Human Rights; it must show that the restriction is required by a compelling social need, and that it is so framed as not to limit freedoms of expression more than necessary or proportionate to achieve a legitimate objective.[327]

Again, even where the word 'reasonable' does not qualify restrictions on the rights and freedoms guaranteed, given the requirement that this test be met both in domestic law and international instruments on Human rights as well as the mandate of the African Commission and Court under Article 60 on applicable principles, which obliges the Commission and the Court to draw inspiration from international law on human and peoples Rights, the Commission 'can' be influenced in its determinations by the jurisprudence of other institutions such as the UN Committee on Human Rights, as well as those, both national and international, engaged in interpreting identical or analogous provisions.

In the Indian case of *State of Madras V.V.G. Row (1952)* SCR 597, 607, construing the constitutional provision on the right to form associations or trade unions guaranteed by Article 19(1)(c) the court held that:

> "The test of reasonableness, whenever prescribed should be applied to each individual statute impugned, and no abstract standard or general pattern of reasonableness can be laid down as applicable to all cases. The nature of the rights alleged to have been infringed, the underlying purpose of the restriction imposed, the extent and urgency of the evil sought to be remedied thereby, the

---

[327] A Lester, Q.C., "Freedom of Expression. Relevant International Principles", Judicial Colloquium in Bangalore, op cit p.27.

disproportion of the imposition, the prevailing conditions at the time, should all enter into judicial verdict".[328]

The African Charter employs in some instances restrictions to rights and freedoms granted such as "abides by the law"; "subject to law and order". Such phrases are not identical but import more or less similar legal consequences as the phrase 'prescribed by law' or 'in accordance with the law'. The European Court of Human Rights in construing this phrase in the Silver Case, concerning restrictions upon prisoners' correspondence, held;

- "One of the principles underlying the Convention is the Rule of law, which implies that interference by the authorities with an individual's rights should be subject to control. This is especially so where, as in the present case, the law bestows on the executive wide discretionary powers, the application whereof is a matter of practice which is susceptible to modification but not to any parliamentary scrutiny".
- The requirements of legal certainty were not met where the prisoners mail was interfered with by prison authorities on basis of unpublished orders and instructions.[329]

In construing the relationship between the phrase 'prescribed by law' and legal certainty and, therefore, the Rule of law, the European Court in *The Sunday Time Case*[330] stated as follows:

"First the law must be adequately accessible, 'the citizen must be able to have an indication that is adequate in the circumstances of the legal rules applicable to a given case. Secondly, a norm cannot be regarded as a 'law' unless it is formulated with sufficient precision to

---

[328] *Ibid.*

[329] *Ibid.* p. 38 (judgement of 25 March 1983, S series A No. 61, 5 EHRR 347). See also *Supra.*

[330] *Ibid.* p. 37.

enable the citizen to regulate his conduct: he must be able-if need be with appropriate advice-to foresee, to a degree that is reasonable in the circumstances, the consequences which a given action may entail" (paragraph 49).

The analysis which proceeded was futuristic in the sense that determination of the Commission were not available at the time[331] we shall now examine how the Commission has dealt with the matter of restrictions and see to what extent it has been influenced by world currents.

An indication of the Commission's position can already be gleaned from the ruling with respect to Article 13 on the right to participate in government. The purpose of the expression "in accordance with the provisions of the law" is surely intended to regulate how the right is to be exercised rather than the law should be used to take away the right". Elaborating further it stated[332]:

"The Commission has argued forcefully that no State Party to the Charter should avoid its responsibilities by recourse to the limitations and "claw-back" clauses in the Charter. It was stated following |developments in other jurisdictions, that the Charter cannot be used to justify violations of sections of it. The Charter must be interpreted holistically and all clauses must reinforce each other. The purpose or effect of any limitation must also be examined, as the limitation of the right cannot be used to subvert rights already enjoyed. Justification, therefore, cannot be derived solely from popular will, as such cannot be used to limit the responsibilities of State Parties in terms of the Charter. Having arrived at this conclusion, it dos not matter whether one person or thirty five percent of Zambians are disenfranchised by the

---

[331] See Osita C. Eze, The African Charter on Human and Peoples' Rights and the Promotion and Enforcement of Duties, *op. cit,* p. 73 *et sequ.*
[332] 211/98 Legal Resources Foundation/Zambia.

measure.That anyone is disenfranchised is not disputed and this constitutes violated of the right"[333]

In communication 140/94/141/94,145/95 the Commission accepted. According to Article 9(2) of the Charter dissemination of opinion may be restricted by law. It construed this as not meaning that national law can set aside the right to express one's opinion guaranteed at the international level, this would make the right to express one's opinion ineffective. To permit national law to take precedence over international law would defeat the purpose of codifying certain rights in international law and indeed the whole essence of treaty making.

Similar line of reasoning is adopted by the Commission in other cases.[334] In effect the Commission rests its argument on three major points: firstly treaty rights cannot be overridden by domestic law despite the 'claw back clauses', secondly the intendment of these 'limitations' is to regulate not to subvert or empty the right of its substance; and thirdly curiously, if taken alone, that the 'limitations' clauses cannot abrogate rights already being enjoyed.

The Commission has had some difficulty dealing with the issue of derogations, which is a 'neighbour' to limitations or draw back clauses and which we shall deal with in the next section. Typically derogations allow states to limit or suspend, for a period, under specified circumstances such as war or other public emergencies rights guaranteed, while draw back clauses permit states to limit   rights guaranteed as specified in the instrument, the latter case, while the state has a measure of appreciation it must be exercised judicially and within the law.

---

[333] Vide UN Human Rights Committee General Comment No 25 (XXXVII/1996) where it states: "Persons who are otherwise eligible to stand for election should not be excluded by unreasonable or discriminatory requirements such as education, residence, or descent, or by reason of political affiliation" (para 15 at p. 127).

[334] See *infra*.

The issue of expansive interpretation of rights and freedoms and restrictive interpretation of limitations will be discussed under the section on the African Commission.[335]

9.4 Derogations and Reservations

9.4.1 Derogations

Derogation clauses in conventions, or even domestic law, normally allow the states in specified circumstances not to fulfill their obligations thereunder during certain contingencies. Derogation is invariably grounded on the exigencies of public emergency.

Article 4 of the Covenant on Civil and Political Rights stipulates that:

In times of public emergency which threatens the life of the nation and the existence of which is officially proclaimed, the States Parties to the present Covenant may take measures derogating from their obligations under the present Covenant to the extent strictly required by the exigencies of the situation, provided that such measures are not inconsistent with their other obligations under international law and do not involve discrimination solely on the ground of race, colour, sex, language, religion or social origin" [Article 4(1)].

No derogation, however, may be made from Articles 6 (the right to life), 7 (freedom from torture, inhuman or degrading treatment), 8(1) and (2) (right not to be held in slavery or servitude), 11 (right not to be imprisoned merely for inability to fulfill a contractual obligation) 15 (prohibition against retrospective penal legislation), 16 (the right to recognition as a person before the law) and 18 (right to freedom of thought, conscience and religion).

---

[335] See *infra.*

Article 15 of the European Convention on Human Rights contains analogous derogation clause but with far less extensive coverage than the Covenant-right to life, proscription of torture or inhuman or degrading treatment, right not be held in slavery or servitude, prohibition of retroactive penal legislation [Articles 2,3,4,(1) and 7].

The American Convention on Human Rights stipulates in its Article 27(1) that rights guaranteed may be suspended in time of war, public danger or other emergency that threatens the independence or security of a State Party" on non discriminatory basis. Article 27(2), however, proscribes the suspension of the following: Article 3 (right to juridical personality); 4 (Right to life); 5 (right to humane treatment); 6 (freedom from slavery); 9 (freedom from *ex post facto* laws); 12 (freedom of conscience and religion). 17 (Rights of the family); 18 (Right to a Name) 19 (Rights of the Child); 20 (Right to nationality); 23 (Right to participate in government), or of the judicial guarantees essential for the protection of such rights.

The African Charter does not make provisions for derogations. In our earlier work we had argued that the Commission has had occasion to rule on violations during periods of emergency. In the instant case which involved the proscription of certain newspapers by the Nigerian military government, the Commission attempted to lay down the rules that should guide limitations under Article 27(2) which apply generally to rights and freedoms guaranteed in the Charter. It stated:

> "In contrast to other international human rights instruments, the African Charter does not contain a derogation clause. Therefore limitations on the rights and freedoms enshrined in the Charter cannot be justified by emergencies or special circumstances. The only legitimate reasons for limitations of the rights and freedoms of the African Charter are found in Article 27(2), that is, that the rights of the Charter "shall be exercised with due regard to the rights of others, collective security, morality and common inter-

est. The justification of limitations must be strictly proportionate with and absolutely necessary for the advantages, which follow. Most important limitation may not erode a right such that the right itself becomes illusory. The government has provided no concrete evidence that the proscription was for any of the above reasons given in Article 27(2). It has failed to prove that proscription of the newspapers was for any reason but simple criticism of the government. if the newspapers had been guilty of libel, for example, they could have individually been sued and called upon to defend themselves. There was no substantive evidence presented that the newspapers were threatening national security of public order." 140/94, 141/94, 145/95, Constitutional Rights Project, Civil Liberties Organisation and Media Rights Agenda/Nigeria.

We had earlier argued that "it is not inconceivable that the Commission would be faced with claims for derogations. If it does, it will most likely have to be guided by the practice at the national and international levels. Derogations in the circumstances may not be allowed with respect to the right to life, freedom from slavery and from discrimination which have come to assume great importance where parties to the Charter are also parties to the Covenant on Civil and Political Rights its derogation clause will apply."[336] The Commission's determination in the instant cases seems to follow a similar trend.

9.4.2 Reservations

A reservation to a treaty is a qualified acceptance of the treaty and therefore a counter offer. No agreement is reached. With respect to a bilateral treaty this is the rule. With respect to multilateral treaties, however, two possibilities exist. Firstly it may be the intention of the parties that such a state can only be a party to the treaty with respect to those

---

[336] Osita C. Eze, *African Charter on Human and Peoples' Rights*, *op. cit.*

states that accept the reservation. Secondly, it may be that a reservation disqualifies a state from becoming a party to the treaty.

It was the practice of the League that "in order that any reservation whatever may be validly made in regard to a clause of the treaty, it is essential that the reservation should be accepted by all contracting parties, as would have been the case if it had been put forward in the course of negotiations. If not, the reservation, like the signature to which it is attached, is null and void".[337]

The League position accords more with the pre Genocide Case practice under customary international law.

The understandings of the Governing Board of the Pan-American Union with respect to the juridical status of treaties ratified with reservations, which have not been accepted, as stated in 1932, are that:

- "The treaty shall be in force, in the form in which it was signed, as between those countries which ratify it without reservation, in the terms in which it was originally drafted and signed.

- It shall be in force as between the Governments which ratify it with reservations and the signatory States which accept the reservations in the form in which the treaty may be modified by the said reservations.

- It shall not be in force between a Government which may have ratified with reservations and another which may have already ratified and which does not accept such reservations"[338].

All three positions follow the customary international law position that the consent of a state is required for it to be bound by a treaty. While the first position insists that reservation excludes a reserving state from being a party to the treaty at all the second position accepts that such a state may be a party if the reservation is accepted and with state

---

[337] Harris, *op. cit*,p. 586.

[338] *Ibid.*

which accepted it. In particular, where the reservation is accepted the terms of the treaty for the parties making and accepting the reservations are modified accordingly. And the third position indirectly confirms the requirement of consent between states, which having previously ratified does not accept a subsequent ratification with reservation by another state.

Reservations to the convention on genocide case[339] introduced liberal dimensions to the issue of reservations. The Genocide Convention did not contain any reservation clause. The kernel of the Court's advisory opinion is that even where there is no express provision for reservations, a state which has made and maintained a reservation which has been objected to by one or more of the parties to the convention but not by others, if such a reservation is compatible with the object and purpose of the treaty can be regarded as a party to the Convention, otherwise that state cannot be regarded as party to the convention. Since the African Charter does not provide for reservations being a "humanitarian convention" (one of the factors that influenced the court's opinion) following this advisory opinion reservations will be admissible provided they are compatible with the 'object and purpose' of the Charter. But would a reservation to such fundamental rights as the freedom of conscience, the profession and free practice of religion (Article 8) elimination of discrimination against women and protection of women and children as subject to Islamic law, right to receive and impart information as subject to Egyptian law. Article 9, (Egypt) and Zambia's modification Article 13(3) to read "Every individual shall have the right of access to any place, services or public property intended for use by the general public" which apparently were made by some states be adjudged compatible with the object and purpose of the convention to allow such states become parties to the Charter?

---

[339] I.C.J. Reports, 1951, p. 15.

But other parties to the convention, as well as its organs, might by permitting such states to conduct themselves in a particular way – accepting communications by or against, receiving reports as required under it –signify acceptance of such states as parties to the convention. Even then it would still be based on, *albeit ex post facto* acceptance – consent.

It would seem that the dissenting opinion of Judges Guerrero, Sir Arnold McNair, Read and Hsu Mo not only accepted the League position as representing the customary law rule on the matter but also insisted that in as much as the representatives of governments who drafted the Genocide Convention wished to see many states become parties to it as possible it was certainly not their intention to achieve universality at any price.

"There is no evidence", it was maintained "that they desired to secure wide acceptance of the convention even at the expense of the integrity or uniformity of its terms, irrespective of the wishes of those states which have accepted all the obligations under it.[340] References to reservations which were compatible or incompatible with the object and purpose of the treaty were said to amount to the propounding of a new rule for which they found no legal basis.

The majority and dissenting advisory opinions represented two tendencies the one liberal and the other orthodox. Both understand the need for state consent before it can be bound for it can be assumed that the test of 'compatibility' is intended to moderate the consequences of a reservation which may be allowed without doing damage to the substance of the treaty.

The formulation of the Vienna Convention on the law of treaties is supportive of the position of the UN General Assembly on the rule in the *Genocide Case,*[341] when it provided in its Article 19(c)

---

[340] *Ibid,* p. 46.

[341] *Ibid,* p. 42.

that:

"a state may when signing, ratifying, accepting, approving or acceding to a treaty formulate reservations unless:- ... the reservation is incompatible with the object or purpose of the treaty".

9.5 Who or What may infringe the Rights Guaranteed under the African Charter

It is often assumed that provisions of Human Rights Conventions are addressed to states (statecentric) which are obliged not only to guarantee but also to respect and ensure the enjoyment of the rights. The very first articles of the African Charter come very close to affirming this position when it provides that:

"The member states of the Organisation of African Unity, parties to this Charter shall recognize the rights, duties and freedoms enshrined in the present Chapter and shall undertake to adopt legislative or other measures to give effect to them".

States Parties are also obliged to promote and ensure through teaching, education and publication the respect of the rights and freedoms contained in the Charter as well as guarantee the independence of Courts and allow the establishment and improvement of appropriate national institutions entrusted with the promotion and protection of the rights and freedoms guaranteed under the Charter (Articles 25 and 26).

It does seem, however, that where a convention confers rights and duties on individuals, that in some cases, such individuals might also be violators of human and peoples' rights. It is conceivable, therefore, that an individual may violate another's right where:

- he exercises his rights without due regard to the rights of others [Article 27(2)];
- acts such as caning may derogate from the rights of the respect of the dignity inherent in a human being (Article 5);

- he restricts the right of another to the freedom of movement

It does seem, however, that the African Charter despite the provisions alluded to above take the traditional position that whether the wrongful act or omission was committed by an individual or a person that in appropriate cases responsibility under international law is a matter for states. Neither the African Charter nor the Rules and Procedures of the African Commission make provision for communications by non-state entities against other non-state entities.

It is not only with respect to infringement of rights and freedoms by individuals that the Charter is silent on how such violation is to be remedied. Where a 'people' violates the right of another 'people' such as those on non-discrimination or independent existence, there is no clear provision on "enforcement".

It would be contrary to the intendment of the Charter if the Commission were to decline the exercise of jurisdiction because there are no express Rules and Procedures for enforcement since as we shall indicate in the next section, the rights guaranteed by the Charter are enforceable. And in any event, people's rights could be vindicated by way of representative action by one of them or even someone acting on their behalf.[342]

Increasingly the issue of rights violations by Transnational Corporations has become the subject of serious discourse. It is possible that such activities could violate the rights to health, food, work, environment, life and even respect for the dignity inherent in the human person yet ordinarily TNCs are not seen as violators. In such circumstances to whom is responsibility attributable? It is normal for the individual(s) as well as the 'corporation' through its principal officers to be held accountable. It is also usual for such acts to have a dual character, depending on the public policy of the State which may provide for civil as well as criminal

---

[342] See the Katanga Case, *supra.*

action. Thus while penal law sanctions the violators, civil action provides the avenue for compensating the victim. Such is the approach adopted by the Nigerian anti-human trafficking Act, even when the Constitution provides for additional civil remedy by proscribing inhuman and degrading treatment as well as treatment that confronts human dignity[343].

What about the duty provisions? With respect to duties owed under the conventions, state parties can petition against a state which has committed a breach of the duty. What about where an individual or peoples are in breach? What happens? It should be noted that with respect to apartheid, crimes against humanity and war crimes etc. that international law imposes responsibility on individuals at least on conventional basis.

There is another sense in which violations could take place within the state. To a large extent, the traditional approach is invariably limited to actual breaches of rights guaranteed or imminently threatened, and invariably requires that a complainant must show interest (locus standi) in the matter. It does not matter that partial emphasis on human rights protected (civil and political rights and the right of private property) and the exclusion of socio-economic rights may constitute concrete material breaches that may not be justiceable; that the ruling class using the instrumentality of the state- parliament, the judiciary and the executive- promotes and reinforces these breaches; that the nature of the socio-economic system which perpetuates minority domination represents instances of violence and permanent breach; and that emphasis on individual rights neglects the validity of group rights.[344]

The question that arises is, is it sufficient to emphasize, in the technistic or technojuristic tradition that violations arise only where formally

---

[343] See *supra.*

[344] Osita C. Eze "Human Rights Issues and Violation" in, Emerging Human Rights, Sherphard Jr. and Anikpo eds op. cit; p. 88.

guaranteed rights are breached? Should we not transcend pure formalism to the exposition of substance that underpins the basic contradictions between what is formally guaranteed and its concrete attainment? In sum, is it not more appropriate to examine what, for want of a better expression, could be categorized as institutionalized permanent non-justiceable breaches which in the end determine and shape the contents and essence of human rights protected? Does this approach, which does not ignore the limited value of "legal" rights guaranteed, not show up their limitations and point in the direction of dynamic transformation of the philosophical basis and material foundations of human rights in a continent that has for centuries experienced, and continues to experience, basic derogations of human rights?[345]

To some extent the African Charter has addressed these issues having formally made the provisions for the three generations rights. And the adoption of enabling laws to bring the Charter into force in the various jurisdictions lays the foundation for evolving appropriate policies and laws that should enhance their actualization. Here the promotional function of the Commission and appropriate national (Governmental and non-governmental) agencies could be invaluable.

9.6 Who are the beneficiaries of rights guaranteed under the African Charter?

It can be deduced from express provisions of the African Charter that individuals and peoples have rights under the Charter. While reference to 'other communications' in contradistinction to reference to 'communications from state', in the context of the African Charter, may be interpreted as reference to individuals and peoples there is no attempt, as already indicated to define 'peoples' as employed in the Charter. If we accept as criteria for determining which group qualifies as peoples,

---

[345] *Ibid.*

groups with identifiable characteristics and core interests'; then national groups with common ancestry, language, culture some measure of economic interaction, may as well qualify. On this score the Ogonis and over two hundred national groups in Nigeria would qualify as peoples with the capacity to have rights and bear obligations as well as the procedural right to enforce such rights under the African Charter. It is also arguable for the same reasons that clans and villages may qualify. But what about special categories such as women, children and disabled persons who have been recognized as deserving of some special treatment? Do these also qualify as peoples under the African Charter? Can States qualify as peoples for the purpose of exercising the right to development at least in relation between States parties to the African Charter?[346]

The states parties to the present Charter shall have the duty to guarantee the independence of the Courts and shall allow the establishment and improvement of appropriate national institutions entrusted with the promotion and protection of the human rights and freedoms guaranteed by the present charter. This explains why as conditionality for the Commission being seized of a matter, in cases of communications from or on behalf non-state entities, there must be evidence that local courts and tribunals have been approached and whatever remedies they have to offer exhausted. The third leg of the enforcement system is not so direct. It is nevertheless deducible from Article 56(7) which excludes the Commission from entertaining disputes where the states have resolved them as provided[347]. It is also possible that the position is the same where the matter is pending before another dispute resolution body. The East African Community has the East African Court of Justice [Article

---

[346] *See* Supra.

[347] That is where such disputes have been settled in accordance with the principles of the United Nations, or the Charter of the Organisation of African Unity or the provisions of the present Charter.

9(e)].[348] It has *inter alia* the competence – original and appellate- in human rights matters [Article 27(2)].

Article 33 of the East African Community Treaty provides that except where jurisdiction is conferred on the court by the treaty disputes to which the community is a party shall not on that ground alone be excluded from the jurisdiction of the national courts of the parties states. In human rights matters the court of justice has both original and appellate jurisdiction. Does this mean that a victim is excluded from access to the domestic court? If the jurisdiction is concurrent, then the court of justice could serve as an appellate court.

ECOWAS Community Court of Justice is established by Article 11 of ECOWAS Treaty, as the principal legal organ of the community. Its constitution, powers and functions are governed by the protocol on the Community Court of Justice, (Article 2).[349]

As originally conceived as individual has no locus before the court. Article 9 of the protocol, on the competence of the court provides:

- The court shall ensure the observance of the law of the principles of equity in the interpretation and application of the provisions of the Treaty.
- The court shall also be competent to deal with disputes referred to it, in accordance with the provisions of Article 56 of the Treaty, by Member
- States or the Authority, when such disputes arise between the Member States or between one or more Member States and the Institutions of the Community in the interpretation or application of the provisions of the treaty.
- A Member State, may on behalf of its nationals institute proceedings against another Member State or Institution of the Community, relating to the interpretation and application of the provi-

---

[348] Treaty Establishing the East African Community, Nov. 1999.

[349] Protocol A/P.1/7/91 on the community court of justice.

sions of the Treaty, after attempts to settle dispute amicably have failed.

- The Court shall have any power conferred upon it, especially by the provisions of the Protocols.

The Court has also the competence to give advisory opinion on questions of the Treaty as prescribed 9Article10). The Court shall apply, as necessary, the body of laws as contained in Article38 of the ICJ Statutes and subject to provisions on review contained in the protocol, its decisions shall be final and immediately enforceable (Article 19). A supplementary Protocol of 2005 has introduced new elements, which are of particular interest for this work.

A new Article 9(4) states clearly that the Court has jurisdiction to determine cases of violation of human right that occur in any Member State. Equally a new Article 10(d) provides that individuals have access to the Court for relief for the violation of their human rights, the submission of application for which shall:

- not be anonymous; nor
- be made whist the same matter has been instituted before another international court.

The Courts of EAC and ECOWAS are international courts. They both guarantee due process and adopt one of the peaceful modes for resolution of disputes envisaged under the Un Charter, the OAU/AU and the African Charter and they come within the ambit of Article 56 (7) of the African Charter expressly mentions only disputes settled by States (as potential violators) we assume that when such disputes are pending before other courts or mechanisms for restoring disputes, that neither the African Commission and Court nor the Courts of Justice of the East African Community and ECOWAS will entertain the dispute, thus putting the parties in double jeopardy.

ECOWAS Court of justice has recovered petitions on right violations but we are yet to get a judgement.[350]

Finally it is important to indicate that because the promotional functions of the Commission are strategic to the actualization of rights, we deem it proper to consider them aside the enforcement system.

---

[350] Supplementary protocol a/sp.1/01/05 amending the preable and articles 1, 2, 9, 22 and 30 of protocol a/p.1/7/91 relating to the community court of justice and article 4 paragraph 1 of the English version of the said protocol.

10

THE AFRICAN COMMISSION AND AFRICAN COURT ON HUMAN AND PEOPLES' RIGHTS

10.1 Background: Nature of the Function of the Commission and Related Matters

This section and the one on the African Court on Human and Peoples' Rights deal with the main African human rights enforcement system and come after laying a sound foundation for it. The system is based on a tripod. The Charter itself requires the domestic courts and tribunals to interpret and apply the rights, freedoms and duties entrenched therein. [Articles 1, 26 and 56(5)]. In particular Article 26 requires that:

> 'States Parties to the present Charter shall have the duty to guarantee the independence of the Courts and shall allow the establishment and improvement of appropriate national institutions entrusted with the promotion and protection of rights and freedoms guaranteed by the present charter".

Other mechanisms such as state reporting missions to states, special Rappoteurs, working groups and NGOs contribute to enforcement of rights.[351]

---

[351] See *infra.*

Before the examination of the functions which the Commission is called upon to perform a word or two on the Commission, its composition - will be in order.

10.1.1 Composition of the Commission

The Commission consists of eleven members chosen from among African personalities with the highest consideration for their high morality, integrity, impartiality and competence in matters of human and peoples' rights, particular consideration being given to persons having legal experience. It does not require that all the members must have a legal experience. The members are to serve in their own personal capacity and are to be elected by secret ballot by the AU Assembly[352] of Heads of State and Government from a list of persons nominated by the states parties to the Charter.[353] Members of the Commission are expected to make a solemn declaration to discharge their duties impartially and faithfully. The Secretary-General of the AU appoints the Secretary of the Commission and provides the staff and services necessary for the effective discharge of the duties of the Commission. Provision is to be made for the emoluments and allowances of the members of the Commission in the Regular Budget of the AU.

Membership of the Commission ends on the death or resignation of a member. It also ends if, in the unanimous opinion of other members of the Commission, a member stops discharging his duties for any reason other than temporary absence or because he is unable to discharge them. While in general the security of tenure is ensured, the manner of appointment of members of the Commission might not be immune from political considerations. It is therefore necessary to ensure, in making

---

[352] Now by AU and appropriate officers.

[353] Under Article 36 the members of the Commission shall be elected foe a six year period and shall be eligible for re-election. The term of office of four of the members elected at the first election shall terminate after two years and the term of office of three others at the end of four years.

such appointments, that there is strict adherence to the criteria set for the choice of nominees. Their solemn declaration to discharge their functions impartially and faithfully would, it is hoped, ensure the integrity of, and therefore respect for, the Commission. The requirement of unanimity for removal will also minimize reliance on extraneous consideration.[354]

It is noteworthy that the African Charter makes provision for the functions of the African Commission. These are:

- to promote Human and Peoples Rights;
- to ensure the protection of Human and Peoples' Rights
- to interpret the provisions of the Charter at the request of a state party, an institution of the OAU or an African Organisation recognized by the OAU and;
- to perform other tasks which may be entrusted to it by the Assembly of Heads of State and Government.

10.1.2. *Human Rights Promotion*

One of the main functions of the Commission is promotional. To some extent this aspect of its work also enhances the protection of human rights. So far as this function is concerned it gathers information, undertakes studies and researches on African problems in the field of human and peoples' rights, organizes seminars, symposia and conferences, disseminates information, encourages national and local institutions concerned with human and peoples' rights and should the need arise, give its views or make recommendations to Governments. (Article 45(1)(a).

Two strategic areas come to mind under this head, that of encouraging institutions concerned with human and peoples' rights and the other of disseminating information. The latter can be accomplished at two levels. Firstly, basic information in the manner of Amnesty

---

[354] Article 31-44.

International's publication – "A guide to the African Charter on Human and Peoples' Rights" with appropriate translations into local languages can be disseminated[355]. Secondly, the process of information sharing should transcend mere mechanical transmission. Symposia, seminars and the media could be employed to explain to African peoples the significance and meaning of these rights, their consequences for their lives and their role in ensuing their protection.

On the institutional side, a more favourable environment could be created in the first instance by encouraging African governments to respect the basic freedoms of expression, of thought, and the rights to movement and association etc. This encouragement will be facilitated if African peoples are mobilized through access to necessary information.

It is also possible to establish National Human Rights Commissions, preferably within the constitutional framework to serve as a watchdog for human and peoples' right violations. The 1992 Constitution of Ghana in its Chapter Eighteen makes provision for the establishment by an Act of parliament, of a Commission on Human and Administrative Justice (s.216) whose members are to be appointed by the President acting in consultation with the Council of state (s.70). It has wide functions - to investigate complaints of violations of fundamental rights and freedoms, concerning the i) administration, (ii) actions of private persons alleged to be violative of human rights and freedoms and (iii) taking appropriate action for remedying any violations through negotiated settlement or legal action (s.218). It can also assist, and indeed become a focal point for educating the people of Ghana on human rights and freedoms (s.218). Whether it will be sufficiently independent to carry out these functions is another matter.

The Nigerian National Human Rights Commission is a product of the Act of the National Assembly even though there are those who advocate that it be grounded in the Constitution. S.1 of the National Hu-

---

[355] London, Amnesty International Publications.

man Rights Commission Decree, No. 22 of 1995 (Now Act) establishes the Commission. The military government that promulgated the decree had among its objectives:

- the facilitation of Nigeria's implementation of its various treaty obligations, including, but not limited to, the Universal Declaration of Human Rights, the International Convention on the Elimination of all forms of Racial Discrimination, and the African Charter on Human and Peoples' Rights;
- creation of an enabling environment for extra-judicial promotion and enforcement of all rights recognized and enshrined in the Constitution of the Federal Republic of Nigeria 1979 as amended and other laws of the land;

It is in furtherance of these objectives that the Commission was established to, among other things, create a forum for dialogue and avoid confrontation over allegations of rights violations by public officers and agencies.

Among the main functions of the Commission are:

- to deal with all matters relating to the protection of human rights as, guaranteed by the Constitution of the Federal Republic of Nigeria 1979, as amended, the African Charter on Human and Peoples' Rights, the United Nations Charter, and the Universal Declaration of Human Rights and other international treaties on human rights to which Nigeria is a signatory,
- to monitor, investigate all alleged cases of human rights violations in Nigeria and make appropriate recommendations to the Federal Government for the prosecution and such other actions as it may deem expedient in each circumstance; and
- assist victims of the human rights violations and seek appropriate redress and remedies on their behalf.

From these provisions it would seem that the Federal Government must authorize litigation (para b). But under paragraph c) assistance to victims includes not only amicable non-judicial modes of settlement, but also support for a victim who has sought redress before the Courts. Therefore, while the Commission can not carry out judicial functions it can assist victims who seek redress in courts. The autonomy of the Commission is somewhat limited by being rooted outside the constitution, the chairman, members of the governing council, as well as the Executive Secretary are approved by the Head of State on the Attorney General's recommendations. The legislative arm (the Senate) is therefore excluded and removal should also go through the same process [S.2(3)(b) and 7(1)]. The nature of the financing provided by government can also undermine the integrity of the Commission being "such sum as may be provided by government of the Federation for the Commission" [S.12(1) and 2(a)]. The autonomy of the Commission is better enhanced if its funding is based on the consolidated revenue fund, and better if it is not under any Ministry and its budget submitted directly to Parliament.

Several African countries have established Human Rights Commissions. These include, Togo (1987), Benin (1989), Morocco (1990), Cameroon (1991), Tunisia, Algeria (1992), Sudan (1994) Chad (1995) South Africa (1994), Kenya (1996), Malawi (1998), Uganda (1995), Liberia (1997), Senegal (1997), Zambia (1996), Mauritania (1998) Rwanda (1998), Central African Republic (1999), Niger (1999), Tanzania (2001)[356].

Human Rights Watch had this to say about these Commissions in 2001:

---

[356] Human Rights Commissions in the Commonwealth: their effectiveness paper presented at the Commonwealth Human Rights Forum at Abuja Nigeria, 3-4 December 2003, by Judge Emile Francis Short Commissioner, Commission on Human Rights and Administrative Justice, Ghana, Ad Litem Judge of the International Criminal Tribunal for Rwanda.

"African national human rights commissions are a mixed bag. Given the needs of their society, to date the performance of most have been disappointing. Many have indeed been formed by governments with poor human rights record, weak state institutions, and little or no history of autonomous state bodies. Some appear largely designed to deflect international criticism of human rights abuses rather than to address those abuses and their causes. Many have been formed with flawed mandates and only weak powers, constraining their ability to effectively investigate and monitor abuses, or make public statements. Others have been undermined by the appointment of commissioners who are unwilling or unable to protest abuses from fear or hope of government favour. Other commissioners may be well-intentioned but have had little or no previous involvement in human rights work or training, and most commissions are under-funded and urban-based. Some commissions work almost behind closed doors and do not make public statements or other documentation available or easily available."

The study however acknowledged that there are encouraging trends. It stated that

"the activities of the more promising commissions are proof that these state bodies have the potential to strengthen a human rights culture and obtaining greater protection against abuses. In this the Ghanaian, South African, and Ugandan commissions stand out. In each case, their members are people of integrity who are not afraid to speak out strongly when confronted with government abuses and to assert their independence in the interest of protecting the rights of their citizens. Although it is still early, the Malawian and Senegalese commissions also show promise."

The Nigerian National Human Rights Commission is currently reviewing its law to enable it be more autonomous, proactive and effective in promoting and protecting Human Rights. And with the current opening of the democratic space (both political and social) in Africa, it will be surprising if other African Human Rights Commissions that have obstacles in their way of effective promotion and protection of human rights are not engaged in the same kind of project..

The African Commission should encourage those African countries where none exists to establish one. The NGOs, the Bar and other bodies concerned with human and peoples' rights could be persuaded to do so.

The role of NGOs in promoting human and peoples' rights has intensified and deepened in recent years, Olisa Agbakoba, the then Chairman of the Civil Liberties Organisations (CLO), one of the leading NGOs, sees the functions of NGOs as developing, promotion and protection of individual and group rights. According to him the various activities with which typical human rights NGO can be involved in the process of protecting individual and groups rights may be outlined as follows:

- To see to it that human rights are laid down, adjusted and extended in international and domestic human rights practice.
- To see to it that legal procedures are laid down to enforce rights and ensure that these rights are made accessible
- To expose human rights violations
- to provide humanitarian assistance to victims of human rights violations
- to create the legal and organisational conditions necessary to give effect to the stated objectives as well as to strengthen the NGO human rights movement".[357]

---

[357] Olisa Agbakoba "What works?" In Managing the Protection of Human Rights op.cit., p. 116. See also Anselm Chidi Odinkalu, Contemporary Human Rights NGO's in West Africa.

The NGOs both African and Non-African have contributed immensely through research and publications to awareness of human rights issues and enforcement.[358] The standard setting functions of the Commission envisaged under Article 45 1(b) could prove very useful particularly where model laws and legislations are acceptable to the people.

The promotional function of the Commission as already indicated also includes that of standard setting. It has the mandate to formulate and lay down principles and rules aimed at solving legal problems relating to human and peoples' rights and fundamental freedoms upon which African Government may base their legislation - model laws (Article 45(I) (b). The work of this Commission in this regard is to be enhanced by its co-operation with other African and international institutions concerned with the promotion and protection of human rights (Article 45 (I) (c).

In what follows, it should be borne in mind tat, National Human Rights Commissions and NGOs play the dual role of promotion and protection of rights.

10.1.3 Protection of Human and Peoples Rights

As already indicated, states and non-state entities can send communications to the Commission.

10.1.4 Communications by States

A state party to the Charter which has a good reason to believe that another state party has violated the provisions of the Charter may by written communication draw the attention of that state to the matter. Within three months of the receipt of the communication, the state to

---

[358] Amnesty International, PIOOM, Civil Liberties Organisation (CLO), Constitutional Rights Projects (CRP), Africa Watch, article 19, Index of Censorship, to mention a few, are NGO's which have made remarkable contributions to the promotion and protection of human and peoples' rights.

which the communication is addressed shall give the enquiring state written explanations or statements elucidating the matter. This should include, as much as possible, information indicating the laws and rules of procedure applied and applicable and the redress already given or pending. Thereafter, if the issue is not settled by bilateral negotiation or other peaceful procedure, either state has the right to submit the matter to the Commission through its Chairman and shall notify the other state involved. This notwithstanding, where a State Party to the Charter considers that another state party has violated the provisions of the Charter it may refer the matter directly to the Commission by addressing a Communication to its Chairman and to the Secretary-General of the OAU and the state concerned (Article 47,48 and 49).

In matters relating to communications, whether by states or non-state entities, the Commission has the power to resort to any appropriate method of investigation. It may also hear from the Secretary General or any other person capable of enlightenment it. (Article 46).

Before the Commission can be seized of a matter submitted to it, it must ensure that local remedies, where they exist, have been exhausted, unless it is obvious that (the procedure is unduly prolonged) (Article 50).

It should be noted that the requirement of the exhaustion of local remedies cannot apply to the state as a sovereign entity as such as it cannot be subjected to the jurisdiction of a foreign court. Where the state intervenes on behalf of its national (or probably on behalf of non-national) then the rule applies to such a person. In fact the offending states' opportunity to make reparations in the first instance – must be exhausted unless it would be futile to pursue local remedies. The Commission has power to ask the states parties concerned to provide it with all relevant information. It is our view that states can only refuse to give such information at their peril, as it would not affect the competence of the Commission to make the appropriate recommendations.[359] States parties concerned may be represented before the Commission and submit written or oral representatives (Article 51). After obtaining from the States Parties concerned and from other sources all the information it deems necessary, and after trying all appropriate means to reach an amicable solution, the Commission shall prepare within a reasonable period a report stating the facts and findings. The report is sent to the states concerned and communicated to the Assembly of Heads of States and Government of the OAU The report to the Assembly may include such recommendations as the Commission deem useful. (Article 53). The Commission is required to submit to each ordinary session of the Assembly of Heads of States and Government a report of its activities (Article 54).

If the experiences of the past are anything to go by then the right of state communication is likely to remain dormant for the foreseeable future as most, if not all African states, being violators of human and peoples' rights and fundamental freedoms are not likely to challenge those with whom they are *in pari delicto.*

10.1.5 Communications by Non-State Entities

The Commission may also receive communications from non-state entities. Even though these are not clearly specified, an integrative interpretation of the Charter will reveal that individuals and peoples are the primary beneficiaries of this procedural right of enforcement [Arts. 55 and 56(1)]. Article 56(1), in particular, refers to "communication relating human and peoples' rights referred to in Article 55 received by the Commission". It does not seem to us, unless a very liberal interpreta-

---

[359] Rules of Procedure of the African Commission on Human and Peoples Rights, see Annex 2. CF. The African Court on Human and Peoples' Court in adopting its Rules of procedure under Article 33 of the Protocol would normally consult with the Commision to ensure that there is harmony between their rules of procedure. See also Thisday, vol. 13, No. 4701, p.54.

tion is adopted importing the epistolary jurisdiction developed by Bhagwati's Indian Supreme Court that NGOs whether African or not can exercise this faculty except where they act on behalf of individuals or peoples alleging that their rights have been violated.

Indeed Rule 114 (1) (a), (now Rule 116), provides that communications may be submitted to the Commission by (a) an alleged victim of a violation by a State Party to the Charter or in his name when it appears that he is unable to submit the communication himself.

It would seem, however, from Rule [114 (1)(b), now rule 116][360] that an organisation alleging, with proof in support, a serious or massive cases of violations of human and peoples' right could send a communication to the Commission even when it is not a victim of right violations. An individual has a similar right under rule 114(1)(b). Rule 114(2) is somewhat problematic. It provides that "the Commission may accept any such communications from any individual or organisation irrespective of where they shall be". It is not clear whether this provision is intended to apply to Rule 114(1)(a) which deals with cases of communication by or on behalf of a victim or human rights violation for in such a case the violation would have to occur in the territory of a state party even when the communication may be sent from outside the territory of the violator state. Rule 114(2) would make sense when read together with Rule 114(b)(i). The individual or the organisation need not be the victim and all that is needed is 'proof' of serious or massive cases of violations of human rights. But how this can directly assist in remedying the wrong done to a victim of right violations is not clear.

It may be, however, that Rule 114(1)(b) is intended to assist the Commission in carrying out its functions under Article 58 of the Charter which requires the Commission to draw the attention of the Assembly of

---

[360] Osita C. Eze, African Charter on Human and People's Rights and the Enforcement of Rights and Duties op. cit.

Heads of Government to the existence of a series of serious or massive violations of human and peoples' rights.[361]

Rule 116 which replaces the old Rule 114 is terse and simply provides that the Commission shall determine questions of admissibility pursuant to Article 56 of the Charter. In effect the new Rule avoids any attempt to interpret Article 56 and leaves it to the Commission to find the appropriate jurisprudence. But in so doing it will no doubt be guided by its determinations on the old Rule 114.[362]

Admissibility Procedures

From the perspective of the African Charter and Rules of Procedure of the Commission two distinctive forms of determination of issue of admissibility are discernable. The first relates to cases where a communication is clearly defective on the face of it viz: where the communication relates to alleged violation(s) by states which are not parties to the African Charter. [Rule 101(2) Rule 102(1).[363] The secretary to the Commission may in such a case 'decide' on the issue of admissibility'.

---

[361] See *infra.*

[362] See 104/93 Centre for the Independence of Judges and Lawyers/Algeria and others. Where the Commission determined with respect to Rule 114(3) and maintained that " in order to decide on the admissibility of a Communication...the Commission shall ensure that the author alleges to be a vicyim of aviolation...that the communication is submitted in the name of an individual who is avictim (or individual who are victims) who would be unable to submit it (paragraph 4). On Rule 114(3)(g) the non-exhaustion of local remedies rendered the communication inadmissible [53/91 Alberto Capitano/Tanzania], also 45/90 Civil Liberties Organization/Nigeria (with respect to Article 56 of the Charter and Rule 114 and 18/88 El Hadj Boubacare Diawara/Benin (article 56(5) Rules 103(1)(f) of the charter.

[363] Article 55 of the African Charter, See also Committee for the Defence of Political Prisoners/Bahrain, 7/88, Wesley Parish/Indonesia, 38/90, Iheanyi-chukwu Ihebereme/USA, 5/88. For African States which had not become parties to the African Charter. See Union Nationale de Liberation de Cabinda v. Angola, 24/89, Austrian Committee Against Torture / Burundi 26/89. For a country

The second refers to cases which deserve some form of consideration. The main provisions that govern this stage are Article 55 and 56 of African Charter, as well as Rules 103 and 111 to 116 (now 113 – 118 of amended Rules) of the Commission's Rules of Procedure.

The cumulative effect of these provisions is the following:

1. On the receipt of individual communications they are listed by the Secretary of the African Commission. It is at this point in time that the first stage of 'admissibility' issue may be decided.[364]

2. All communications which have passed the first stage are listed and submitted to the next session of the African Commission for consideration. Individual Commissioners are assigned some communications to ascertain whether they satisfy in effect the conditionality for admissibility which limit the jurisdiction of the Commission.

These are:

- The communication has to be against a state which has ratified the Charter
- A communication may only be made in relation to violations of a right guaranteed in the Charter and must be sufficiently 'particularized or substantiated' in order to disclose a claim. It has been suggested that communications may refer to violations of other human rights not explicitly guaranteed under the Charter. Firstly, this second category of rights includes those derivable from rights guaranteed under the African Charter. Secondly, as made more explicit in the protocol establishing the Human Rights

---

like Morocco which withdrew from the OAU because of the recognition of Western Sahara by the OAU. See Austrian Committee Against Torture/ Morocco, 20188, Andre Hourer/ Morocco, 41/90, see also Mohammed El-Nekheily/OAU.

[364] For decision on Rule 103(1)(f) and Article 56(5). See fn 28 Supra. See also 8/88 Nzicoa Buyingo/Uganda where a communication was dismissed pursuant to Article 56(5) of the African Charter and Rule 103(1)(f).

Court they include rights which States Parties have undertaken to guarantee outside the African Charter on human and peoples rights.[365]

- A Communication should state the name, address, age and profession of the author (whether individual or peoples or groups). Once a communicator has satisfied these requirements he can request anonymity and the Commission may not disclose his/her identity to the state alleged to have violated human or people's rights.

- It must state the name of the state complained against which, as earlier indicated, must be a state which has ratified the convention.

- A communication should indicate what legal measures have been taken at the national level showing that the requirement of exhaustion of local remedies has been met.

The formulation of this provision/requirement raises certain problems of interpretation. Article 56(5) of the African Charter states that communications relating to human and peoples' rights shall be considered if they "are sent after exhaustion of local remedies, if any, unless it is obvious that this procedure is unduly, delayed". It would seem that the phrase 'if any' implies there is no local remedy to exhaust. Even when 'remedies' exist does the local exhaustion of remedy rule apply where the available remedy is patently unjust or it will be futile to exhaust it? (*Robert E. Brown Case)* 6 R.I.A.A., 120, 129 (1923); *Finish Ships Arbitration* (3.R.1 A.A. 1479 (1934): *EL Oro Mining and Railway Co Case* (5.R.1.A.A. 191) (1931).

The Commission has on several occasions as already indicated ruled on exhaustion of local remedies.

---

[365] Article 3 and 7 of the protocol to the African Charter on the Establishment of the African Court on Human and People's Rights.

Three major criteria could be deduced from the practice of the Commission in determining the rule namely: the remedy must be available, effective and sufficient.

A remedy is considered available if the petitioner can pursue it without impediment, it is deemed effective if it offers a prospect of success, and it is found sufficient if it is capable of redressing the complaint.

In the words of the Commission, in the Dawda K. Jawara Communication, (147/95 and 149/966):

"This rule is one of the most important conditions for admissibility of communications, there is no doubt therefore, that in almost all the cases, the first requirement looked at by the Commission and the state concerned is the exhaustion of local remedies. The rational of the local remedies rule both in the Charter and other international instruments is to ensure that before proceedings are brought before an international body, the State concerned must have had the opportunity to remedy the matter through its own local system. This prevents the Commission from acting as a court of first instance rather than a body of last resort. Three major criteria could be deduced from the practice of the Commission in determining this rule, namely: the remedy must be available, effective and sufficient. A remedy is considered available if the petitioner can pursue it without impediment, it is deemed effective if it offers a prospect of success, and it is found sufficient if it is capable of redressing the complaint. The government's assertion of non-exhaustion of local remedies will therefore be looked at in this light. As aforementioned, a remedy is considered available only if the applicant can make use of it in the circumstance of his case. The applicants in cases Nos. ACHPR/60/91, ACHPR/87/93, ACHPR/101/93 and ACHPR/129/94 had their communications declared admissible by the Commission because the competence of the ordinary courts had been ousted either by decrees or the establishment of special tribunals). The Commission has stressed that, remedies, the availability of which is not evident, cannot be invoked by the State to the detriment of the complainant. Therefore, in a situation where the jurisdiction of the courts have been ousted by decrees whose validity cannot be challenged or questioned, as is the position with the case under consideration, local remedies are deemed not only to be unavailable but also non-existent. The existence of a remedy must be sufficiently certain, not only in theory but also in practice, failing which, it will lack the requisite accessibility and effectiveness. Therefore, if the applicant cannot turn to the judiciary of his country because of generalized fear for his life (or even those of his relatives), local remedies would be considered to be unavailable to him".

vi. The communication does not deal with cases which have been settled by the states involved in accordance with the principles of the Charter of the United Nations or the Charter of the Organisation of African Unity or the provisions of the Present Charter. The authority of the African Commission to resort to peaceful modes of resolving conflicts otherwise than by 'judicial' process between states on the one hand and individual and groups on the other, is not expressly granted as is the case with inter state disputes.

Article 55 of the African Charter when read together with Article 56(7) of the Charter is indicative of the fact that, states parties to the African Charter intended that prior to the ordinary course of consideration of individual or group petitions that the Commission may take steps to resolve the 'conflict'. Such steps can only in the circumstances mean non-contentious peaceful modes of settlement of disputes. It is to be noted that Rule 114(3)(f) of the Commission deviates somewhat from the express provisions of Article 56(7) of the African Charter which excludes from the competence of the Commission 'cases which have been settled' by stipulating that for admissibility purposes, the Commission shall ensure *inter alia* that the issue is not already being considered by another international investigation or settlement body.

It does not seem, as has been argued by some that (Art. 29(7)[366] since it imposes a duty on the individual, provides the legal basis for the exercise of this faculty, since it refers to relations with other members of society, not states. Where the violation of the right of an individual or group(s) by an individual or group(s) is imputable to a state and the state did nothing to stop it or the state failed to take measures to punish those responsible for the act(s) there is a violation.

The African Commission affirmed the responsibility of a state party for non-state actors, in 207/97 Africa Legal Aid/The Gambia, citing with approval its previous determination in 74/92 Commission Nationale des Droits de l'Homme des Libertes/Chad where it ruled:

"The Charter specifies in Article 1 that the States Parties shall not only recognize the rights, duties and freedoms adopted by the Charter, but they should also "undertake measures to give effect to them" in other words, if a state neglects to ensure the rights in the African Charter, this constitute a violation even if the state or its agents are not the immediate cause of the violation. The African Charter unlike other human rights instruments does not allow for state parties to derogate from their treaty obligations during emergency situations. Thus even a war in Chad cannot be used as an excuse by the state violating or permitting violation of rights in the African Charter."[367]

The principle of State responsibility stated in 74/92 above was already part of international law: *Home Missionary Society Claim* (U.S.V.

---

[366] Article 27(9) provides that the individual has the duty "to preserve and strengthen positive cultural African values in his relations with other members of society in the spirit of tolerance, dialogue…" and consultation.

[367] But see supra for some qualification to this apparent rigid position.

Great Britain) (1920 R.1.A.A. 42, *Corfu Channel Cases* (Merits) I.C.J. Report, 1949; p.4). In case of default by the state or its agency amounting a breach of a minimum standard of international law viz denial or delay of justice, and his state of nationality takes up his case, then amicable methods of conflict resolution should be employed between the complainant state and the violator state.

While it is arguable that 'the Commission should be in a position to seek' amicable settlement in case of non state communications and for this purposes authorize individual Commissioners with respect to communications originating from or concerning countries assigned to them to, in appropriate cases, initiate discussions with a view to amicable settlement between authors of individual communications or their duly authorised representatives and states parties,[368] it must be pointed out that the method may be more suited to peaceful resolution of inter-state conflicts rather than individuals-state conflicts and that the Commission might have to work hard to persuade State parties to accept mediation, conciliation and good offices as means of resolving conflicts between them and individuals.

The Commission has however, indicated that on several occasions, it has employed these modes for the settlement of state/individual conflicts.

Under the regime of the American Convention on Human Rights, any person or group of persons, or any non-governmental entity legally recognized in one or more of the member states may lodge petitions with Commission containing denunciations or complaints of the violation of the convention by a State Party (Article 44).

More relevant to our present discussion is Article 48(I)(f) which stipulates:

---

[368] See Odinkalu and An-main "Enhancing the procedure of the African Commission on Human and Peoples' Rights with Respect to individual Communications".

"The Commission shall place itself at the disposal of the parties concerned with a view to reaching amicable settlement of the matter on the basis of respect for the human rights recognized in this Convention."[369]

This approach may be a further step in enhancing the status of individuals and peoples as subjects of international law. Beyond this the Commission is expected, where the subject matter of any communication has been settled, not be seized of it. (Article 56(7). Art5(2) (a) of the Optional Protocol to the International Covenant on Civil and Political Rights provides that:

"The Committee shall not consider any communication from any individual unless it has ascertained that: (a)   The same is not being examined under another procedure of international investigation or settlement."

The provision of the African Charter deals with cases which have been settled 'while the similar provision of the optional protocol is concerned with matters 'not being examined' Ironically Rule 114(2) (F) of Rules of Procedure of African Commission adopts a form similar to that of the Optional Protocol.

The Commission in Njoku/Egypt, 40/90 where the complainant submitted a petition to United Nations Commission on Human Rights, which the UN body did not act on and was subsequently referred to the African Commission, found that the matter had not been settled as required by Article 56(7) and therefore declares it admissible.

In another communication Mpaka-Nsusu Andre Al Phuse/Zaire 15/88 referral to the UN Human Rights Committee was sufficient to render the communication inadmissible.[370]

It is important to note the difference between these two communications. In Njoku's case the matter was not dealt with, while in

---

[369] American Convention on Human Rights, Articles 44 and 48 (f).
[370] See also Amnesty International/Tunisia, 69/92.

the second of Alphunse the matter was still pending. The determinations have not helped in resolving the extending the conventional scope of this requirement from 'settled' to 'not being examined' imported by the Commissions Rules of Procedure. It further, even though the tendency is to add rather diminish advantages attached to rights, raises the issues as to what extent rules of procedure can add to or modify clear provisions of a convention.

The Commission needs to clarify its position in this regard even though we dare suggest that where there is concurrent jurisdiction it would make little sense, all things are equal, for more than one of the organisations or bodies having such competence to be seized of the matter at the same time.

vii. Additionally communications will not be considered if they are written in insulting language[371], are based exclusively[372] on news disseminated through the mass media are not submitted within a reasonable period from the time local remedies have been exhausted.

Consideration of Communications

Before each session of the Commission the Secretary to the Commission makes a list of communications by individuals, persons and non-state entities and transmits them to the members of the Commission [Article 55(1)]. Under Rule 102, the secretary to the Commission is not only required to communicate the full text of each communication referred to the commission to each member of the Commission on request, he is also required to attach to the list of communications transmitted to

---

[371] Ligue Camerounaise des Droits de L'Homme/Cameroon, where an NGO painted a graphic picture of serious and massive violations, torture and dictatorship. The Commission declared the communication inadmissible.

[372] Emphasis mine. cf Sir Dawda K. Jawara/Gambia/147/95, 149/96 where the Commission stated: " While it would be dangerous to rely exclusively on news dissemination from the mass media, it would be equally damaging of the Commission were to reject a communication because some aspects are based on news disseminated through the mass media.

members of the Commission, a brief summary of their contents. He is also under an obligation to ensure that these lists are regularly distributed to the members of the Commission. (Rule 102(1) and (2). No communication concerning a state which is not a party to the Charter shall be received by the Commission or placed on a list under Rule 102 [Rule 101(3)].

Article 55(2) which stipulates that 'a communication shall be considered by the Commission if a simple majority of its members so decide" is not without difficulty of interpretation. Does this apply to the issues preliminary to the determination of admissibility, the issue of admissibility itself or to the substantive consideration of the matter after the issue of admissibility has been decided?

Once it is accepted that the idea of admissibility may not be determined until the alleged violator state is given the opportunity to comment on the allegations against it as well as where necessary after clarification which may be needed either from the communicator of petitioner or the state, then Article 55(2) would appear relevant after these stages have been gone through. At this stage the Commission can by a simple majority of its members determine whether the communication satisfies the conditions for admissibility laid down in Article 56 of the charter and therefore whether it is admissible or not. [Rule 115(1)] now Rule 117.[373]

This line of reasoning is supported by the Rule of Procedure of the Commission which stipulates that "a communication may be declared admissible *only on condition that the State Party concerned has received the text of the communication and that it has been given the op-*

---

[373] It is possible that Article 55(2) or at least a similar procedure is applicable to the issue of listing which communications may be considered by the Commission for the purpose of admissibly. The Commission needs to clarify this.

portunity to submit the information and observations pursuant to paragraph 1 of this rule" [Rule 115(2)].[374]

This is further buttressed by Rule 115(3), now Rule 117, which states that: "a request made under paragraph 1 of this Rule (Rule 115) should indicate clearly that the request does not mean that a decision whatsoever has been taken on the issue of admissibility".

Where a determination of inadmissibility has been made, the author of the communication is so informed as early as possible by the Commission through the Secretary-General. [Rule 116(1)], now Rule 118. The Commission may reconsider its decision on inadmissibility at a later date if it is seized by the interested individual or on his behalf, of a written request containing information to the effect that the ground for inadmissibility have ceased to exist [Rule 116(2)].

If the Commission decides that the communication is admissible the author of the communication and the alleged violator state are so informed [Rule 117(1)], now Rule 119. The State Party to the Charter concerned shall within the ensuing four months submit, in writing to the commission, explanations or statements elucidating the issue under consideration and indicating, if possible, measures it was able to take to remedy the situation [Rule 117(2)].

All explanations or statements by a state under Rule 117(2) above shall be communicated to the author of the communication who may submit in writing additional information and observations within a time limit fixed by the Commission [Rule 117(3)].

At this stage based on the information gathered both from the State Party concerned and the individual the Commission may reverse its decision on admissibility. If it does not, and having satisfied the requirements of Article 57 of the Charter making the consideration of the substantive matter dependent on the prior transmission of all communi-

---

[374] Emphasis Mine.

cations to the state, concerned, the Commission may then proceed with its final decision' on the matter. [Rule 118(1)] now Rule 120.

The Commission may refer a communication to a working group[375] composed of three of its members at most, which shall submit recommendations to it on which it may base its observations. The observations of the Commission are transmitted to the Assembly which may authorize its publication [Rule 118(1) and (2)].

This requirement for confidentiality of the deliberations of the Commission on communications till authorised by the Assembly of Heads of State and Government, has come under severe criticism for unduly shielding violator states and removing the sanction that adverse publicity would ordinarily import.[376]

Article 59 (1) of the African Charter provides that all matters relating to Communications procedure "shall remain confidential until such time as the Assembly of Heads of State and Government shall otherwise decide". The Commission may, however, issue press releases on activities concluded in private sessions. It is not clear, whether the communiqué will be detailed enough to guide would be communicators and counsels. Even when as is the case with the Committee of Human Rights under the Optional Protocol, proceedings of the African Commission are held in private, both bodies publish reports of their proceedings albeit that the latter does so after 'clearance' by the OAU Heads of State and Government. It is not clear apart from its competence, to authorize publication, what the role of the OAU Heads of State and Government is in this regard. It is not clear for instance whether it is a form of 'appellate jurisdiction' "with the power to confirm, override or modify the view of

---

[375] Under Rule 113. The Commission may not set up one or several working groups composed of three of its members at most to submit recommendations on the conditions of admissibility stipulated in Article 56 of the Charter. See also general power to establish Committee or working groups under Rule.

[376] See *infra* Fn. 249.

the Commission". And despite the absence of a stipulation to that effect, the Assembly may well in determining the scope of its competence, *competence de la competence,*[377] decide that it possessed such powers? If the objective is to shield violator states from embarrassment then it not only undermines the efficacy of the African Commission with respect to its protective functions but also removes a critical pressure factor that should encourage States Parties to the African Charter to fulfill their obligations thereunder.[378]

Based on our discussion above we suggest that:

- The Commission should clarify the nature of the function which the Assembly of Heads of State and Governments plays with respect to observations and views sent to it by the Commission on individual and group communications;

- Reference to the Assembly of Heads of State and Government be dispensed with, if it is not an extension of the 'judicial' function of the Commission and that accordingly the requirement of confidentiality be dispensed with; and

- The Commission might well borrow a leaf from the pattern of the Annual Report of the UN Committee on Human Rights which is sufficiently detailed to serve as a guide on matters of jurisprudence, procedure and substantive law to victims of human rights violations and other parties having interest in matters of human and peoples' rights.[379] Some progress has been made but much more needs to be made. And the Court when it commences busi-

---

[377] This is the principle according to which an international organization can determine its own competence.

[378] U.O. Umozurike "Five Years of the African Commission" *op cit,* 1992, Osita C. Eze, "The Place of the African Charter in the Enforcement of Rights" *op. cit.*

[379] Rosalyn Higgins "The Relationship Between International and Regional Human Rights norm and Domestic Law"(1992) 18 CLB, Lallah, *op. cit.*

ness is expected to enrich the jurisprudence under the African Charter.

Article 58 Jurisdiction

Article 58(1) stipulates: "when it appears after deliberations of the Commission that one or more communications apparently relate to special cases which reveal the existence of a series of serious or massive violations of human and peoples' rights, the Commission shall draw the attention of the Assembly of Heads of State and Government to these special cases. The Assembly of Heads of State and Government may then request the Commission to undertake an in-depth study of these cases and make a factual report accompanied by its findings and recommendations (Article 58(2).

What amounts to the existence of a series of serious or massive violations of human rights or an in depth-study will no doubt be decided by the Commission according to the circumstances of each case. We do not believe that much can be achieved by attempting to define them in abstract.

What should be of the immediate concern is whether and to what extent the African Charter has subverted the domestic jurisdiction clause contained in both the UN Charter and the Charter of the Organisation of African Unity as well as the Constitutive Act of the AU That the Commission can consider and make observations with respect to violations of human and peoples' rights is not in doubt. That this faculty has whittled down the domestic jurisdiction clause already alluded to is not in doubt either. But does this also mean that the Commission can enter into the territory of a state party to carry out any form of investigation without its consent? Will refusal to allow visitation be interpreted as failure to take advantage of an opportunity offered to a state to defend itself? It is our considered view that a state party is under an obligation, subject to any limitation imposed by the Charter, to allow investigation in Loco.

The practice of the Commission indicates not only that consent must be obtained from the host government before a visit whether with respect to resorting to any appropriate method of investigation "(Article 46) or under Article 58, but also that findings might not have contributed to determinations of particular petitions. In many cases visits are regarded as promotional.[380]

The commission needs to clarify this as well as elaborate on procedures for visitations.

It is true that the African Charter in its Article 7 obliquely guarantees the right to fair hearing for it selects and affirms elements of fair hearing such as the right of an accused to be presumed innocent until found guilty, the right to counsel, and to be tried within a reasonable time by an impartial court or tribunal and prohibition against retroactive legislation.

By way of contrast Article 14 of the UN Covenant on Civil and Political Rights and Article 8 of the Inter-American Convention on Human Rights, as earlier indicated, are not only explicit on the right to fair hearing but on their constituent elements as are evidenced by the practice of an overwhelming majority of States.

It should be noted that the right to fair hearing to the extent that it is guaranteed under the African Charter and the Covenant on Civil and Political Rights refer to the exercise of that right at the national level.

---

[380] Malawi African Association/Mauritanian, 54/91, Amnesty International/Mauritania, 61/91, Ms Sarre Diop Union Interfricaine des Droitsde L'ltomme RADDITO/Mauritania 164/97, Collech of des venves et Ayants droits/ Mauritania 164/97, Amnesty International/ Sudan, 48/90 Comite Loosli Bachelard/ Sudan/ 50/91, Lawyers Committee for Human Rights/ Sudan, 52/91, Association of Members of Episcopal Conference of East Africa/ Sudan, 89/93. See also Murray, R. on-site visits by the African Commission on Human and People's Rights: A case study and comparison with Inter-American Commission on Human Rights, African Journal of International and Comparative Law, 1999, Vol.11, p.3

Failure of States Courts or tribunals to comply with this requirement could lead to the Commission taking the view that an individual communicator, who has suffered as a consequence, has been denied justice.

If the Commission expects state courts and tribunals to comply with the principles of fair trial it would seem not only odd but also contrary to well established principles of international law, if it did not itself apply the same principles in performing its protective task which is judicial in character.

The Commission in interpreting Article 7 of the African Charter should adopt an expansive approach so as to include those elements of fair trial that have become general principles of law recognized by civilized nations as well as principles to which it may have recourse under Articles 60 and 61 of the African Charter.

Indeed to reaffirm the principles of natural justice, which may be presumed to be part of the rule on fair hearing, Rule 107(1) proscribes a member of the Commission from taking part in the consideration of the case if he has any personal interest in the case, if he has participated in any capacity in the adoption of any decision relating to the case or which is the subject of the communication. Hopefully the decision referred to will not apply to issues of listing and determination of admissibility.

Despite the possibility of inferring the right to oral presentation in matters of communications by non state entities from Article 46 of the African Charter which authorizes the Commission to resort to "any appropriate method of investigation" it is clearly desirable, in order to enhance the capacity of non-state entities, which are in a weaker position than the states, that the Commission incorporates in it Rules of Procedure a comparable provision as Rule 99 (now Rule 100), which confers that privilege in cases of inter-state communications.

It should be noted, however, that in the African context where most of the victims of human and peoples' rights violations are invariably the poor that the issue of the cost of transporting the victim or his legal representative to the locus where the Commission is meeting could create a serious obstacle to the exercise of this faculty. Nevertheless, it should be there for those who wish to use it and can afford it.

With respect to on-the-site missions Art. 46 of the Charter, as already indicated, provides the legal authority for carrying out such activities. The Rules of Procedure of the African Commission do not contain any provisions on how this faculty may be exercised. We, therefore, accept the proposal that.

The Commission should adopt and develop guidelines on on-site missions, including directives for taking testimonies during such missions as well as mechanisms for releasing reports of such missions.[381]

The adhoc approach which invariably results in press releases, after such missions seems rather inadequate.

Interim or Provisional Measures and the Inter-Sessional Period

Rule 109 (now Rule 111) of the Rules of Procedure of the African Commission provides that:

"Before making its final views known to the Assembly on the communication the Commission may inform the state party concerned of its views on the appropriateness of taking provisional measures to avoid irreparable prejudice being caused to the victim of the alleged violation. In so doing, the Commission shall inform the State Party that the expression of its view on the adoption of those provisional measures does not imply a decision on the substance of the communication".[382] While Rule 109 might well prove adequate in dealing with matters, including

---

[381] Odinaku and An-Naim, *op. cit*, pp.6-7.

[382] In communication, 60/91. Constitutional Rights Project/Nigeria where the complainant NGO submitted a petition on behalf of individuals sentenced to death and awaiting execution, the Commission applied the old Rule 109 (now 111) requesting the Nigerian Government, because of the emergency nature of the case, top as before the execution until it had fully considered the substance of the case. See also Constitutional Rights Project/ Nigeria; 139/94, Constitutional Rights Projects/ Nigeria, 140/94.

those arising from emergency situations during the period of sitting of the commission, it does not address situations, whether arising out of emergency or not, that call for the Commission's attention during the period when it is not in formal session. Article 58(3) authorizes the Commission to report a case of emergency duly noticed by it to the Chairman of the Assembly of Heads of State and Government who may request an in-depth study. In the absence of a clear provision on what the Commission can do during the intersession period, Article 58(3) may only be applicable while the Commission is sitting.

A project prepared by the International Commission of Jurists (ICJ) states that:

"In cases of urgency you should immediately bring the matter to the attention of the Chairman and the Secretariat of the ACHPR, giving the reasons why the case needs urgent treatment".

The project then continues: It is not clear yet if (like in the case of other regional commissions) the Chairman may act in the period between the sessions of the ACHPR on such a communication". Clearly there is an element of uncertainty in this area of the Commission's work, even when the Rules of Procedure make provisions for extra sessions as well as extraordinary or special sessions which may be obviated by the Commission adopting appropriate rules in this regard. The practice of the UN Committee on Human Rights in this regard is instructive.

We had suggested earlier that:

- The Commission may have more regular sessions and or extend the duration during which it sits.
- The Commission may consider instituting a pre-sessional working group that should have the following functions;
- examining communications; and making
- recommendations on their admissibility or merit;

Indeed the practice of the Human Rights Committee shows that such a working group can by a unanimous decision decide on matters of admissibility. But it cannot even by unanimity, decide that a petition is inadmissible[383].

iii. the Commission might consider the appointment of a special Rapporteur empowered to request interim measures, in appropriate cases, to seek information from the authors of communication and States Parties concerned regarding question of admissibility and, to recommend directly to the (Commission) the inadmissibility of communications which are clearly inadmissible.[384]

These criticisms have been taken care of by the amended Rules. For Rule 111, had added two new paragraphs to the old Rule 109 which now deal with the matter thus:

> "The Commission, or when it is not in session, the Chairman, in consultation with other members of the Commission, may indicate to the parties any interim measure the adoption of which seems desirable in the interest of the parties or the proper conduct of the proceedings before it. In case of urgency when the Commission is not in session, the Chairman, in consultation with other members of the Commission, may take any necessary action on behalf of the Commission. As soon as the Commission is again in session, the Chairman shall report to it on any action taken."

The Commission has since the early 90s adopted the practice of appointing rappotteurs with defined mandates. The NGOs were partly responsible for this development. The mandate has varied from being charged with some thematic areas or a country.

Thus there have been Special Rapporteurs:

- on Extra Judicial, Summary and Arbitrary Executions,
- on Prisons and conditions of detentions in Africa,

---

[383] See Lallah, *op. cit.*

[384] *Ibid.*

- on Freedom of Expression in Africa,
- on Rights of Women in Africa,
- on Human Rights Defenders in Africa, and
- on Refugees, Asylum seekers and internally displaced persons
- prevention of torture, cruel, inhuman and degrading punishment and treatment,
- Workng Group on the situation of indigenous populations[385]

Advisory Opinion

The Commission is also required to interpret all the provisions of the Charter at the request of a state party, an institution of the OAU or an African organisation recognized by the OAU [Article 45(3)]

Article 45(3) confers on the Commission, therefore, the competence to give advisory opinion on legal issues relating to the Charter. Advisory opinions are not normally regarded as binding,[386] in the manner of decisions or determinations. Recommendations or observations' in the context of the African Charter, as already indicated, have some binding effect. This not withstanding, parties seeking advisory opinion under Article 45(3) are expected to accept and honour them, for as Osieke pointed out"... a determination of the International Court of Justice, even by Advisory Opinion, on a question or dispute about the interpretation of the ILO Constitution, will constitute a most important and impar-

---

[385] Except foe the Rapporteuron Extra Judicial, Arbitrary and Summary execution, the others presented their reports on the activities carried out during the intersession at the 35th Ordinary Session of the Commission held in Banjul The Gambia, from 21st May to 4 th June 2004, Final Communique, 4th June 2004. The African Commission at the same session adopted resolutions on the following: Protection of Human Rights Defenders in Africa, Situation of Human Rights in Cote d'Ivore, Situation of Human Rights in Nigeria, Situation in the Darfur of Sudan, Situation of women and children in Africa.

[386] Ebere Osieke, Constitutional Law and Practice in the International Labour Organisation, Dordrech, Martinus Nijhoff Publishers, 1985, p. 184.

tial pronouncement on the matter and should not be set aside".[387] As to parties which have the capacity to seek advisory opinion there arises some difficulty of interpretation, with respect to the phrase 'Organisations recognized by the O.A.U'. Since the African Commission is a body established by the OAU it would seem that, within the limits of its competence, that is to say, the promotion and protection of human and peoples' rights guaranteed in the Charter, that recognition of NGOs or other organisations which confers upon them the capacity to seek advisory opinion is in order.

Finally it may be maintained that the advisory jurisdiction which the African Commission exercises serves the double function of promoting human and peoples' rights, by clarifying the legal issues in doubt, and protecting the same where parties accept such opinions and implement them in specific cases.

It may be convenient at this point to mention Article 45(4) which even though, is not part of the advisory jurisdiction of the Commission, is nevertheless one that impacts on the scope of its functions. Article 45(4) stipulates that the Commission shall perform any other tasks which may be entrusted to it by the Assembly of Heads of State and Government.

Nature of the Protective Function

There is no explicit statement in the Charter as to whether the Commission can make binding decisions. It can be inferred from the absence of such explicit provision and references to the competence of the Commission to make recommendations with respect to state communications and in cases of a series of massive violations of human and peoples' rights which might be deduced from individual petitions that the Commission's function of ensuring the protection of human and peo-

---

[387] Op. cit. p.204. See also S. Rosenne, The World Court What it is and How it Works, Leiden, Sijhoof, 1975, p.80.

ples' rights guaranteed under the Charter involves the determination of the compatibility of state laws and actions, including administrative judicial decision with provisions of the African Charter, that its work in this regard is judicial in character. The mandate of the Human Rights Committee under the International Covenant on Civil and Political Rights and its Optional Protocol which under Article 5(4) of the latter empowers it, in relation to individual petitions, to forward its views to the state party concerned has been interpreted by members of the Committee to import the faculty to act judicially. In the words of Rosalyn Higgins:

> "The Covenant... is silent on the binding quality or otherwise of its decisions under the Optional Protocol. For that reason and because it performs other non adjudicative functions, it is commonly described as a quasi-judicial organ"

10.2 African Court on Human and Peoples Rights

It is important to have an insight into the nature of the Court in terms of its structure, composition and guiding principles before examining its mandate and how it is intended to carry it out.[388]

---

[388] Probably to streamline the institutional framework of the AU and its organs, a decision was taken by the Assembly of Heads of State and Government of the African Union at its 3rd Ordinary session in July 2004 to merge the AU Court of Justice and the African Court of Human and Peoples Rights. Whatever be the result of this merger, it is hoped that it will strengthen rather dimish the capacity and competence of the African Human Rights Court/Chamber to carry out its mandate in particular, it may be considered if time has not come to make the right of individual petition independent of state approval and whether there should not be a clear affirmation of right of petition against persons especially transnational corporations operating or having branches in Africa.

Composition

The Court shall consist of eleven judges, nationals of member states of the O.AU. (now AU) elected on an individual basis from among jurists of high moral character and of recognized practical judicial or academic experience. They should also be experienced in the field of human and peoples' rights. No two judges shall be nationals of the same State (Article II).

As formulated the requirement for appointment, in contrast to the position under the Commission, insists on legal qualifications as a minimum precondition. While the non insistence on legal qualification may be tolerable at the level of the Commission, the requirement for membership of the Court is explicit on the minimum requirement of legal qualification and experience for membership of the court for the task of crafting the jurisprudence of the court, given the manner in which the rights, freedoms and duties enshrined therein has been drafter requires the highest professional skills.

Provisions are made for nomination of candidates, election, tenure and related matters. A State Party to the Protocol may nominate up to three candidates, at least two which shall be nationals of that state. This means that such a state can nominate up to three candidates. Due consideration is to be given, in making such nominations, to adequate gender representation. By making the issue of gender explicit, it is not only ahead of the Commission in this regard (Article 12), but it has, by affirmative action, fulfilled the gender equality guaranteed by the Charter[389].

The Secretary General of the OAU, sets in motion the process of compiling the list, 90 days after the coming into force of the Protocol and ensure that member states get a copy of the list thirty days before the next session (Article 13). Election is by secret ballot by the Assembly. In the election, however, in addition to the qualifications already

---

[389] see supra. See also Articles 2 and 18(3).

stated, the Assembly shall ensure that there is representation of the main regions of Africa and of their principal legal traditions and an adequate gender representation (Article 14).

The judges of the Court are to be elected for a term of six years and are to be re-elected only once. The term of four judges elected at the first election shall expire at the end of four years, and the term of four other judges shall expire at the end of four years. The judges whose tenure will end at the end of the initial periods of two years and four years shall be chosen by ballot to be drawn by the Secretary General of the OAU immediately after the first election has been completed. All judges except the President of the court shall perform their duties on a part time basis. However, the Assembly may change this arrangement as it deems fit. (Article 15)[390].

After their election, the judges of the Court shall make a solemn declaration to discharge their duties impartially and faithfully (Article 16). It is also stipulated that the position of judge of the Court is incompatible with any activity that might interfere with the independence or impartiality of such a judge or the demands of the office, as determined in the Rules of Procedure of the Court. (Article 18).

"The Independence of the judges shall be fully ensured in accordance with international law. No judge may hear any case in which the same judge has previously taken part as agent, counsel or advocate for one of the parties or as a member of a national or international court of a commission of enquiry or in any other capacity. Any doubt on this point shall be settled by decision of the Court. The judges of the Court shall enjoy, from the moment of their election and throughout their term of office, the immunities extended to diplomatic agents in accordance with

---

[390] Article 15(3) provides that a judge elected to replace a judge whose tenure has not expired shall hold office for the reminder of the predecessor's term.

international law.[391] At no time shall the judges of the Court be held liable for any decision or opinion issued in the exercise of their functions" (Article 17).

A judge shall not be suspended or removed from office unless, by the unanimous decision of the other judges of the Court, the judge concerned has been found to be no longer fulfilling the required conditions to be a judge of the Court. Such a decision of the Court shall become final unless it is set aside by the Assembly at its next session, (Article 19).

Finally, the Court shall examine cases brought before it, if it has a quorum of at least seven judges. (Article 23).

On matters of evidence it is provided in Article 26 that:

- The Court shall hear submissions by all parties and if deemed necessary, hold an enquiry. The States concerned shall assist by providing relevant facilities for the efficient handling of the case.
- The Court may receive written and oral evidence including expert testimony and shall make its decision on the basis of such evidence.

---

[391] See Vienna Convention on Diplomatic Relations, 1961, Vienna Convention on Consular Relations and Optional Protocols, 1963 – Diplomatic immunity is also governed by Customary international law. See also Shasore, O. Jurisdiction and Sovereignty in Nigerian Commercial Law, Lagos, Nigerian Institute of International Affairs, 2007p. 49 *et sequ;* See also U. S. Diplomatic and Consular Staff in Tehran Case (US v. Iran) I.C.J. Reports, 1980, p3, This was a case where several hundred Iranian students and other demonstrators occupied the US Embassy in Tehran by force.US Consulates elsewhere in Iran were similarly occupied. They were protesting against the admission of the deposed Shah of Iran into US for medical treatment. The Iranian security forces rather confront them melted away from the scene. The Court decided "that the Islamic Republic of Iran has violated obligations under international conventions in force between the two countries, as well as under long established rules of general international law".

If the Court finds that there has been a violation of a human or peoples' right, it shall make appropriate orders to remedy the violation, including the payment of fair compensation or reparation.   In cases of extreme gravity and urgency, and when necessary to avoid irreparable harm to persons, the Court shall adopt such provisional measures as it deems necessary. [Article 27].

The mandate of the Court with respect to the nature of remedies is therefore very clear, unlike the position under the Commission.

- The Court shall render its judgment within ninety (90) days of having completed its deliberations.
- The judgment of the Court decided by majority shall be final and not subject to appeal.
- Without prejudice to sub-article 2 above, the Court may review its decision in the light of new evidence under conditions to be set out in the Rules of Procedure.
- The Court may interpret its own decision
- The judgment of the Court shall be read in open court, due notice having been given to the parties.
- Reasons shall be given for the judgment of the Court.
- If the judgment of the Court does not represent, in whole or in part, the unanimous decision of the judges, any judge shall be entitled to deliver a separate or dissenting opinion [Article 28].

Article 29 makes provision for notification of Judgment

- The parties to the case shall be notified of the judgment of the Court and it shall be transmitted to the Member States of the OAU/AU and the Commission.
- The Council of Ministers shall also be notified of the judgment and shall monitor its execution on behalf of the Assembly.

Execution of Judgment

As for the execution of judgments the States parties to the present protocol undertake to comply with the judgment in any case to which they are parties within the time stipulated by the Court and to guarantee its execution.

From the above it can be seen that the court is unfettered in the exercise of the judicial functions with the competence to make binding decisions and award appropriate remedies.

The Court is required to submit to each regular session of the Assembly, a report on its work during the previous year. The report shall specify, in particular, the cases in which a State has not complied with the Court's judgment.

Expenses of the Court, emoluments and allowances for judges and the budget of its registry shall be determined and borne by the OAU/AU in accordance with criteria laid down by the OAU/AU in consultation with the Court. [Article 32].

General

A protocol established an African Court on Human and Peoples Rights within the Organization of African Unity (Article 1). The Court is to complement the protective functions of the African Commission. From what follows, it is evident that the court is a form of 'appellate' jurisdiction from the Commission.

The Court has jurisdiction to hear all cases and disputes concerning the interpretation and application of the Charter, the protocol itself and any other relevant human rights instrument ratified by the States concerned. The court has the competence to determine its own jurisdiction (competence de la competence) (Art. 3). In carrying out its protective assignment the court shall apply the provisions of the Charter and any other relevant human rights instruments ratified by the states concerned (Art. 7). This gives a lot of room to the Court but its exact scope needs to be determined by the Court itself.

The Court has also the competence to give advisory opinion at the request of a member state of the OAU/AU, any of its organs, or any African Organisation recognized by the OAU/AU. The Advisory opinion may be on any legal matter relating to the Charter or any other relevant human rights instruments, provided that the subject matter of the opinion is not related to a matter being considered by the Commission. The court is required to give reasons for its advisory opinions, provided that every judge shall be entitled to deliver a separate or dissenting opinion (decision) (Act 4). The word 'decision' rather than advisory opinion is used to describe the determination given by the court under its advisory jurisdiction. The latter would clearly be preferred in the circumstances.

Who can Access the Court?

Article 5 provides that the following can access the Court:

- The Commission
- The State Party which has lodged a complaint to the Commission;
- The State Party against which the complaint has been lodged at the Commission.
- The state party whose citizen is a victim of human rights violation;
- African Intergovernmental Organisations.

When a State Party has an interest in a Case, it may submit a request to the Court to be permitted to join.

The Court may entitle relevant Non-Governmental Organisations (NGOs) with observers status before the Commission, and individuals to institute cases directly before it, in accordance with Article 34(6) of the Protocol.

Article 34(6) requires a state party to make a declaration accepting the right of individual petition before the individual can access the court directly [Article 5(3)].

It seems that individual cases may go to the Court through the Commission or through a State Party whose citizen is a victim of rights violation. But neither the Commission nor the individual may be compelled to do so. The Court has discretion to allow individuals to institute proceedings directly before the Court in accordance with Article 34(6) of the Protocol. This may occur where a State party who is the alleged violator has at the time of ratification or thereafter opted for the competence of the court to receive cases under Article 5(3).

An individual petition may therefore proceed through the State or Commission, depending on whether either is willing to do so or via Article 34(6) against violator state which has accepted the competence of the Court to receive individual petitions.

Issue of Admissibility

The court in deciding on the issue of admissibility shall take into account the provisions of Article 36 of the Charter. In considering admissibility with respect to cases instituted under Article 5(3) of the Protocol, it may request the opinion of the Commission which shall give it as soon as possible. The Court may consider or refer them to the Commission. [Article 6].

Nature of Proceedings

Proceedings are to be in public unless otherwise provided by the Rules. Parties to a case are entitled to be represented by legal representatives of its choice. Free legal representation may be provided when the interests of justice so required. Any person, witness or representative of a party who appears before the Court shall enjoy protection and all facilities, in accordance with international law, necessary for discharging of their functions, tasks and duties in relation to the court (Article 10).

Settlement of Disputes

The Court may try to reach an amicable settlement in a case before it in accordance with the provisions of the Charter.

When a case is before the Court, it shall hear submissions by all parties and if deemed necessary hold an enquiry. The states concerned are required to assist by providing relevant facilities for the efficient hearing of the case. The Court may receive written or oral evidence including expert testimony and shall make its decision on the basis of such evidence. (Article 26).

The Court has the power to make binding decisions and grant appropriate remedies. Where it finds that there has been a violation of human or peoples rights, it shall make appropriate orders to remedy the violation, including the payment of fair compensation or reparation. In effect, it has the power to grant appropriate reparation under international law, as indicated above. There is also provision for interim measures in appropriate cases. In cases of extreme gravity and urgency and when necessary to avoid irreparable harm to persons, the court shall adopt such provisional measures as it deems necessary (Art. 27).

Applicable Law

The Charter is a treaty – an international agreement governed by international law. It is, therefore, to be presumed that whatever additional aids to interpretation might be provided by the Charter, that the corpus of international law both conventional and customary law on the law of treaties will apply. More specifically, the formal sources of international law, treaties, customary international law and general principles of law recognized by civilized nations will be applicable.

So will the subsidiary law determining agencies such as judicial decisions (both international and national) and teachings of mostly highly qualified publicists. Not to forget that the mention of subsidiary law determining agencies implies that states remain the principal law determining agencies.

More specifically the Vienna Convention on the Law of Treaties (1969) governs together with relevant customary international law the interpretation of treaties between states in written form. And the African Charter on Human and Peoples' Rights and the Protocol are such instruments.[392]

The African Charter adopts what might appear to be 'other' sources of law which should be of assistance to the African Commission in its task of ensuring the enforcement of the Charter either under its functions of making recommendations or observations with respect to state or non-state communications or in its advisory capacity. Chapter IV titled 'Applicable principles' is somewhat unclear since while it includes two Articles (60 and 61) which could be categorized as 'principles' it contains one provision on a duty imposed on states to submit two yearly periodic reports (Article 62) and the other on the mode of coming into force of the African Charter (Article 63). We are, however, more directly concerned, at this juncture, with Articles 60 and 61.

Article 60 provides that the Commission shall draw inspiration from international law on human and peoples' rights, particularly from the provisions of the various African instruments on human and peoples' rights, the Charter of the United Nations,[393] the Charter of the Organization of African Unity, the Universal Declaration of Human Rights, and other instruments adopted by the United Nations and African countries in the field of human and peoples' rights as well as from the provisions

---

[392] Article, 2. Vienna Convention on the Law of Treaties which defines a treaty as an international agreement concluded between states in written form and governed by international law, whether embodied in a single instrument or two or more related instruments and whatever it particular designation—' Article 3 of the Convention provides for treaties which are otherwise valid under customary international law". See also Harris D. J. Cases and Materials on International Law, *op. cit*, p.768.

[393] Article 38 of the ICJ Statute.

of various instruments adopted within the Specialized Agencies of the United Nations of which the parties to the Charter are members.

It would seem that the instruments enumerated above, the list of which is not intended to be exhaustive are more than a guide as the word inspiration signifies a higher level of commitment' than the word 'guide'. For instance the African Commission would be expected to adopt the interpretations of analogous provisions on refugees that are found in the African Refugees convention, and the 1951 U.N. convention as amended by the protocol of 1971. So will it be expected, in its interpretation of the provisions of the African Charter on fair hearing, which, as has already been indicated is rather lean, to pray in aid of the connotations of that phrase in the Universal Declaration of Human Rights and the International Covenant on Civil and Political Rights. Indeed it is arguable, since the provisions of the Charter on Human Rights practice economy of words, that the Commission, while evolving its own jurisprudence, will be expected to extract from these various instruments both principles and substance of the rights and freedoms guaranteed.

Even though the Charter does not specifically mention judicial decisions, whether national or international, as subsidiary sources of law, it is arguable that decisions of national courts on provisions of the African Charter might provide useful guide for the Commission. Under the Charter states are not only required to adopt legislative and other measures to give effect to the rights, duties and freedom guaranteed thereunder, (Article 1) but also to guarantee the independence of the courts which should adjudicate on rights violations.

National human rights jurisprudence is increasingly enriched by cross borrowings between the courts of various nations and between them and international adjudicatory or determining bodies.

The increasing tendency of national courts to be influenced by judicial interpretation of international Human Rights has been affirmed by the Bangalore Principles,[394] the Bangalore Judicial Colloquium on the Domestic Application of International Human Rights Norms which have been reaffirmed by the Harare Declaration on Human Rights (1989),[395] Banjul affirmation (1990)[396] and the Abuja Confirmation of the Domestic Application of International Human Norms (1991).[397]

The relevant principles contained in the summary of the conclusions of the Bangalore Colloquium include the following:

- Fundamental Human Rights and Freedoms are inherent in all human kind and find expression in constitutions and legal systems throughout the world and in the international human rights instruments.

- These international human rights instruments provide important guidance in cases concerning fundamental human rights and freedoms.

- While it is desirable for the norms contained in the International Rights Instruments to be still more widely recognized and applied by national courts this process must take fully into account local laws, traditions, circumstances and needs.

- "It is within the proper nature of the judicial process and well established judicial functions for national courts to have regard to the international obligations which a country undertakes whether or not they have been incorporated into domestic law for the purpose of removing ambiguity or uncertainty from national constitutions, legislation or common law".[398]

---

[394] Colloquium in Bangalore *op. cit* pp ix - x

[395] For text see Journal of Human Rights and Practice, vol. 2 Nos 1 & 2, Nov. 1992 pp 86-91.

[396] *Ibid*, pp. 91-96.

[397] *Ibid*, pp. 97-105.

[398] Cit, paras 1,2,6 and 7 see also Osita C. Eze "Constitutional Protection and legal Limits in Conflict Reporting" *op.cit.*

Article 61 which could also be construed as a source of law for the Commission requires it to take into consideration as subsidiary measures to determine the principles of law, other general or international conventions, laying down rules expressly recognized by Member States of the Organisation of African Unity, African practices consistent with international norms on human and peoples' rights, customs generally accepted as law, general principles of law recognized by African states as well as legal precedents and doctrines.

It would therefore seem, given the applicability of Article 38 of the ICJ statute as well as Articles 60 and 61 of the African Charter that the Commission and the Court can draw from a wide corpus of jurisprudence of state and international practices if they are to give flesh and substance to the skeletal provisions of the Charter relative to rights, duties and freedoms. But it must start by clearing its own stable. It must first determine what it considers are the sources of law which it must apply when dealing with specific cases or rendering advisory opinions.

Indeed our analysis is eloquently supported by a number of rulings by the Commission.

The extent of reliance of the Commission on the possibility offered by Article 61 and 62 is best illustrated by its ready reliance on such standard setting documents as Fundamental Principles on Independence of the Judiciary, Declaration on the Protection of all Persons against Forced Disappearance, adopted by General Assembly Resolution 47/133 of 18 December 1992 (22/88 International PEN/Burkina Faso (paragraphs 38 and 44)[399].

---

[399] See 212/98 Amnesty International/Zambia, paragraph 50. See 54/91, 61/91, 98/93, 164/97 and 210/98 paragraph 123) where the Commission relied on Art, 23(3) of the Universal Declaration of Human Rights on right to just and favourable remuneration and Article 7 of International Covenant on Economic Social and Cultural Rights on the same subject.

Remedies

The Charter does not specify what the Commission may include in its recommendations. But it may be difficult to conceive of rights and duties enforcement without remedies no matter how ineffective. It can be presumed that the Commission's recommendations will include a determination as to whether the conduct of a state party concerned is or is not in breach of the rights guaranteed or duties imposed. They may, in addition require the state to adopt interim measures under Rule 109 or to stop acts or abrogate the laws or policies that are in confrontation with the African Charter.

At another level, since it is a well established rule of public international law that a breach of an international obligation imports an obligation to make reparation, *Chorzow Factory Case (Indemnity) (Merits)*[400] in that case the P.C.I.J. stated:

"... it is a principle of international law, and even a general conception of law, that any breach of an agreement involves an obligation to make reparation. In Judgment No. 8... the Court has already said that reparation is the indispensable complement of a failure to apply a convention, and *there is no necessity for this to be stated in the Convention itself*".[401]

Since under the Charter duty is owed to the individual, peoples or other non-state entities, not to violate their rights would they be entitled to reparation when their rights are violated? Judicial and arbitral decisions and opinions have elaborated the forms which reparation may take in international law. These include:

---

[400] (Germany v. Poland) P.C.I.J. Reports, series A No 17, pp. 46-48.

[401] I' m Alone Case, 3RIAA, 1609, 29AJIL, 326(1935), The Borchgrave Case, P.C.I.J. Reports Series A/B, No. 72 at p. 165 (19377) See also Osita C. Eze, Legal Aspects of Reparation, Arguments for and Against, *op. cit.*

- monetary compensation for actual injury or damage suffered whether material or non-material
- Satisfaction, including apologies, and
- Restitution in kind or restoration of the status quo *ante*

If the African Commission has the competence to 'grant' these remedies, and we think it has, since there is no express limitation of its competence in this regard, then it may recommend the remedies as are appropriate in each case. It has in fact done so in a number of occasions.

The Court as we have already indicated has amplitude of power to 'make appropriate orders to remedy violation of rights including the payment of fair compensation or reparation. (Article 27). Both the Commission and the Court can give interim orders in situations of urgency and to avoid irreparable damage.

The Commission had assigned responsibility for reparation in 64/92/68/92 and 78/92/Malawi and implied it in many other cases. But it fell short of being in most cases, explicit as to what exactly is entailed.

Related Matters

In this section we shall examine certain areas which may impact on the ultimate performance of the Commission as a promoter and protector of human and peoples' rights such as consideration of report from states parties and resources of the Commission including the efficacy of its secretariat.

10.3 Reports of the Commission

Article 62 of the Charter requires each state to submit every two years, from the date the Charter comes into force, a report on the legislative or other measures taken with a view to giving effect to the rights and freedoms recognized and guaranteed by the Charter.

Even though the Rules of Procedure of the Commission in its Chapter VXV, (Rules 81 – 86) place this supervisory function of the Commission under promotional activities it does more than promote for laws and policies adopted as a consequence may have the direct consequence of securing the actualization of the rights guaranteed.

Rule 81(1) reinforces the provision of Article 62 which stipulates that the reports shall include measures which States Parties would have taken to give effect to the rights. The reports should indicate, where possible, the factors and difficulties impeding the implementation of the provisions of the Charter.

As of July 1992 only ten States out of 46 states parties had submitted their report. Not only are reports from most of the states overdue but except for probably one country most country reports have tended to report on laws etc. promulgated without discussing whether they are being implemented and their implications for human and peoples' right promotion and protection. Furthermore, the guaranteed independence of members of the Commission not withstanding, it would appear from observations of parties to the deliberations of the Commission on such reports that some Commissioners might be tempted to shield their governments from embarrassment that could result from a negative assessment of government's performance.

Since the *raison d'etre* for the adoption of the Charter is the promotion and protection of human and peoples' rights the removal of these inadequacies would facilitate the attainment of the aims and objectives of the Charter. in this regard we share the view expressed by Badawi El Sheikh, President, African Commission on Human and Peoples' Rights, when he asserts that:

"Without intensive reporting and effective consideration of them (i.e. reports) the Commission's ability to assess and encourage respect of human rights would be negatively affected".[402]

Yet the Rules of Procedure of the African Commission, have made provisions for the implementation of the reporting system by: whenever the Commission requests States Parties to submit reports, fixing the date for the presentation of these reports, if the state fails to comply with Article 63 [Rule 81(2)], informing the States Parties, through the Secretary General of its wishes regarding the form and contents of the reports (Rule 81(3), ensuring that the reports provide all necessary information pursuant to provisions of Rule 81 of the Rules of Procedure and requesting further information where this requirement is not met [Rule 85(1) and (2)].

Where following the consideration of the reports and information submitted by a State Party the Commission decides that the State has not discharged some of its obligations it may address general observation to the State concerned as it may deem necessary.

"All these notwithstanding it is our view that the Commission, in order to facilitate its work in this areas needs to produce, if it hasn't done so, a standard form that would elicit all necessary information from States Parties."[403]

The initial set of guidelines set by the Commission in 1988 proved inadequate because of its complexity. It required a foundation report which would as it were part a true picture of human rights situation in the state including inter-alia its laws and institutions, judicial and

---

[402] Human Rights and Challenges for their implementation in Africa" Badawi El Sheik, In Africa New Lease of Life, Kenya Symposium, 1993, OMCT/SOS TORTURE, op. cit. pp 207-209.
[403] See Eze Osita C. Ume Umana Chair Lecture, *op. cit.*

administrative decisions. Periodic reports which would follow would enable the Commission to assess the degree of progress or lack of it.

A more simplified guideline was issued in 1998 and even though these have some improvement there continues to be defaults. The Amended guidelines provide: [404]

1. An initial report (the first report) should contain a brief history of the state, it's form of government, the legal system and the relationship between the arms of government.

2. The initial report should also include basic documents such as the constitution, the Criminal Code and Procedure and landmark decisions on human rights.

3. The major human rights instruments to which the state is a party and the steps taken to internalize them should be set out.

4. How well is the party implementing the following rights protected by charter: a) civil and political rights; b) Economic, social and cultural rights; and c) Group rights.

5. What is the state doing to improve the condition of the following groups mentioned in the charter a) women; b) children and c) disabled?

6. What steps are being taken to protect the family and encourage its cohesion?

7. What is being done to ensure that individual duties are observed?

8. What are the problems encountered in implementing the charter having regard to the political, economic or social circumstances of the state?

---

[404] Amendment of the General Guidelines for the Periodic Reports by State Parties Doc/OS.27 (XXIII).

9. How is the state as an interested party, using the charter in its international relationship, particularly in ensuring respect for it.

10. How is the state as an interested party, using the charter in its international relationship, particularly in ensuring respect for it.

11. Any other relevant information relating to the implementation and promotion of the charter.

The amended Rules have added Rule 87 to this part which reads:

- The Commission shall adopt and carry out a programme of action which gives effect to its obligations under the Charter particularly Article 45(1).
- The Commission shall carry out the promotional activities in member States and elsewhere on a continuing basis;
- Each member of the Commission shall file a written report on his/her activities at each session including countries visited and organisations contacted.
- No doubt these new activities are intended to deepen the promotional activities of the Commission.

11

CONCLUSIONS

It is nearly fourteen years since the African Charter Came into force. To date about 46 out of the 52 member states of the OAU (now AU) have ratified the Charter. The African Commission on Human and Peoples' Rights has been in existence since 1987. Its Rules of procedure were adopted in February 1988. And have since been revised. It is, therefore, in comparison with other regional human rights institutions – Europe and the Americas – relatively young. Yet much is expected from it for peoples who for the past four centuries – first through the slave trade, then through legitimate but unequal trade, colonialism and now neo-colonialism with its new variant of 'a world order' managed by the World Trade Organisation, (WTO), the World Bank and International Monetary Fund through the instrumentality of agencies of powerful governments and transnational corporations[405] continue to suffer deprivations of their human and peoples' rights and fundamental freedoms and in particular economic, social and cultural rights. And we should not forget the devastations caused by African dictators, whether civilian or military, that literally in the Fanonian sense stepped into the shoes of the colonial officers and even worse in many cases.

Yet in order to ascertain to what extent the hopes borne out of the Charter can be actualized it is necessary to address some of the problematic that may pose obstacles in this regard.

---

[405] Perkins J., *Confessions of an Economic Hitman*, *op. cit.*

The African Charter has the singular merit of anchoring the rights guaranteed and duties imposed on African values and traditions of African civilization and can, therefore, be said to be responsive to Africa's needs, - respect for the family, the elders, society as well as ensure guarantee of group rights (peoples rights). In the same vein it covers, the three generations rights emphasizing their interconnectedness and interdependence. This in itself is a major achievement but it is fraught with problems both for the individual and peoples on the one hand and the Commission and the Court on the other. For the Commission the problem that is posed, given that the Charter provisions on rights and duties of whatever generation are couched in prescriptive terms, is how they are to be enforced, particularly given that the Commission does not seem to have the power to make binding decisions even when parties may be expected to comply in good faith with its recommendations. In any event even the ECOSOC rights can now be enforced based on principles established by the practice of institutions charged with their implementation as elaborated in the Maastricht guidelines and supplemented by emergent African Constitutional experience. And in this regard the Commission's cautious steps in giving its imprimatur to the justiceability of ECOSOC rights are a very welcome development.

The Court, will be at home, in dealing with the interpretation of Charter provisions on rights and duties, and building on encouraging, though modest beginning made by the Commission. In particular it has the competence to make binding decisions. Even then quite a number of African countries could, given proper management of their resources and guided by the centrality of the philosophy of man-centred development and the Common Good be in a position to comply with the Charter's imperatives on the right to education and health. The Court has in any event, the competence and opportunity to develop and deepen the jurisprudence of rights, particularly in the areas of ECOSOC and peoples rights.

For the individual the problems that are posed are: the Charter provisions on human and peoples' rights are so general that he/she might not be able to determine precisely what the rights are; foresee the likely breaches and their consequences and be in a position; to plan accordingly. The near absence of the rule of certainty that the limitations to these rights import for the most part-viz in 'conformity with the law', etc. results in the same defects. This is despite of the fact that the Commission has generally adopted an expansive approach in the interpretation of rights provisions and also insisted that a state which imposes limitations, apparently authorised by the Charter strictly proves that the limitations fall within the ambit of what is permissible and in particular that such limitations cannot be employed to undermine the enjoyment of the rights guaranteed. While the determinations of the Commission so far follow this pattern they are not readily available to the people to whom they are addressed, that is to say potential victims, counsels, NGOs and States.

For "peoples" there is a crisis of identity. The Charter does not define what the word means although this may not present a serious problem as it allows the Commission or the Court to develop proper jurisprudence on the matter. What is more the Rules of Procedure of the Commission do not make any provision as to how peoples can assert their rights. Yet it is quite clear right from the preamble to the Charter through its dispositive provisions that 'peoples' are bearers of rights and obligations and have been accorded appropriate procedural rights under the provisions of 'other communication". Peoples may, however, communicate in a representative capacity. The Protocol does not make the matter any clearer. In one instance where the Commission had the occasion to pronounce on it, it obliquely accepted that 'peoples' can be subjects of rights and duties under international law (subjects of international law). [406]

---

[406] 75/92 Congress du Peuple Katangais/Zaire. See also *supra.*

Short of determinations that may be made by the Commission it is envisaged that other peaceful modes of settlement of disputes such as mediation and conciliation may be employed in resolving matters arising from individual, peoples' and other non-state communications. This faculty is clearly provided for in the case of state communications. It is only left to be inferred in the case of non-state entities with respect to the Commission. We suggest that this deficiency should be remedied by an affirmative action of the Commission for one of the benefits of granting individuals and peoples some measure of international personality, such as is the case under the African Charter, is to put all parties on an equal footing. And in matters of human rights it properly accords with two cardinal principles of equality before the law and that of non-discrimination.

At a more substantive level, we are not sure what remedies are available to victims of human rights violations. In other words does a recommendation to a state party concerned (a violator state) include how the victims should be compensated (satisfied) or is simply framed in general terms advising the state to abrogate whatever law or policy or stop whatever acts that may confront rights guaranteed or even in terms of just making reparations. If this be the case, and we hope it is not, then what passes for protection under the Charter would in all probability be categorized as promotional. The Court, with it competence to make binding decisions is an eminent position to develop much needed case law in this area.

The promotional work of the Commission is strategic and central to the effectiveness of the Charter. It provides avenues for generating and sharing information on human and peoples' rights. It is understood that the Commission, apart from the extensive space it has to cover, can act more as a facilitator and that NGOs and other mass or popular organisations, as well as, the larger civil society can provide the building blocks for this joint enterprise for the promotion and securing of Human Rights.

In particular a National Human Rights Commission, that is as independent of government as possible, supported by the bar, labour unions, NGO's and other mass organisations should spring up to mobilize the peoples of Africa for democracy and respect for human and peoples' rights.

The Secretariat of the Commission which is ill staffed and funded and the Commission which meets twice a year and for about two weeks[407] cannot fulfill both its promotional and protective functions. There is need for better staffing and funding.

As for the protective functions of the Commission, the seat of the Commission in Banjul may appear rather remote. There may be need to encourage NGOs to serve as transmission points for national petitioners. In making donations to Human Rights NGOs, therefore, due account should be taken of this added function. Additionally, the Rules of Procedure of the Commission should be modified into *inter alia* provide for oral evidence in appropriate cases as well as clarify the processes for *in loco* investigations. With respect to the matter, it is our view that the State Party concerned is under an obligation not only to allow visits *in loco* but also to facilitate them otherwise one would be led to an absurd situation where the provisions on fact finding and in-depth study, which is the Commission may be required to make or may decide to make, would be mere decorations. There is also the need to modify the Rules of Procedure to grant legal aid in appropriate cases[408]. The obligation to

---

[407] Rule 2.2.; Rule 3 provides that the Commission may decide to hold extraordinary sessions, when the Commission is not in session, such an extraordinary session may be convened by the Chairman in consultation with members of the Commission. The Chairman shall also convene extraordinary sessions: a, At the request of the majority of the members of the Commission or b, At the request of the current Chairman of the organization of African Unity/African Union.

[408] See Article 10(2) of the Protocol Establishing the African Court on Human and Peoples' Rights which makes provision for this. "Where the interest of justice so require." See also *supra.*

do so, in any event, derives from the right to fair hearing. The hearing will not be fair if you do not have adequate means to properly prepare your case, and move the Commission.

So far we have been concerned with programmes of the Commission. We are aware that human and peoples' rights are better actualized within the framework of democracy and the Rule of Law which are at one and the same time based on equitable access to resources and means of producing them and that without social and economic democracy it is futile to talk of democracy in its true sense.

It also implies that peoples, empowered control both the polity and the socio-economic system and that the authority of the rulers derives from and its legitimacy depends on the sovereignty of the people.

And at a more practical level it connotes the idea of accountability and responsibility to peoples (sovereign) with the consequence, once peoples are understood to include the ancestors, those living and those yet to be born, a sort of 'PERSON' in perpetuity, that punishment of grave crime against the peoples cannot be time bared. We cannot on the one hand fight for reparations for the consequences of the slave trade as well as colonialism and on the other hand introduce the right against retrospective criminal legislation as a bar to the punishment of serious crimes committed before our very eyes. In recent times International Criminal Tribunal has been set up to deal with serious (criminal) cases violative of rights institutionalized within the framework of the UN.

Furthermore, a proper reading of the *Judgment of the Nuremberg International Military Tribunal* [1946.41 A.J.I.L., 172 (1947)] would show that the tribunal by, *inter alia*, construing the principle *of nullum crimen sine lege nulla poena sine lege* as a principle of justice and not a limitation on state sovereignty, concedes that in cases of outrageously immoral and unconscionable crimes an exception to the principle could be justified. Acts of rulers which lead to persistent underdevelopment – reckless use or theft of public resources- and denial of basic right to life, food, shelter, health etc. would most probably qualify as such exceptions. And if increasing state practice-Canada, Australia and U.S.A.- of recognizing the rights of indigenous peoples to reparations for crimes committed against them in the past is any indication of current state practice then it lends support to the Nuremberg principle admitting of exceptions in special cases. And there has been growing of movement for the enhancement of the rights of indigenous peoples with the United Nations. [409]

In the alternative, nearly all the crimes the subject of our discussion are already proscribed by the criminal law of most countries. Establishing international or national criminal tribunals to try such cases may only be retrospective, therefore, with respect to the mode of trial which may be changed and the punishment imposed. This approach does not seem to contradict the provisions of Article 7(2) of the African Charter which stipulates:

"No one may be condemned for an act or omission which did not constitute a legally punishable offence at the time it as committed. No penalty may be inflicted for an offence for which no provision was made at the time it was committed. Punishment is personal and can be imposed only on the offender".

We are aware of all this yet it seems that there is something central to the whole question of human rights without which our ideals of human and peoples' rights and democracy and the Rule of Law which are part of the same thing, may continue to remain illusive.

This idea, this right is captured in Article 5 of the African Charter as in other international instruments on human and peoples' rights. It is the right of every individual to the respect of the dignity, inherent in a human being.

---

[409] World Conference on Human Rights – Vienna Declaration and Programme of Action on Human Rights, 1993, paragraphs 28-32.

It marks out the human person as a special being deserving special treatment from the hordes of mammals. Although one is aware that in some industrialized societies animals have the protection against cruel treatment.

In concluding this work, we emphasize the responsibility of those who govern, determine the basis on which they govern, with what powers and limitations, all in understanding that their authority deriving from the sovereignty of the people must correspond with that mandate and therefore seek the common good.

We also recognize the challenges posed by the new global architecture which is essentially undemocratic and immoral that feeds on an unjust social economic order in which third world countries like Nigeria are victims. A way must be found of meeting this challenge if the rights guaranteed in the charter are to be substantially actualized. For in the end the state has the primary responsibility for the security and welfare of its people.

- ❖ Therefore, whenever, life is made intolerable, or there is mass poverty because, in spite of available resources, we are denied the means of livelihood – food, water, shelter, education, health care or scanty resources are not equitably utilized to serve these ends;
- ❖ Whenever, some dictator, whether military or civilian, tells us how and what to think, what to say and how to say it, where to go and with whom to consort, whether to worship one God, or two gods, or none at all, how to lead our private lives;
- ❖ Whenever we loose our liberty for no just cause and in order to gratify the ruler intent on further humiliating us;
- ❖ Whenever the loss of our liberty is compounded by being interned in, overcrowded, unsanitary and not so properly lit or ventilated prison or police 'death' chambers and without sufficient access medi-care;

❖ Whenever, rulers carry on public affairs which undermine the environment, without due regard to those who inhabit it or in such a manner as to lead to conflicts between and within peoples within the state,

❖ Whenever, any of these, some of these or most of these happen(s), we are degraded and our dignity is diminished and so is the dignity (if they have any left) of those responsible for denying us our dignity and worth as human beings.

If there is a general acceptance that there is some intrinsic value in the respect for the dignity inherent in the human person and his/her worth as a human being these things would rarely happen and if and when they do happen there would be automatic censure and remedy.

Human and peoples' rights attach to us because being *homines sapienntes* we have dignity and because we must have dignity. Because we have dignity we must insist on respect for fundamental rights and freedoms and resist any attempt by dictators, who have the audacity to tutor us on democracy, human rights, and Rule of Law, to foist them on us, here, there and everywhere. Otherwise we run a great risk of loosing our dignity and our rights and freedoms with it.

TABLE OF CASES

The State v. NTN Pty Ltd & MBN Ltd, Supreme Court of Papua New Guinea, 7 April, 1887, (No.Sc. 323.), 230

Sunday Times Case, Judgment of 26 April, 1979, Series 4, No 30, 121, 232, 234

Thomas v. Collins (1944), 126

Togo v. Judges of the District Court of New South Wales and others (Appeal no 259 of 1987), 111

Torcaso   Watkins 367 U.S. 488, 116

Tyrer v. United Kingdom, 1978 [2 EHRR.1], 86

Union Inter Africaine des Droits de l'Homme and others/Angola, 159/96, 138, 193

Union Nationale de Libération du Cabinda/Angola, 24/89, 264

US Diplomatic and Consular Staff in Tehran (US v. Iran) I.C.J. Reports 1980, p.3. 144, 290

Welsh v. United States 394 US 344 (1970), 112

Wight v. Madagascar, (115/82), 110

Yesufu Garba & Ors v. The University of Maiduguri & Ors (1986) 1NWLR, 550, 122

Zaire Case 10/93, 210/98, 186

Zwaan de Vriez v. The Netherlands 182/84, 72

INTERNATIONAL INSTRUMENTS

1. The Universal Declaration on Human Rights, adopted and roclaimed General Assembly Resolution 217 A (III) of 10 December, 1948

2. International Covenant on Civil and Political Rights, General Assembly Resolution 2200A , entered into force March 23, 1976

3. European Convention on Human Rights, Rome, 4th November, 1950.

4. American Convention on Human Rights, (signed at Inter-American Specialized Conference on Human Rights, San Josi; Costa Rica, 22 November, 1969)

5. The Charter of the United Nations, signed on 26th June 1945 in San Francisco, came into force on 24th October, 1945.

6. The Covenant of the League of Nations, 1919.

7. UN Declaration of the Rights of People Belonging of National, Ethnic, Religious or Linguistic Minorities adopted by the U.N. General Assembly resolution 47/135, 18 December 1992

8. The UN Convention on the Elimination of All forms of Racial Discrimination (1995)

9. The Convention of the Elimination of All forms of Discrimination Against Women (1976).

10. Constitution of the Republic of Nigeria, Lagos, Government Printer, 1999.

11. Constitution of the Republic of Ghana, 1992

12. Constitution of the Republic of Uganda, 1995

13. Constitution of the Republic of South Africa, Government Gazette, Cape Town, 18 December, 1996

14. United Nations Protocol to Prevent, Suppress and Punish Trafficking in Persons especially Women and Children, Supplementing the United Nations Convention against Transnational Organized crime (2001)

15. United Nations Convention against Transnational Organized Crime (2000)

16. UN Protocol against the Smuggling of Migrants by Land, Sea and Air, Supplementing the

17. United Nations Convention against Transnational Organized Crime (2000).

18. Trafficking in Persons (Prohibition) Law Enforcement and Administration Act 2003, Federal Republic of Nigeria Official Gazette, No 89, Vol.90, 2003

19. UN Convention Against Torture Dec. 10 1984

20. The Vienna Declaration and Programme of Action on Human Rights (1993).

21. The U.N. Convention Relating to the Status of Refugees, 1951.

22. U.N. Protocol Relating to the Status of Refugees of 31st January 1967.

23. The OAU Convention Governing Specific Aspects of Refugee problems in Africa of September 1969

24. Vienna Convention on Diplomatic Relations, 1961

25. UN Declaration on Territorial Asylum adopted by General Assembly Resolution 2312 (XXII) of 14th December, 1967.

26. European Convention for the Protection of Human Rights and Freedoms, 1950

27. European Social Charter, 1960

28. UN Declaration on the Granting of Independence to Colonial Countries and Peoples (1960), res. 1514 (XV)
29. National Human Rights Commission Act, No 22 of 1995.

BIBLIOGRAPHY

Adeyemi, A. A " Death Penalty in Nigeria: Criminology Perspective"
in Narcotics Law and Politics, Federal Ministry Of Justice
Vol. 8

Abdalla" He trogeneeity and Differrenciation- The End of the of the
Third World" Development Dialogue 11, 1978

Academic Freedom and Human Rights Abuses in Africa, An African
Watch Report, New York, 1991.

Adione-Egom, Luke Globalization at the crossroads, capitalism or
communalism, Lagos: Global Market Associates, 2002.

Afigbo, Adiele Ropes of Sand: Studies in Igbo History and Culture,
Ibadan and London: University Press and Oxford University Press, 1981 (1984), 387p

Ake, Caude Social Science as imperialism: the theory of political
development, Ibadan, University Press, 1979.

Amoako, K. Y. Perspectives on Africa's Development , United
Nations, Economic Commission of Africa, United
Nations, 2000

Application of International Human Rights Law in Nigeria. Paper
presented at a seminar and Domestic Application
of Human Rights Law held in Banjul the Gambia, 29th-30th
July 2000.

Badawi, El Sheik Human Rights and challenges for their implementation in Africa. In: Africa a New Lease on Life, Kenya
Symposium, 1993.

Barran, "The Commitment of the Intellectual" in his The *Longer view New York*, New York Monthly Reviews 1966

Bello E. G. " The Africa Charter on Human and People's Rights: A Legal Analysis*," Recueil de Cours* Vol 194 (1986)

British Council in West Africa, *Managing the Protection of Human Rights*, Document from an International Seminar held in Abuja, Nigeria 28 February – 4 March 1994.

Cervenka, Z The Organization of African Unity and its charter. (London C. Hurst & Co, 1968).

Collection of International Conventions, Agreements and other texts concerning Refugees, New York, LUN HRC, 1971.

Common Good and the Catholic Social Teaching: A Statement by the Catholic Bishops Conference of England and Wales.

Chand H. Fundamental Human Rights in Nigeria, Jos Unico Press 1980

Constitutional protection and legal limits in conflict reporting, vol.1, 1992.

Crisis of Public International Law and regulation of private foreign investment: the quest for a new legal order. *Nigerian Journal of International Studies* vol. 5&6, 1981.

Dialo I. Les Réfugiers en Afrique Cadre International et Régionale de Règlement, Vienna, Wilhelm Braimatter, 1971.

Dissent in a democratic polity options in a presidential system. In : Democracy and the Rule of Law. Lagos, Federal Ministry of Justice, 1992.

Elias, T.O. Background Paper for the UN Seminar on the Establishment of Regional Commission on Human Rights with

Special Reference to Africa (Monrovia: Liberia 10-12 September, 1979).

Eze, Osita.C. Africa, New World Order, Human Rights and Democracy, 1992 Inaugural Lecture, Imo State University (Now Abia State University) UTURU.

Fargal, M. H. African Unity and Liberation (M.A. Thesis, University of Dar-es-Salaam, 1968).

Farrar, Introduction to Legal Method (London, Sweet and Maxwell, 1977).

Fitzmaurice, "The General Principles of Law considered from the Standpoint of the Rule of Law" 92, Hague Recueil.

Gluckman M. Judicial process Among the Barotse of Northern Rhodesia, 2nd enlarged edition, Manchester University Press, 1967.

Gonidec P. F. Les Droits Africains: Évolution et Source, Paris, R. Pichon.

Green, R. H. "Participatory Pluralism and Pervasive Poverty: Some Reflections. Third World Legal Studies, 1989.

Gupta A. The Rhodesia Crisis and the Organisation of African Unity *International Studies* (New Delhi), Vol. 9, no 1, July 1967.

Harris D. J. Case and Materials on International, 5th & 9th Ed., London, Sweet and Maxwell, 1998

Higgins, Rosalyn. The Relationship between International and Regional Human Rights Norm and Domestic Law (1992) 18 CLB

Human Rights: a Compilation of International Instruments, Vol, 1
(First Part, Universal Instruments, New York, United Nations, 1993)

Human Rights Studies in Universities, J. E. McCarty, J. B. Marrie, S. P. Mark's under the supervision of Karei Vasak (Paris UNESCO 1973).

Human Rights in Africa: some selected problems, Lagos NIIA/Macmillan, 1984, 314p

Human Rights, Peace and Rerum Novarum of Leo XIII. In: Catholic Social Teachings En-Route in Africa, Obiora F. Ike Ed. Enugu CIDJAP, 1991.

Hunt A. The Sociological Movement in Law, London, Macmillan Press Ltd, 1978, pp.150-151.

Joseph, Richard A. Democracy and Pre-Colonial Politics in Nigeria, the Rise and Fall of the second republic Ibadan, Spectrum Books Ltd, 1991.

Legal Aspect of Preparation of Reparation, Arguments For and Against in Conveyancer and Property Contemporary Law Journal (Maiden Issue)

Legal Status of Foreign Investment in the East African Common Market Leiden, Nijhoff, 1975

Legal Structure for the Resolution of International Problems in the Domain of Private Foreign Investments; a Third World Perspective Now and in the Future, *Georgia Journal of International Comparative La*w, vol. 9, 1979.

Mair, L. P. Native Politics in Africa, London, Routledge

Mobogunje, A.L. The Development Perspective a Spatial Perspective (London: Hutchinson University Library 1980).

Morchan A. Human Rights and International Relations, Moscow Progress Publishers, 1982.

Mubilia Muky, La mise en demeur du droit des réfugies et des personnes déplacées en Afrique: Problématique et Perspectives, undated (forthcoming).

Ndiaye. B « La place des droits de l'homme dans la Chartre de L'Organization de l'Unité Africaine » in : Les dimensions internationales des droits, Paris, 1978

Nigeria and the World Trade Organization, Nigerian Institute of International Affairs, 2004.

Njenka, F. X. N. Contrast between the Effects of Laws of the European Constituent Territories, East African Law Journal, 1968.

Nussbaum, A. A Concise History of the Law of Nations, New York, Macmillan.

Nzimiro I.The Crisis in the Social Sciences: the Nigerian Situation. *The World Forum Occasional Paper No. 2.* Oguta, Pan African Publishers, 1986, 89p.

Non-Discrimination and its application to matters of racism and racial discrimination and discrimination based on religion and xenophobia. *In*: Judicial Excellence: Essays in honours of Hon. Justice Anthony I. Iguh. Eds. Irukwu, J.O and Umezulike I.A. Enugu, SNAAP Press Ltd. 2004.

OAU faces Rhodesia. *The African Review*, vol. 5, no 1 1975: pp 51-54.

Ojo A. Constitutional Law and Military Law in Nigeria. Ibadan, Evans Brothers, 1987.

Okagbue Isabella, "Death Penalty as an Effective Deterent to Drug Abuse and Drud Trafficking" in Narcotics Law and Policy in Nigeria, Eds. A Kalu and Y. Osinbajo, Lagos Federal Ministry of Justice, Vol. 8.

Okpaluka C. Judicial Approach to Constitutional Interpretation in Nigeria, Enugu, MaH Madek and Co. 1992.

Ollawa, P.E. Participatory Democracy in Zambia: the Political Economy of National Development, Elmscourt, Arthur H Stockwell Ltd, 1979, chapter 2.

Organisation de L'Unité Africaine in : Les Dimensions Internationales Des Droits de L'Homme (Paris, UNESCO, 1978)

Osieke, Ebere Constitutional Law and Practice in the International Labour Organisation, Dordrecht, Boston, London: Martinus Nijhoff Publishers, 1985.

Quashigah, E.K. Human Rights in Traditional and Modern Africa: an Analytical and Comparative Study. Ph.D thesis in Law for the Faculty of Law, University of Nigeria 1989.

Raham, M.D. The Roles and Significance of participatory organization of the rural poor, alternative strategies of rural development theory and experience – an overview. *Third World Legal Studies*, 1982.

Read, J. S. "Bill of Rights in 'The Third World, Some Commonwealth Experiences" in Verfassung und Recht in Übersee/ Law and Politics in Africa, Asia and Latin America, Vol. 6, No. 1 (1973), Quartal.

Rodney, W. How Europe Underdeveloped Africa, (Tanzania Publishing House, 1972).

Rosenne, S. The World Court: What It Is and How It Works? Leiden: M. Nijhoff, 1975.

Ross " The Common Market Tribunal. The Solution between International and Domestic Law in East Africa" I.C. L. Vol. Part 2, April 1972, pp 361-374.

Rubin, M. Africa and Refugees. *African Affairs*, vol 73, 1974.

Rule of Law and Human Rights, Principles and Definitions. International Commission of Jurists, Geneva, 1966

Schapera Government in Politics in Tribal Societies (London, C. A. Watts and Co. Ltd), 1963

Schwarzenberger G. Frontiers of International Law (London, Stevens and sons, 1962)

Seaton and Maliti, Tanzania Treaty Practice (London, Oxford University Press, 1973).

Shasore O. Jurisdiction and Sovereign Immunity in Nigerian Commercial Law, Lagos, Nigerian Institute of International Affairs, 2007

Sherpard G. W. "African People's Rights, The Third Generation in a Global Perspective" in: Sherppard G. W. and Anikpo M. Eds.

Sieghart P. International Law of Human Rights, Oxford University Press 1985.

Starke, J.S. Introduction to International Law, 9th edition (London Butterworths, 1984).

Solving the Intellectual Property Rights Deadlock. Paper presented at a Discussion Panel at a Conference Organised by the

Foundation for Democracy in Africa, International Conference Centre, Abuja, 25-28 February 2002.

Sulivan, Dennis G. and Others, How America is Ruled, New York, John Wiley & Sons, 1980.

Szego, Hannah Bokor, New States and International Law, Budapest Akademia Kiado, 1970.

The Crisis of International Law and Regulation of Private Foreign Investments; the Quest for a New Legal Order. *Nigerian Journal of International Studies*, Vol. 5-7, 1981.

The Organisation of African Unity, Twenty-five Years After. *Nigerian Journal of International Affairs*, Vol 14, No.1, 1988.

Theoretical Perspectives and Problematic. In: Society and the Rule of Law, Osita C. Eze ed. (Owerri: Publishers Ltd, 1987).

The Place of the African Charter in the Enforcement of Rights, Presented at the Seminar on Managing the Protection of Human Rights.

The Police, Rule of Law and Human Right – Public Perspective. Forthcoming in Policing Nigeria Project.

The Quest for Communication Freedom and Consequences for National Development. In: Philosophy and Dimensions of National Communication Policy. Vol 12. Eds. Unaemeka T, Uvieghare E, and Uyo Didi. Lagos, Centre for Africa Avis and Civilization,1989.

United Nations and Decolonization in Southern Africa. *Nigerian Journal of International Affairs, Vol* 3, No 1 & 2, 1977. and Onyepere Eze, Study on Rights to Health in Nigeria, in: Nigeria, Shelter Initiative, 2001

Umozurike, U.O. Five Years of the African Commission on Human
and Peoples Rights. NSIA Lecture series No 2, 1992
"Autochthony in the African Charter on Human and People's Rights."

United Nations Training Manual, Projects of the Governments of Benin, Nigeria and Togo, United Nations Office on Drugs
and Crime (undated).

Vasak. K. "Problems Concerning the Setting up of a Regional Commission on Human Rights with Special Reference to Africa". Background paper for the United Nations Seminar on
the Establishment of Regional Commission on Human
Rights with Special Reference to Africa, Cairo, 1969.

Vatican Council II the Concillar and Post Concillar Documents,
General editor, Austin Flannery, O. P., 1988, Revised Edition, Dublic, Dominican Publications, 1988

Viorst M. The Great Document of Western Civilization, London,
Chilton Books Company, 1965.

Wako A. "Social Dimension of Structural Adjustment Programmes in
Africa. Anew Lease of Life"

Weis P. The Convention of the Organisation of African Unity
Governing the Specific Aspects of Refugee Problems in
Africa. *Human Rights Journal*, vol. III: 1970.

Wilmot P. Sociology: A New Introduction (London: Collins International Text Books, 1985).

ANNEX I

Protocol to the African Charter on Human and Peoples` Rights on the Establishment of an African Court on Human and Peoples` Rights.

The Member States of the Organization of African Unity hereinafter referred to as the OAU, States Parties to the African Charter on Human and Peoples` Rights. Considering that the Charter of the Organization of African Unity recognizes that freedom, equality, justice, peace and dignity are essential objectives for the achievement of the legitimate aspirations of the African Peoples; Noting that the African Charter on Human and Peoples` Rights reaffirms adherence to the principles of Human and Peoples` Rights, freedoms and duties contained in the declarations, conventions and other instruments adopted by the Organization of African Unity, and other international organizations; Recognizing that the twofold objective of the African Commission on Human and Peoples` Rights is to ensure on the one hand promotion and on the other protection of Human and Peoples` Rights, freedom and duties; Recognizing further, the efforts of the African Charter on Human and Peoples` Rights in the promotion and protection of Human and Peoples` Rights since its inception in 1987; Recalling resolution AHGéRes.230 (XXX) adopted by the Assembly of Heads of State and Government in June 1994 in Tunis, Tunisia, requesting the Secretary-General to convene a Government experts` meeting to ponder, in conjunction with the African Commission, over the means to enhance the efficiency of the African commission and to consider in particular the establishment of an African Court on Human and Peoples` Rights; Noting the first and second Government legal experts` meeting held respectively in Cape Town, South Africa (September, 1995) and Nouakchott, Mauritania (April 1997), and the third Government Legal Experts meeting held in Addis Ababa, Ethiopia (December, 1997), which was enlarged to include Diplomats; Firmly convinced that the attainment of the objectives of the African Charter on Human and Peoples' Rights requires the establishment of an African Court on Human and Peoples' Rights to complement and reinforce the functions of the African Commission on Human and Peoples' Rights.

Have agreed as follows:

Article 1 Establishment of the Court

There shall be established within the Organization of African Unity an African Court Human and Peoples' Rights hereinafter referred to as "the Court", the organization, jurisdiction and functioning of which shall be governed by the present Protocol.

Article 2 Relationship between the Court and the Commission

The Court shall, bearing in mind the provisions of this Protocol, complement the protective mandate of the African Commission on Human and Peoples' Rights hereinafter referred to as "the Commission", conferred upon it by the African Charter on Human and Peoples' Rights, hereinafter referred to as "the Charter".

Article 3 Jurisdiction

1. The jurisdiction of the Court shall extend to all cases and disputes submitted to it concerning the interpretation and application of the Charter, this Protocol and any other relevant Human Rights instrument ratified by the States concerned.
2. In the event of a dispute as to whether the Court has jurisdiction, the Court shall decide.

Article 4 Advisory Opinions

1. At the request of a Member State of the OAU, the OAU, any of its organs, or any African organization recognized by the OAU, the Court may provide an opinion on any legal matter relating to the Charter or any other relevant human rights instruments, provided that the subject matter of the opinion is not related to a matter being examined by the Commission.

2. The Court shall give reasons for its advisory opinions provided that every judge shall be entitled to deliver a separate of dissenting decision.

Article 5 Access to the Court

1. The following are entitled to submit cases to the Court: the commission; State Party which had lodged a complaint to the Commission; State Party against which the complaint has been lodged at the Commission; State Party whose citizen is a victim of human rights violation; African Intergovernmental Organizations

2. When a State Party has an interest in a case, it may submit a request to the Court to be permitted to join.

3. The Court may entitle relevant Non Governmental organizations (NGOs) with observer status before the Commission, and individuals to institute cases directly before it, in accordance with article 34 (6) of this Protocol.

Article 6 Admissibility of Cases

1. The Court, when deciding on the admissibility of a case instituted under article 5 (3) of this Protocol, may request the opinion of the Commission which shall give it as soon as possible.

2. The Court shall rule on the admissibility of cases taking into account the provisions of article 56 of the Charter.

3. The Court may consider cases or transfer them to the Commission.

Article 7 Sources of Law

The Court shall apply the provision of the Charter and any other relevant human rights instruments ratified by the States concerned.

Article 8 Consideration of Cases

The Rules of Procedure of the Court shall lay down the detailed conditions under which the Court shall consider cases brought before it, bearing in mind the complementarities between the Commission and the Court.

Article 9 Amicable Settlement

The Court may try to reach an amicable settlement in a case pending before it in accordance with the provisions of the Charter.

Article 10 Hearings and Representation

1. The Court shall conduct its proceedings in public. The Court may, however, conduct proceedings in camera as may be provided for in the Rules of Procedure.

2. Any party to a case shall be entitled to be represented by a legal representative of the party's choice. Free legal representation may be provided where the interests of justice so require.

3. Any person, witness or representative of the parties, who appears before the Court, shall enjoy protection and all facilities, in accordance with international law, necessary for

the discharging of their functions, tasks and duties in relation to the Court.

Article 11 Composition

1. The Court shall consist of eleven judges, nationals of Member States of the OAU, elected in an individual capacity from among jurists of high moral character and of recognized practical, judicial or academic competence and experience in the field of human and peoples` rights.
2. No two judges shall be nationals of the same State.

Article 12 Nominations

1. States Parties to the Protocol may each propose up to three candidates, at least two of whom shall be nationals of that State.
2. Due consideration shall be given to adequate gender representation in nomination process.

Article 13 List of Candidates

1. Upon entry into force of this Protocol, the Secretary-general of the OAU shall request each State Party to the Protocol to present, within ninety (90) days of such a request, its nominees for the office of judge of the Court.
2. The Secretary-General of the OAU shall prepare a list in alphabetical order of the candidates nominated and transmit it to the Member States of the OAU at least thirty days prior to the next session of the Assembly of Heads of State and Government of the OAU hereinafter referred to as "the Assembly".

Article 14 Elections

1. The judges of the Court shall be elected by secret ballot by the Assembly from the list referred to in Article 13 (2) of the present Protocol.

2. The Assembly shall ensure that in the Court as a whole there is representation of the main regions of Africa and of their principal legal traditions.

3. In the election of the judges, the Assembly shall ensure that there is adequate gender representation.

Article 15 Terms of Office

1. The judges of the Court shall be elected for a period of six years and may be re-elected only once. The terms of four judges elected at the first election shall expire at the end of two years, and the terms of four more judges shall expire at the end of four years.

2. The judges whose terms are to expire at the end of the initial periods of two and four years shall be chosen by lot to be drawn by the Secretary-General of the OAU immediately after the first election has been completed.

3. A judge elected to replace a judge whose term of office has not expired shall hold office for the remainder of the predecessor's term.

4. All judges except the President shall perform their functions on a part-time basis. However, the Assembly may change this arrangement as it deems appropriate.

Article 16 Oath of Office

After their election, the judges of the Court shall make a solemn declaration to discharge their duties impartially and faithfully.

Article 17 Independence

1. The independence of the judges shall be fully ensured in accordance with international law.

2. No judge may hear any case in which the same judge has previously taken part as agent, counsel or advocate for one of the parties or as a member of a national or international court or a commission of enquiry or in any other capacity. Any doubt on this point shall be settled by decision of the Court.

3. The judges of the Court shall enjoy, from the moment of their election and throughout their term of office, the immunities extended to diplomatic agents in accordance with international law.

4. At no time shall the judges of the Court be held liable for any decision or opinion issued in the exercise of their functions.

Article 18 Incompatibility

The position of judge of the court is incompatible with any activity that might interfere with the independence or impartiality of such a judge or the demands of the office as determined in the Rules of Procedure of the Court.

Article 19 Cessation of Office

1. A judge shall not be suspended or removed from office unless, by the unanimous decision of the other judges of the Court, the judge concerned has been found to be no longer fulfilling the required conditions to be a judge of the Court.

2. Such a decision of the Court shall become final unless it is set aside by the Assembly at its next session.

Article 20 Vacancies

1.   In case of death or resignation of a judge of the Court, the President of the Court shall immediately inform the Secretary General of the Organization of African Unity, who shall declare the seat vacant from the date of death or from the date on which the resignation takes effect.

2.   The Assembly shall replace the judge whose office became vacant unless the remaining period of the term is less than one hundred and eighty (180) days.

3.   The same procedure and considerations as set out in Articles 12, 13 and 14 shall be followed for the filling of vacancies.

Article 21 Presidency of the Court

1.   The Court shall elect its President and one Vice-President for a period of two years. They may be re-elected only once.

2.   The President shall perform judicial functions on a full-time basis and shall reside at the seat of the Court.

3.   The functions of the President and the Vice-President shall be set out in the Rules of Procedure of the Court.

Article 22 Exclusion

If the judge is a national of any State which is a party to a case submitted to the Court, that judge shall not hear the case.

Article 23 Quorum

The Court shall examine cases brought before it, if it has a quorum of at least seven judges.

Article 24 Registry of the Court

1. The Court shall appoint its own Registrar and other staff of the registry from among nationals of Member States of the OAU according to the Rules of Procedure.

2. The office and residence of the Registrar shall be at the place where the Court has its seat.

Article 25 Seat of the Court

1. The Court shall have its seat at the place determined by the Assembly from among States parties to this Protocol. However, it may convene in the territory of any Member State of the OAU when the majority of the Court considers it desirable, and with the prior consent of the State concerned.

2. The seat of the Court may be changed by the Assembly after due consultation with the Court.

Article 26 Evidence

1. The Court shall hear submissions by all parties and if deemed necessary, hold an enquiry. The States concerned shall assist by providing relevant facilities for the efficient handling of the case.

2. The Court may receive written and oral evidence including expert testimony and shall make its decision on the basis of such evidence.

Article 27 Findings

1. If the Court finds that there has been violation of a human or peoples' rights, it shall make appropriate orders to remedy the violation, including the payment of fair compensation or reparation.

2. In cases of extreme gravity and urgency, and when necessary to avoid irreparable harm to persons, the Court shall adopt such provisional measures as it deems necessary.

Article 28 Judgment

1. The Court shall render its judgment within ninety (90) days of having completed its deliberations.
2. The judgment of the Court decided by majority shall be final and not subject to appeal.
3. Without prejudice to sub-article 2 above, the Court may review its decision in the light of new evidence under conditions to be set out in the Rules of Procedure.
4. The Court may interpret its own decision.
5. The judgment of the Court shall be read in open court, due notice having been given to the parties.
6. Reasons shall be given for the judgment of the Court.
7. If the judgment of the court does not represent, in whole or in part, the unanimous decision of the judges, any judge shall be entitled to deliver a separate or dissenting opinion.

Article 29 Notification of Judgment

1. The parties to the case shall be notified of the judgment of the Court and it shall be transmitted to the Member States of the OAU and the Commission.
2. The Council of Ministers shall also be notified of the judgment and shall monitor its execution on behalf of the Assembly.

Article 30 Execution of Judgment

The States Parties to the present Protocol undertake to comply with the judgment in any case to which they are parties within the time stipulated by the Court and to guarantee its execution.

Article 31 Report

The Court shall submit to each regular session of the Assembly, a report on its work during the previous year. The report shall specify, in particular, the cases in which a State has not complied with the Court's judgment.

Article 32 Budget

Expenses of the Court, emoluments and allowances for judges and the budget of its registry, shall be determined and borne by the OAU, in accordance with criteria laid down by the OAU in consultation with the Court.

Article 33 Rules of Procedure

The Court shall draw up its Rules and determine its own procedures. The Court shall consult the Commission as appropriate.

Article 34 Ratification

1. This Protocol shall be open for signature and ratification or accession by any State Party to the Charter.
2. The instrument of ratification or accession to the present Protocol shall be deposited with the Secretary-General of the OAU.
3. The Protocol shall come into force thirty days after fifteen instruments of ratification or accession have been deposited.
4. For any State Party ratifying or acceding subsequently, the present Protocol shall come into force in respect of that State on the date of the deposit of its instrument of ratification or accession.
5. The Secretary-General of the OAU shall inform all Member States of the entry into force of the present Protocol.

6.   At the time of the ratification of this Protocol or any time thereafter, the State shall make a declaration accepting the competence of the Court to receive cases under article 5 (3) of this Protocol. The Court shall not receive any petition under article 5 (3) involving a State Party which has not made such a declaration.

7.   Declarations made under sub-article (6) above shall be deposited with the Secretary-General, who shall transmit copies thereof to the State parties.

Article 35 Amendments

1.   The present Protocol may be amended if a State Party to the Protocol makes a written request to that effect to the Secretary-General of the OAU. The Assembly may adopt, by simple majority, the draft amendment after all the State Parties to the present Protocol have been duly informed of it and the Court has given its opinion on the amendment.

2.   The Court shall also be entitled to propose such amendments to the present Protocol as it may deem necessary, through the Secretary-General of the OAU.

3.   The amendment shall come into force for each State Party which has accepted it thirty days after the Secretary-General of the OAU has received notice of the acceptance.

ANNEX II

*Rules of Procedure of the African Commission
on Human and Peoples' Rights*

Adopted on 6 October 1995

(Document made available through the Danish Centre for Human Rights). The African Commission on Human and Peoples' Rights, Having Considered the African Charter on Human and Peoples' Rights, Acting in accordance with Article 42.2 of the Charter, Has adopted the present revised Rules of Procedure:

General Provisions - Organisation of the Commission
Chapter I
Sessions

Rule 1 - Number of Sessions The African Commission on Human and Peoples' Rights (hereinafter referred to as "the Commission" shall hold the sessions which may be necessary to enable it to carry out satisfactorily its functions in conformity with the African Charter on Human and Peoples' Rights (hereinafter referred to as "The Charter").

Rule 2 - Opening Date 1. The Commission shall normally hold two ordinary sessions a year each lasting for about two weeks. 2. The ordinary sessions of the Commission shall be convened on a date fixed by the Commission on the proposal of its Chairman and in consultation with the Secretary General of the Organisation of African Unity (OAU) (hereinafter referred to as "The Secretary General"). 3. The Secretary General may change under exceptional circumstances, the opening date of a session, in consultation with the Chairman of the Commission.

Rule 3 - Extraordinary session 1. The Commission may decide to hold extraordinary sessions, When the Commission is not in session, and the Chairman may convene extraordinary sessions in consultation with the members of the Commission. The Chairman of the Commission shall also convene extraordinary sessions:

1. At the request of the majority of the members of the Commission or
2. At the request of the current Chairman of the Organisation of African Unity.
3. Extraordinary sessions shall be convened as soon as possible on a date fixed by the Chairman, in consultation with the Secretary General and the other members of the Commission.

Rule 4 - Place of meetings The sessions shall normally be held at the Headquarters of the Commission. The Commission, in consideration with the Secretary General decides to hold a Session elsewhere.

Rule 5 - Notifications of the Opening Date of the Sessions. The Secretary of the commission (hereinafter referred to as the Secretary, shall inform members of the Commission of the date and venue of the first meeting of each session. This notification shall be sent, in the case of an Ordinary Session, at least eight (8) weeks, if possible, before the Session.

Chapter II

Agenda

Rule 6 - Drawing up the Provisional Agenda

1. The Provisional Agenda for each Ordinary Session shall be drawn up by the Secretary in consultation with the Chairman of the Commission in accordance with the provisions of the Charter and these Rules.

2. The Provisional Agenda shall include if necessary, items on: "Communications from States", and "Other Communications" in conformity with the provisions of Article 55 of the Charter. It should not contain any information relating to such communications.

3. Except as specified above on the communications, the Provisional Agenda shall include all the items listed by the present Rules of Procedure as well as the items proposed by.

4. The items to be included in the provisional agenda under sub paragraphs b, c, f and g of paragraph 3 must be communicated to the Secretary, accompanied by essential documents, not later than eight (8) weeks before the Opening of the Session.

5. a) All national liberation movements, specialised institutions, intergovernmental or non-governmental organisations wishing to propose the inclusion of an item in the Provisional Agenda must inform the Secretary at least ten (10) weeks before the opening of the meeting. Before formally proposing the inclusion of an item in the Provisional Agenda, the observations likely to be made by the Secretary must duly be taken into account; b) All proposals made under the provisions of the present paragraph shall be included only in the Provisional Agenda of the Commission, if at least two thirds (2/3) of the members present and voting so decide.

6. The Provisional Agenda of the Extraordinary Session of the Commission shall include only the item proposed to be considered at that Extraordinary Session.

Rule 7 - Transmission and Distribution of the Provisional Agenda

1. The Provisional Agenda and the essential documents relating to each item shall be distributed to the members of the Commission by the Secretary who shall endeavour to transmit them tot

members at least six (6) weeks before the opening of the Session.

2. The Secretary shall communicate the Provisional Agenda of that session and have the essential documents relating to each Agenda item distributed at least six weeks before the opening of the Session of the Commission to the members of the Commission, member States parties to the Charter, to the current Chairman of the Organisation of African Unity and observers.

3. The draft agenda shall also be sent to the specialised agencies, to non governmental organisations and to the national liberation movements concerned with the agenda.

4. In exceptional cases the Secretary may, while giving his reasons in writing, have the essential documents relating to some items of the Provisional Agenda distributed at least four (4) weeks prior to the opening of the Session.

Rule 8 - Adoption of the Agenda At the beginning of each session, the Commission shall if necessary, after the election of officers in conformity with rule 17, adopt the agenda of the Session on the basis of the Provisional Agenda referred to in Rule 6.

Rule 9 - Revision of the Agenda The Commission may, during the Session, revise the Agenda if need be, adjourn, cancel or amend items. During the Session, only urgent and important issues may be added to the Agenda.

Rule 10 - Draft Provisional Agenda for Next Session The Secretary shall, at each session of the Commission, submit a Draft Provisional Agenda for the next session of the Commission, indicating with respect to each item, the documents to be submitted on that item and the decisions of the deliberative organ which authorized their preparation so as to enable the Commission to consider these documents as regards the contribution they make to its proceedings, as well as their urgency and relevance to the prevailing situation.

Chapter III

Members Of The Commission

Rule 11 - Composition of the Commission The Commission shall be composed of eleven (11) members elected by the Assembly of Heads of State and Government hereinafter referred to as "the Assembly", in conformity with the relevant provisions of the Charter.

Rule 12 - Status of the Member

1. The members of the Commission shall be eleven (11) personalities appointed in conformity with the provisions of Article 31 of the Charter.

2. Each member of the Commission shall sit on the Commission in a personal capacity. No member may be represented by another person.

Rule 13 - Term of Office of the Members

1. The term of office of the members of the Commission elected on 29 July 1987 shall begin from that date. The term of office of the members of the Commission elected at subsequent elections shall take effect the day following the expiry date of the term of office of the members of the Commission they shall replace.

2. However, if a member is re-elected at the expiry of his or her term of office, or elected to replace a member whose term of office has expired or will expire, the term of office shall begin from that expiry date.

3. In conformity with Article 39 (3) of the Charter, the member elected to replace a member whose term has not expired, shall complete the term of office of his or her predecessor, unless the

remaining term of office is less than six (6) months. In the latter case, there shall be no replacement.

Rule 14 - Cessation of Functions

1. If in the unanimous opinion of the other members of the Commission, a member has stopped discharging his duties for any reason other than a temporary absence, the Chairman of the Commission shall inform the Secretary General of the Organisation of African Unity, who shall then declare the seat vacant.

2. In case of the death or resignation of a member of the Commission, the Chairman shall immediately inform the Secretary General who shall declare the seat vacant from the date of the death or from that on which the resignation took effect. The member of the Commission who resigns shall address a written notification of his or her resignation directly to the Chairman or to the Secretary General and steps to declare his or her seat vacant shall only be taken after receiving the said notification. The resignation shall make the seat vacant.

Rule 15 - Vacant sea.t Every seat declared vacant in conformity with Rule 14 of the present Rules of Procedure shall be filled on the basis of Article 39 of the Charter.

Rule 16 - Oath Before coming into office, every member of the Commission shall make the following solemn commitment at a public sitting. "I swear to carry out my duties well and faithfully in all impartiality".

Chapter IV

Officers

Rule 17 - Election of Officers

1. The Commission shall elect among its members a Chairman and Vice-Chairman.

2. The elections referred to in the present Rule shall be held by secret ballot. Only the members present shall vote, the member who shall obtain the two-thirds majority of the votes of the members present and voting shall be elected.

3. If no member obtains this two-thirds majority in a second, third and fourth ballot, the member having the highest number of votes at the fifth ballot shall be elected.

4. The officers of the Commission shall be elected for a period of two (2) years. They shall be eligible for re-election. None of them, may, however, exercise his or her functions if he or she ceases to be a member of the Commission.

Rule 18 - Power of the Chairman The Chairman shall carry out the functions assigned to him by the Charter, the Rules of Procedure and the decisions of the Commission. In the exercise of his functions the Chairman shall be under the authority of the Commission.

Rule 19 - Absence of the Chairman

1. The Vice Chairman shall replace the Chairman during a session if the latter is unable to attend a whole or part of a sitting of a session.

2. In the absence of both the Chairman and Vice Chairman, members shall elect an acting Chairman.

Rule 20 - Functions of the Vice Chairman The Vice Chairman, acting in the capacity of the Chairman, shall have the same rights and the same duties as the Chairman.

Rule 21 - Cessation of the Functions of an Officer If any of the officers ceases to carry out his or her functions or declares that he or she is no longer able to serve as an officer or exercise the functions of a member of the Commission, a new officer shall be elected for the remaining term of office of his or her predecessor.

Chapter V

Secretariat

Rule 22 - Function of the Secretary General

1. The Secretary General or his representative may attend the meeting of the Commission. He shall neither participate in the deliberations, nor in the voting. He may, however, be called upon by the Chairman of the Commission to make written or oral statements at the sittings of the Commission.
2. He shall appoint, in consultation with the Chairman of the Commission, a Secretary of the Commission.
3. He shall, in consultation with the Chairman provide the Commission with the necessary staff, means and services for it to carry out effectively the functions and missions assigned to it under the Charter.
4. The Secretary General acting through the Secretary shall take all the necessary steps for the meetings of the Commission.

Rule 23 - Functions of the Secretary to the Commission The Secretary of the Commission shall be responsible for the activities of the Secretariat under the general supervision of the Chairman, and particularly:

a) He/she shall assist the Commission and its members in the exercise of their functions;

b) He/she shall serve as an intermediary for all the communications concerning the Commission;

c) He/she shall be the custodian of the archives of the Commission;

d) The Secretary shall bring immediately to the knowledge of the members of the Commission all the issues that will be submitted to him/her.

Rule 24 - Estimates Before the Commission approves a proposal entailing expenses, the Secretary shall prepare and distribute, as soon as possible, to the members of the Commission, the financial implications to the proposal. It is incumbent on the Chairman to draw the attention of the members to those implications so that they discuss them when the proposal is considered by the Commission.

Rule 25 - Financial Rules The Financial Rules adopted pursuant to the provisions of Articles 41 and 44 of the Charter, shall be appended to the present Rules of Procedure.

Rule 26 - Financial responsibility The Organisation of African Unity shall bear the expenses of the staff and the facilities and services placed at the disposal of the Commission to carry out its functions.

Rule 27 - Records of Cases A special record, with a reference number and initialed, in which shall be entered the date of registration of each petition and communication and that of the closure of the procedure relating to them before the Commission, shall be kept at the Secretariat.

Chapter VI

Subsidiary Bodies

Rule 28 - Establishment of Committees and Working Groups

1. The Commission may during a session, taking into account the provisions of the Charter establish, if it deems it necessary for the exercise of its functions, committees or working groups, composed of the members of the Commission and send them any agenda item for consideration and report.

2. These committees or working groups may, in consultation with the Secretary General, be authorized to sit when the Commission is not in session.

3. The members of the committees or working groups shall be appointed by the Chairman subject to the approval of the absolute majority of the other members of the Commission.

Rule 29 - Establishment of Sub-Commissions

1. The Commission may establish Sub Commissions of experts after the prior approval of the Assemble.

2. Unless the Assembly decides otherwise, the Commission shall determine the functions and composition of each Sub Commission.

Rule 30 - Offices of the Subsidiary bodies Unless the Commission decides otherwise, the subsidiary bodies of the Commission shall elect their own officers.

Rule 31 - Rules of Procedure The Rules of Procedure of the Commission shall apply, as far as possible to the proceedings of its subsidiary bodies.

Chapter VII

Public Sessions and Private Sessions

Rule 32 - General principle The sittings of the Commission and of its subsidiary bodies shall be held in public unless the Commission decides otherwise or it appears from the relevant provisions of the Charter that the meeting shall be held in private.

Rule 33 - Publication of Proceedings At the end of each private or public sitting, the Commission or its subsidiary bodies may issue a communiqué.

Chapter VIII

Languages

Rule 34 - Working Languages The working languages of the Commission and of all its institutions shall be those of the Organisation of African Unity.

Rule 35 - Interpretation

1. The address delivered in one of the working languages shall be interpreted in the other working languages.
2. Any person addressing the Commission in a language other than one of the working languages, shall, in principle, ensure the interpretation in one of the working languages. The interpreters of the Secretariat may take the interpretation of the original language as source language for their interpretation in the other working languages.

Rule 36 - Languages to be used for Minutes of Proceedings The summary minutes of the sittings of the Commission shall be drafted in the working languages.

Rule 37 - Languages to be used for resolutions and other official decisions All the official decisions and documents of the Commission will be rendered in the working languages.

Rule 38 - Tape recordings of the Session The Secretariat shall record and preserve the tapes of the sessions of the Commission. It may also record and conserve the tapes of the sessions of the committees, working groups and sub-commissions if the Commission so decides.

Rule 39 - Summary Minutes of the Sessions The Secretariat shall draft the summary minutes of the public and private sessions of the Commission and of its subsidiary bodies. It shall distribute them as soon as possible in a draft form to the members of the Commission and to all other participants in the session. All those participants may, in the thirty (30) days following the receipt of the draft minutes of the session, submit corrections to the Secretariat. The Chairman may, under special circumstances, in consultation with the Secretary-General, extend the time for the submission of the corrections. In case the corrections are contested, the Chairman of the Commission or the Chairman of the subsidiary body whose minutes they are, shall resolve the disagreement after having listened to, if necessary, the tape recordings of the discussions. If the disagreement persists, the Commission or the subsidiary body shall decide. The corrections shall be published in a distinct volume after the closure of the session.

Rule 40 - Distribution of the Minutes of the Private Sessions and Public Sessions

1. The final summary minutes of the public and private sessions shall be the document intended for general distribution unless, the Commission decides otherwise.

2.   The minutes of the private sessions of the Commission shall be distributed forthwith to all members of the Commission.

Rule 41 - Reports to be submitted after each session The Commission shall submit to the current Chairman of the Organisation of African Unity, a report on the deliberations of each session. This report shall contain a brief summary of the recommendations and statements on issues to which the Commission would like to draw the attention of the current Chairman and member States of the Organisation of African Unity.

Rule 42 - Submission of official decisions and reports The text of the decisions and reports officially adopted by the Commission shall be distributed to all members of the Commission as soon as possible.

Chapter X
Conduct of the Debates

Rule 43 - Quorum The quorum shall be constituted by seven (7) members of the Commission,, as specified in Article 42 (3) of the Charter.

Rule 44 - Additional Powers of the Chairman

1.   In addition to the powers entrusted to him/her under other provisions of the present Rules of Procedure, the Chairman shall have the responsibility to open and close each session; he/she shall direct the debates, ensure the application of the present Rules of Procedure, grant the use of floor, submit to a vote matters under discussion and announce the result of the vote taken.

2.   Subject to the provisions of the present Rules of Procedure, the Chairman shall direct the discussions of the Commission

and ensure order during meeting. The Chairman may during the discussion of an agenda item, propose to the Commission to limit the time allotted to speakers, as well as the number of interventions of each speaker on the same issue and close the list of speakers

3. He/she shall rule on the points of order. He/she shall also have the power to propose the adjournment and the closure of debates as well as the adjournment and suspension of a sitting. The debates shall deal solely with the issues submitted to the Commission and the Chairman may call a speaker, whose remarks are irrelevant to the matter under discussion, to order.

Rule 45 - Points of Order

1. During the debate of any matter a member may, at any time, raise a point of order and the point of order shall be immediately decided by the Chairman, in accordance with the Rules of Procedure. If a member appeals against the decision, the appeal shall immediately be put to the vote and if the Chairman's ruling is not overruled by the majority of the members present, it shall be maintained.

2. A member raising a point of order cannot, in his or her comments, deal with the substance of the matter under discussion.

Rule 46 - Adjournment of Debates During the discussion on any matter, a member may move the adjournment of the debate on the matter under discussion. In addition to the proposer of the motion one member may speak in favour of and one against the motion after which the motion shall be immediately put to the vote.

Rule 47 - Limit the Time accorded to Speakers The Commission may limit the time accorded to each speaker on any matter, when the time allotted for debates is limited and a speaker spends more time than the time accorded, the Chairman shall immediately call him to order.

Rule 48 - Closing the list of speakers The Chairman may, during a debate, read out the list of speakers and with the approval of the Commission, declare the list closed. Where there are no more speakers, the Chairman shall, with the approval of the Commission, declare the debate closed.

Rule 49 - Closure of Debate A member may, at any time, move for the closure of the debate on the matter under discussion, even if the other members or representatives expressed the desire to take the floor. The authorisation to take the floor on the closure of the debate shall be given only to two speakers before the closure, after which the motion shall immediately be put to the vote.

Rule 50 - Suspension or Adjournment of the Meeting During the discussion of any matter, a member may move for the suspension or adjournment of the meeting. No discussion on any such motion shall be permitted and it shall be immediately put to the vote.

Rule 51 - Order of the Motions Subject to the provisions of Rule 45 of the present Rule of Procedure the following motions shall have precedence in the following order over all the other proposals or motions before the meeting.
- a) To suspend the meeting
- b) To adjourn the meeting
- c) To adjourn the debate on the item under discussion
- d) For the closure of the debate of the item under discussion.

Rule 52 - Submission of Proposals and Amendment of Substance. Unless the Commission decides otherwise the proposals, amendments or motions of substance made by members shall be submitted in writing to the Secretariat; they shall be considered at the first sitting following their submission.

Rule 53 - Decisions on Competence Subject to the provisions of Rule 45 of the Procedure, any motion tabled by a member for a decision on the competence of the Commission to adopt a proposal submitted to it shall immediately be put to the vote.

Rule 54 - Withdrawal of a Proposal or a Motion The sponsor of a motion or a proposal may still withdraw it before it is put to the vote, provided that it has not been amended. A motion or a proposal thus withdrawn may be submitted again by another member.

Rule 55 - New Consideration or a Motion When a proposal is adopted or rejected, it shall not be considered again at the same session, unless the Commission decides otherwise. When a member moves the new consideration of a proposal, only one member may speak in favour of and one against the motion, after which it shall immediately be put to the vote.

Rule 56 - Interventions

1. No member may take the floor at a meeting of the Commission without prior authorisation on the Chairman. Subject to Rules 45, 48, 49 and 50 the Chairman shall grant the use of the floor to the speakers in the order in which it has been requested.

2.   The debates shall deal solely with the matter submitted to the Commission and the Chairman may call to order a speaker whose remarks are irrelevant to the matter under discussion.

3.   The Chairman may limit the time accorded to speakers and the number of the interventions which each member may make on the same issue, in accordance with Rule 44 of the present Rules.

4.   Only two members in favour and two against the motion of fixing such time limits shall be granted the use of the floor after which the motion shall immediately be put to the vote. For questions of procedure the time allotted to each speaker shall not exceed five minutes, unless the Chairman decides otherwise. When the time allotted discussions is limited and a speaker exceeds the time accorded the Chairman shall immediately call him to order.

Rule 57 - Right to Reply The right of reply shall be granted by the Chairman to any member requesting it. The member must, while exercising this right, be as brief as possible and take the floor preferably at the end of the sitting at which this right has been requested.

Rule 58 - Congratulations The congratulations addressed to the newly elected members to the commission shall only be presented by the Chairman or a member designated by the latter. Those addressed to the newly elected officers shall only be presented by the outgoing Chairman or a member designated by him.

Rule 59 – Condolences shall be exclusively presented by the Chairman on behalf of all the members. The Chairman may, with the consent of the Commission, send a message of condolence.

Chapter XI

Vote and Elections

Rule 60 - Right to Vote Each member of the Commission shall have one vote. In the case of equal number of votes the Chairman shall have a casting vote.

Rule 61 - Asking for a Vote A proposal or a motion submitted for the decision of the Commission shall be put to the vote if a member so requests. If no member asks for a vote, the Commission may adopt a proposal or a motion without a vote.

Rule 62 - Required majority

1.   Except as otherwise provided by the Charter or other Rules of the present Rules of Procedure, decisions of the Commission shall be taken by a simple majority of the members present and voting.

2.   For the purpose of the present Rules of Procedure, the expression "members present and voting" shall mean members voting for or against. The members who shall abstain from voting shall be considered as non-voting members.

3.   Decisions may be taken by consensus, failing which, Commission shall resort to voting.

Rule 63 - Method of Voting

1.   Subject to the provisions of Rule 68, the commission, unless it otherwise decides, shall normally vote by show of hands, but any member may request the roll-call vote, which shall be taken in the alphabetical order of the names of the members of the Commission beginning with the member whose name is drawn by lot by the Chairman. In all the votes by roll-call each

member shall reply "yes", "no" or "abstention". The Commission may decide to hold a secret ballot.

2.	In case of vote by roll-call, the vote of each member participating in the ballot shall be recorded in the minutes.

Rule 64 - Explanation of Vote Members may make brief statements for the only purpose of explaining their vote, before the beginning of the vote or once the vote has been taken. The member who is the sponsor of a proposal or a motion cannot explain his vote on that proposal or notion except if it has been amended.

Rule 65 - Rules to be observed while voting A ballot shall not be interrupted except if a member raises a point of order relating to manner in which the ballot is held. The Chairman may allow members to intervene briefly, whether before the ballot beginning or when it is closed, but solely to explain their vote.

Rule 66 - Division of Proposals and Amendments Proposals and amendments may be separated if requested. The parts of the proposals or of the amendments which have been adopted shall later be put to the vote as a whole; if all the operative parts of a proposal have been rejected, the proposal shall be considered to have been rejected as a whole.

Rule 67 - Amendment An amendment to a proposal is an addition to, deletion from or revision of part of that proposal.

Rule 68 - Order of Vote on amendments When an amendment is moved to a proposal, the amendment shall be voted on first.

When two or more amendments are moved to a proposal, the Commission shall first vote on the amendment furthest removed in substance from the original proposal and then on the amendment next furthest removed therefrom and so on until all the amendments have been put to the vote. Nevertheless when the adoption of an amendment implies the rejection of another amendment, the latter shall not be put to the vote. If one or several amendments are adopted, the amended proposal shall then be put to the vote.

Rule 69 - Order of Vote on the Proposals
1. If two or more proposals are made on the same matter, the Commission, unless it decides otherwise, shall vote on these proposals in the order in which they were submitted.
2. After each vote the Commission may decide whether it shall put the next proposal to the vote. 3. However, the motions which are not on the substance of the proposals shall be voted upon before the said proposals.

Rule 70 - Elections shall be held by secret ballot unless the election is for a post for which only one candidate has been proposed and that candidate has been agreed upon by the members of the Commission.

Chapter III

Participation of Non-Members of the Commission

Rule 71 - Participation of States in the deliberations
1. The Commission or its subsidiary bodies may invite any State to participate in the discussion of any issue that shall be of particular interest to that State.
2. A State thus invited shall have no voting right, but may submit proposals which may be put to the vote at the request of any member of the Commission or of the subsidiary body concerned.

Rule 72 - Participation of other Persons or Organisations The Commission may invite any organisation or persons capable of enlightening it to participate in its deliberations without voting rights.

Rule 73 - Participation of Specialised Institutions and Consultation with the latter

1. Pursuant to the agreements concluded between the Organisation of African Unity and the Specialised Institutions, the latter shall have the right to: a) Be represented in the public sessions of the Commission and its subsidiary bodies; b) Participate, without voting rights, through their representatives in deliberations on issues which shall be of interest to them and to submit, on these issues, proposals which may be put to vote at the request of any member of the Commission or the interested subsidiary body.

2. Before placing on the provisional agenda issues submitted by a Specialised Institution, the Secretary General should initiate such preliminary consultations as may be necessary, with this institution.

3. When an issue proposed for inclusion in the provisional agenda of a session, or which has been added to the agenda of a session pursuant to Rule 5 of the present Rules of Procedure, contains a proposal requesting the Organisation of African Unity to undertake additional activities relating to issues concerning directly one or more specialised institutions, the Secretary General should enter in to consultation with the institutions concerned and inform the Commission of the ways and means of ensuring coordinated utilisation of the resources of the various institutions.

4. When at a meeting of the Commission, a proposal calling upon the Organisation of African Unity to undertake additional ac-

tivities relating to issues directly concerning one or several specialised institutions, the Secretary General, after consulting as far as possible, the representatives of the interested institutions, should draw the attention of the Commission to the effects of that proposal.

5. Before taking a decision on the proposals mentioned above, the Commission shall make sure that the institutions concerned have been duly consulted.

Rule 74 - Participation of other Inter-Governmental Organisations

1. The Secretary shall inform, not later that 4 weeks before a session, non-governmental organisations with observer status of the days and agenda of a forthcoming session.

2. Representatives of Inter-Governmental Organisations to which the Organisation of African Unity has granted permanent observer status and other Organisations recognised by the Commission, may participate, without voting rights, in the deliberations of the Commission on issues falling within the framework of the activities of these organisations.

Chapter XIII

Relations with and Representation of Non-Governmental Organisations

Rule 75 - Representation Non-governmental organisations, granted observer status by the Commission, may appoint authorised observers to participate in the public sessions of the Commission and of its subsidiary bodies.

Rule 76 - Consultation The Commission may consult the non-governmental organisations either directly or through one or several committees set up for this purpose. These consultations may be held at the invitation of the Commission or at the request of the organisation.

Chapter XIV

Publication and Distribution of the Reports and Other Official Documents of the Commission

Rule 77 - Report of the Commission Within the framework of the procedure of communication among States parties to the Charter, referred to in Articles 47 and 49 of the Charter, the Commission shall submit to the Assembly a report containing, where possible, recommendations it shall deem necessary. The report shall be confidential. However, it shall be published by the Chairman of the Commission after reporting unless the Assembly directs otherwise.

Rule 78 - Periodical Reports of Member States Periodical Reports and other information submitted by States parties to the Charter as requested under Article 62 of the Charter shall be documents for general distribution. The same thing shall apply to other information supplied by a State party to the Charter, unless the Commission decides otherwise.

Rule 79 - Reports on the Activities of the Commission

1. As stipulated in Article 54 of the Charter, the Commission shall each year submit to the Assembly, a report on its deliberations, in which it shall include a summary of the activities.
2. The report shall be published by the Chairman after the Assembly has considered it.
3.

Rule 80 - Translation of reports and other documents The Secretary shall endeavour to translate all reports and other document of the Commission into the working languages.

Part Two - Provisions Relating to the Functions of the Commission

Chapter XV
Promotional Activities

Report Submitted By States Parties To The Charter Under Article 62 Of The Charter

Rule 81 - Contents of Reports

1. States parties to the Charter shall submit reports in the form required by the Commission on measures they have taken to give effect to the rights recognised by the Charter and on the progress made with regard to the enjoyment of these rights. The reports should indicate, where possible, the factors and difficulties impeding the implementation of the provisions of the Charter.

2. If a State party fails to comply with Article 62 of the Charter, the Commission shall fix the date for the submission of that State party's report.

3. The Commission may, through the Secretary-General, inform State parties to the Charter of its wishes regarding the form and contents of the reports to be submitted under Article 62 of the Charter.

Rule 82 - Transmission of the Reports

1. The Secretary may, after consultation with the Commission, communicate to the specialised institutions concerned, copies of all parts of the reports which may relate to their areas of competence, produced by member States of these institutions.

2. The Commission may invite the specialised institutions to which the Secretary has communicated parts of the report, to

submit observations relating to these parts within a time limit that it may specify.

Rule 83 - Submission of Reports The Commission shall inform, as early as possible, member States parties to the Charter, through the Secretary, of the opening date, duration and venue of the Session at which their respective reports shall be considered. Representatives of the States parties to the Charter may participate in the sessions of the Commission at which their reports shall be considered. The Commission may also inform a State party to the Charter from which it wanted complementary information, that it may authorise its representative to participate in a specific session. This representative should be able to reply to questions put to him/her by the Commission and make statements on reports already submitted by this State. He may also furnish additional information from his State.

Rule 84 - Non-submission of Reports

1. The Secretary shall, at each session, inform the Commission of all cases of non-submission of reports or of additional information requested pursuant to Rules 81 and 85 of the Rules of Procedure. In such cases, the Commission may send, through the Secretary, to the State party to the Charter concerned, a report or reminder relating to the submission of the report or additional information.

2. If, after the reminder referred to in paragraph 1 of this Rule, a State party to the Charter does not submit the report or the additional information requested pursuant to Rules 81 and 85 of the Rules of Procedure, the Commission shall point it out in its yearly report to the Assembly.

Rule 85 - Examination of information contained in reports

1. When considering a report submitted by a State party to the Charter under Article 62 of the Charter, the Commission should first make sure that the report provides all the necessary information including relevant legislation pursuant to the provisions of Rule 81 of the Rules of Procedure.

2. If, in the opinion of the Commission, a report submitted by a State party to the Charter, does not contain adequate information, the Commission may request this State to furnish the additional information required, by indicating the date on which the information needed should be submitted.

3. If, following the consideration of the reports, and the information submitted by a State party to the Charter, the Commission decides that the State has not discharged some of its obligations under the Charter, it may address all general observations to the State concerned as it may deem necessary.

Rule 86 - Adjournment and Transmission of the Reports

1. The Commission shall, through the Secretary, communicate to States parties to the Charter for comments, its general observations made following the consideration of the reports and the information submitted by States parties to the Charter. The Commission may, when necessary fix a time limit for the submission of the comments by the States parties to the Charter.

2. The Commission may also transmit to the Assembly, the observations mentioned in paragraph 1 of this Rule, accompanied by copies of the reports it has received from the States parties to the Charter as well as the comments supplied by the latter if possible.

Rule 87 - Promotional Activities

1. The Commission shall adopt and carry out a program of action which gives effect to its obligations under the Charter, particularly Article 45 (1).

2. The Commission shall carry out other promotional activities in member states and elsewhere on a continuing basis.

3. Each member of the Commission shall file a written report on his/her activities at each session including countries visited and organisations contacted.

Chapter XVI

Protection Activities Communications from the States Parties to the Charter

Section I - Procedure for the consideration of communications received in conformity with article 47 of the charter: procedure for communications-negotiations

Rule 88 - Procedure

1. A communication under Article 47 of the Charter should be submitted to the Secretary General, the Chairman of the Commission and the State party concerned.

2. The communication referred to above should be in writing and contain a detailed and comprehensive statement on the actions denounced as well as the provisions of the Charter alleged to have been violated.

3. The notification of the communication to the State party to the Charter, the Secretary General and the Chairman of the Commission shall be done through the most practicable and reliable means.

Rule 89 - Register of Communications The Secretary shall keep a permanent register for all communications received under Article 47 of the Charter.

Rule 90 - Reply and time limit

1. The reply of the State party to the Charter to which a communication is addressed should reach the requesting State party to the Charter within 3 months following the receipt of the notification of the communication.
2. It shall be accompanied particularly by: a) Written explanations, declarations or statements relating to the issues raised; b) Possible indications and measures taken to end the situation denounced; c) Indications on the law and rules of procedure applicable or applied; d) Indications on the local procedures for appeal already used, in process or still open.

Rule 91 - Non-Settlement of the Issue

1. If within three (3) months from the date the notification of the original communication is received by the addressee State, the issue has not been settled to the satisfaction of the two interested parties, through the selected channel of negotiation or through any other peaceful procedure selected by common consent of the parties, the issue shall be referred to the Commission, in accordance with the provisions of Article 48 of the Charter.
2. The issue shall also be referred to the Commission if the addressee State party to the Charter fails to react to the request made under Article 47 of the Charter, within the same 3 months' period of time.

Rule 92 - Seizing of the Commission At the expiration of the 3 months' time limit referred to in Article 47 of the Charter, and in the absence of a satisfactory reply or in case the addressee State party may submit the communication to the Commission through a notification addressed to its Chairman, the other interested State party and the Secretary General.

Section II

Procedure for the consideration of the communications received in conformity with articles 48 and 49 of the charter: procedure for communication-complaint

Rule 93 - Seizing of the Commission

1. Any communication submitted under Articles 48 and 49 of the Charter may be submitted to the Commission by any one of the interested States parties through notification addressed to the Chairman of the Commission, the Secretary General and the State party concerned.

2. The notification referred to in paragraph 1 of the present Rule shall contain information on the following elements or accompanied particularly by a) Measures taken to try to resolve the issue pursuant to Article 47 of the Charter including the text of the initial communications and any future written explanation from the interested States parties to the Charter relating to the issue; b) Measures taken to exhaust local procedure for appeal; c) Any other procedure for the international investigation or international settlement to which the interested States parties have resorted.

Rule 94 - Permanent Register of Communications The Secretary shall keep a permanent register for all communications received by the Commission under Articles 48 and 49 of the Charter.

Rule 95 - Seizing of the Members of the Commission The Secretary shall immediately inform the members of the Commission of any notification received pursuant to Rule 91 of the Rules of Procedure and shall send to them, as early as possible, a copy of the notification as well as the relevant information.

Rule 96 - Private Session and Press Release

1. The Commission shall consider the communications referred to in Articles 48 and 49 of the Charter in closed session.
2. After consulting the interested States parties to the Charter, the Commission may issue through the Secretary, release on its private sessions for the attention of the media and the public.

Rule 97 - Consideration of the Communication The Commission shall consider a communication only when: a) The procedure offered to the States parties by Article 47 of the Charter has been exhausted; b) The time limit set in Article 48 of the Charter has expired; c) The Commission is certain that all the available local remedies have been utilised and exhausted, in accordance with the generally recognized principles of international law, or that the application of these remedies is unreasonably prolonged or that there are no effective remedies.

Rule 98 Amicable Settlement Except the provisions of the present Rules of Procedure, the Commission shall place its good offices at the disposal of the interested States parties to the Charter so as to reach an amicable solution on the issue based on the respect of human rights and fundamental liberties, as recognized by the Charter.

Rule 99 - Additional Information The Commission may through the Secretary, request the States parties or one of them to communicate additional information or observations orally or in writing. The Commission shall fix a time limit for the submission of the written information or observations.

Rule 100 - Representation of States Parties
1. The States parties to the Charter concerned shall have the right to be represented during the consideration of the issue by the Commission and to submit observations orally and in writing or in either form.
2. The Commission shall notify, as soon as possible, the States parties concerned, through the Secretary of the opening day, the duration and the venue of the session at which the issue will be examined.
3. The procedure to be followed for the presentation of oral or written observations shall be determined by the Commission.

Rule 101 - Report of the Commission
1. The Commission shall adopt a report pursuant to Article 52 of the Charter within 12 months, following the notification referred to in Article 48 of the Charter and Rule 90 of the present Rules of Procedure.
2. The provisions of paragraph 1 of Rule 99 of these Rules of Procedure shall not apply to the deliberations of the Commission relating to the adoption of the report.
3. The report referred to above shall concern the decisions and conclusions that the Commission will reach.
4. The report of the Commission shall be communicated to the States parties concerned through the Secretary.
5. The report of the Commission shall be sent to the Assembly through the Secretary General, together with the recommendations that it shall deem useful.

Chapter XVII

Other communications procedure for the consideration of the communications received in conformity with article 55 of the charter

Section I

Transmission of Communications to the Commission

    Rule 102 - Seizing of the Commission

1. Pursuant to these Rules of Procedure, the Secretary shall transmit to the Commission the communications submitted to him for consideration by the Commission in accordance with the Charter.

2. No communications concerning a State which is not a party to the Charter shall be received by the Commission or placed in a list under Rule 103 of the present Rules.

    Rule 103 - List of Communications

1. The Secretary of the Commission shall prepare lists of communications submitted to the Commission pursuant to Rule 101 above, to which he/she shall attach a brief summary to their contents and regularly cause the lists to be distributed to members of the Commission. Besides, the Secretary shall keep a permanent register of all these communications which shall be made public.

2. The full text of each communication referred to the Commission shall be communicated to each member of the Commission on request.

    Rule 104 - Request for Clarifications

1. The Commission, through the Secretary, may request the author of a communication to furnish clarifications on the applicability of the Charter to his/her communication, and to

specify in particular: (a) His name, address, age and profession by justifying his very identity, if ever he/she is requesting the Commission to be kept anonymous; (b) Name of the State party referred to in the communication; (c) Purpose of the communication; (d) Provision(s) of the Charter allegedly violated; (e)The facts of the claim; (f) Measures taken by the author to exhaust local remedies, or explanation why local remedies will be futile; (g) The extent to which the same issue has been settled by another international investigation or settlement body.

2. When asking for clarification or information, the Commission shall fix an appropriate time limit for the author to submit the communication so as to avoid undue delay in the procedure provided for by the Charter.

3. The Commission may adopt a questionnaire for the use by the author of the communication in providing the above-mentioned information.

4. The request for clarification referred to in paragraph 1 of this rule shall not prevent the inclusion of the communication on the lists mentioned in paragraph 1 of Rule 102 above.

Rule 105 - Distribution of Communications For each communication recorded, the Secretary shall prepare as soon as possible, a summary of the relevant information received, which shall be distributed to the members of the Commission.

Section II
General provisions governing the consideration of the communications by the commission or its subsidiary bodies.

Rule 106 - Private Session The sessions of the Commission or its subsidiary bodies during which the communications are examined as provided for in the Charter shall be private.

Rule 107 - Public Sessions The sessions during which the Commission may consider other general issues, such as the application procedure of the Charter, shall be public.

Rule 108 - Press Releases The Commission may issue, through the Secretary and for the attention of the media and the public, releases on the activities of the Commission in its private session.

Rule 109 - Incompatibility

1.   No member shall take part in the consideration of a communication by the Commission a) If he/she has any personal interest in the case, or b) If he /she has participated, in any capacity, in the adoption of any decision relating to the case which is the subject of the communication.
2.   Any issue relating to the application of paragraph 1. above shall be resolved by the Commission.

Rule 110 - Withdrawal of a Member If, for any reason, a member considers that he/she should not take part or continue to take part in the consideration of a communication, he/she shall inform the Chairman of his/her decision to withdrawal.

Rules 111 - Provisional Measures

1.   Before making its final views know to the Assembly on the communication, the Commission may inform the State party concerned of its views on the appropriateness of taking provisional measures to avoid irreparable damage being caused to

the victim of the alleged violation. In so doing, the Commission shall inform the State party that the expression on its views on the adoption of those provisional measures does not imply a decision on the substance of the communication.

2.	The Commission, or when it is not in session, the Chairman, in consultation with other members of the Commission, may indicate to the parties any interim measure, the adoption of which seems desirable in the interest of the parties or the proper conduct of the proceedings before it.

3.	In case urgency when the Commission is not in session, the Chairman in consultation with other members of the Commission, may take any necessary action on behalf of the Commission. As soon as the Commission is again in session, the Chairman shall report to it on any action taken.

Rule 112 Prior to any substantive consideration, every communication should be made known to the State concerned through the Chairman of the Commission, pursuant to Article 57 of the Charter

Section III

Procedures to determine Admissibility

Rule 113 - Time Limits for Consideration of the Admissibility The Commission shall decide, as early as possible and pursuant to the following provisions, whether or not the communication shall be admissible under the Charter.

Rule 114 - Order of Consideration of the Communication

1.	Unless otherwise decided, the Commission shall consider the communications in the order they have been received by the Secretariat.

2.   The Commission may decide, if it deems it good, to consider jointly two or more communications.

Rule 115 - Working Groups The Commission may set up one or more working groups; each composed of three of its members at most, to submit recommendations on admissibility as stipulated in Article 56 of the Charter.

Rule 116 - Admissibility of the Communications The Commission shall determine questions of admissibility pursuant to Article 56 of the Charter.

Rule 117 - Additional Information

1.   The Commission or a working group set up under Rule 113, request the State party concerned or the author of the communication to submit in writing additional information or observations relating to the issue of admissibility of the communication. The Commission or the working group shall fix a time limit for the submission of the information or observations to avoid the issue dragging on too long.

2.   A communication may be declared admissible if the State party concerned has been given the opportunity to submit the information and observations pursuant to paragraph 1 of this Rule.

3.   A request under paragraph 1 of this Rule should indicate clearly that the request does not mean any decision whatsoever has been taken on the issue of admissibility.

4.   However, the Commission shall decide in the issue of admissibility if the State party fails to send a written response within three (3) months from the date of notification of the text of the communication.

Rule 118 - Decision of the Commission on Admissibility

1. If the Commission decides that a communication is inadmissible under the Charter, it shall make its decision known as early as possible, through the Secretary to the author of the communication and, if the communication has been transmitted to a State party concerned, to that State.

2. If the Commission has declared a communication inadmissible under the Charter, it may reconsider this decision at a later date if it receives a request for reconsideration.

Section IV

Procedures for the Consideration of Communications

Rule 119 - Proceedings

1. If the Commission decides that a communication is admissible under the Charter, its decision and text of the relevant documents shall as soon as possible, be submitted to the State party concerned, through the Secretary. The author of the communication shall also be informed of the Commission's decision through the Secretary.

2. The State party to the Charter concerned shall, within the 3 ensuing months, submit in writing to the Commission, explanations or statements elucidating the issue under consideration and indicating, if possible, measures it was able to take to remedy the situation.

3. All explanations or statements submitted by a State party pursuant to the present Rule shall be communicated, through the Secretary, to the author of the communication who may submit in writing additional information and observations within a time limit fixed by the Commission.

4. States parties from whom explanations or statements are sought within specified times shall be informed that if they fail

to comply within those times the Commission will act on the evidence before it.

Rule 120 - Final Decision of the Communication

1. If the communication is admissible, the Commission shall consider it in the light of all the information that the individual and the State party concerned has submitted in writing; it shall make known its observations on this issue. To this end, the Commission may refer the communication to a working group, composed of 3 of its members at most, which shall submit recommendations to it.

2. The observations of the Commission shall be communicated to the Assembly through the Secretary General and to the State party concerned.

3. The Assembly or its Chairman may request the Commission to conduct an in-depth study on these cases and to submit a factual report accompanied by its findings and recommendations, in accordance with the provisions of the Charter. The Commission may entrust this function to a Special Rapporteur or a working group.

Final Chapter

Amendment and Suspension of the Rules of Procedure

Rule 121 - Method of Amendment Only the Commission may modify the present Rules of Procedure.

Rule 122 - Method of Suspension The Commission may suspend temporarily, the application of any Rule of the present Rules of Procedure, on condition that such a suspension shall not be incompatible with any applicable decision of the Commission or the Assembly or with any relevant provision of the Charter and that the proposal shall have been submitted 24 hours in advance. This condition may be set aside if no member opposes it. Such a suspension may take place only with a specific and precise object in view and should be limited to the duration necessary to achieve that aim

Deliberated and adopted by the commission at its 18th session held in Praia, Cape Verde.

INDEX

Globethics.net Publications

The list below is only a selection of our publications. To view the full collection, please visit our website.

All products are provided free of charge and can be downloaded in PDF form from the Globethics.net library and at www.globethics.net/publications. Bulk print copies can be ordered from publictions@globethics.net at special rates for those from the Global South.
Paid products not provided free of charge are indicated*.
The Editor of the different Series of Globethics.net Publications is Prof. Dr Obiora Ike, Executive Director of Globethics.net in Geneva and Professor of Ethics at the Godfrey Okoye University Enugu/Nigeria.

Contact for manuscripts and suggestions: publications@globethics.net

African Law Series

Ghislain Patrick Lessène, *Code international de la détention en Afrique*, 2013, 620pp. ISBN: 978-2-940428-70-0

D. Brian Dennison/ Pamela Tibihikirra-Kalyegira (eds.), *Legal Ethics and Professionalism. A Handbook for Uganda*, 2014, 400pp. ISBN 978–2–88931–011–1

Pascale Mukonde Musulay, *Droit des affaires en Afrique subsaharienne et économie planétaire*, 2015, 164pp. ISBN: 978–2–88931–044–9

Pascal Mukonde Musulay, *Démocratie électorale en Afrique subsaharienne: Entre droit, pouvoir et argent*, 2016, 209pp. ISBN 978–2–88931–156–9

Pascal Mukonde Musulay, *Droits, libertés et devoirs de la personne et des peuples en droit international africain Tome I Promotion et protection*, 282pp. 2021, ISBN 978-2-88931-397-6

Pascal Mukonde Musulay, *Droits, libertés et devoirs de la personne et des peuples en droit international africain Tome II Libertés, droits et obligations démocratiques*, 332pp. 2021, ISBN 978-2-88931-399-0

Ambroise Katambu Bulambo, *Règlement judiciaire des conflits électoraux. Précis de droit comparé africain*, 2021, 672pp., ISBN 978-2-88931-403-4

Osita C. Eze, *Africa Charter on Rights & Duties, Enforcement Mechanism*, 2021, 406pp, ISBN 978-2-88931-414-0

Focus Series

Bosco Muchukiwa Rukakiza, *Résilience et transformation des conflits dans les États des Grands Lacs africains: Théorie, démarches et applications*, 2021, 126pp. ISBN 978-2-88931-405-8

Global Series

Carol Cosgrove Sacks/ Paul H. Dembinski (eds.), *Trust and Ethics in Finance. Innovative Ideas from the Robin Cosgrove Prize*, 2012, 380pp. ISBN: 978–2–940428–41–0

Nicolae Irina / Christoph Stückelberger (eds.), *Mining, Ethics and Sustainability*, 2014, 198pp. ISBN: 978–2–88931–020–3

Philip Lee and Dafne Sabanes Plou (eds), *More or Less Equal: How Digital Platforms Can Help Advance Communication Rights*, 2014, 158pp. ISBN 978–2–88931–009–8

Sanjoy Mukherjee and Christoph Stückelberger (eds.) *Sustainability Ethics. Ecology, Economy, Ethics. International Conference SusCon III, Shillong/India*, 2015, 353pp. ISBN: 978–2–88931–068–5

Amélie Vallotton Preisig / Hermann Rösch / Christoph Stückelberger (eds.) *Ethical Dilemmas in the Information Society. Codes of Ethics for Librarians and Archivists*, 2014, 224pp. ISBN: 978–288931–024–1.

Prospects and Challenges for the Ecumenical Movement in the 21st Century. Insights from the Global Ecumenical Theological Institute, David Field / Jutta Koslowski, 256pp. 2016, ISBN: 978–2–88931–097–5

Christoph Stückelberger, Walter Fust, Obiora Ike (eds.), *Global Ethics for Leadership. Values and Virtues for Life*, 2016, 444pp. ISBN: 978–2–88931–123–1

Dietrich Werner / Elisabeth Jeglitzka (eds.), *Eco-Theology, Climate Justice and Food Security: Theological Education and Christian Leadership Development*, 316pp. 2016, ISBN 978–2–88931–145–3

Obiora Ike, Andrea Grieder and Ignace Haaz (Eds.), *Poetry and Ethics: Inventing Possibilities in Which We Are Moved to Action and How We Live Together*, 271pp. 2018, ISBN 978–2–88931–242–9

Christoph Stückelberger / Pavan Duggal (Eds.), *Cyber Ethics 4.0: Serving Humanity with Values*, 503pp. 2018, ISBN 978–2–88931–264-1

Texts Series

Principles on Sharing Values across Cultures and Religions, 2012, 20pp. Available in English, French, Spanish, German and Chinese. Other languages in preparation. ISBN: 978–2–940428–09–0

Ethics in Politics. Why it Matters More than Ever and How it Can Make a Difference. A Declaration, 8pp, 2012. Available in English and French. ISBN: 978–2–940428–35–9

Religions for Climate Justice: International Interfaith Statements 2008–2014, 2014, 45pp. Available in English. ISBN 978–2–88931–006–7

Ethics in the Information Society: The Nine 'P's. A Discussion Paper for the WSIS+10 Process 2013–2015, 2013, 32pp. ISBN: 978–2–940428–063–2

Principles on Equality and Inequality for a Sustainable Economy. Endorsed by the Global Ethics Forum 2014 with Results from Ben Africa Conference 2014, 2015, 41pp. ISBN: 978–2–88931–025–8

Water Ethics: Principles and Guidelines, 2019, 41pp. ISBN 978–2–88931-313-6, available in three languages.

Praxis Series

Christoph Stückelberger, *Responsible Leadership Handbook: For Staff and Boards,* 2014, 116pp. ISBN :978-2-88931-019-7 (Available in Russian)

Angèle Kolouchè Biao, Aurélien Atidegla (éds.,) *Proverbes du Bénin. Sagesse éthique appliquée de proverbes africains,* 2015, 132pp. ISBN 978-2-88931-068-5

Elly K. Kansiime, *In the Shadows of Truth: The Polarized Family,* 2017, 172pp. ISBN 978-2-88931-203-0

Christopher Byaruhanga, *Essential Approaches to Christian Religious Education: Learning and Teaching in Uganda,* 2018, 286pp. ISBN: 978-2-88931-235-1

Christoph Stückelberger / William Otiende Ogara / Bright Mawudor, *African Church Assets Handbook,* 2018, 291pp. ISBN: 978-2-88931-252-8

Oscar Brenifier, *Day After Day 365 Aphorisms,* 2019, 395pp. ISBN 978-2-88931-272-6

Education Ethics Series

Obiora F. Ike, Justus Mbae, Chidiebere Onyia (Eds.), *Mainstreaming Ethics in Higher Education: Research Ethics in Administration, Finance, Education, Environment and Law Vol. 1*, 2019, 779pp. ISBN 978-2-88931-300-6

Ikechukwu J. Ani/Obiora F. Ike (Eds.), *Higher Education in Crisis Sustaining Quality Assurance and Innovation in Research through Applied Ethics*, 2019, 214pp. ISBN 978-2-88931-323-5

Deivit Montealegre / María Eugenia Barroso (Eds.), *Ethics in Higher Education, a Transversal Dimension: Challenges for Latin America. Ética en educación superior, una dimensión transversal: Desafíos para América Latina*, 2020, 148pp. ISBN 978-2-88931-359-4

Obiora Ike, Justus Mbae, Chidiebere Onyia, Herbert Makinda (Eds.), *Mainstreaming Ethics in Higher Education Vol. 2*, 2021, 420pp. ISBN: 978-2-88931-383-9

Christoph Stückelberger/ Joseph Galgalo/ Samuel Kobia (Eds.), *Leadership with Integrity. Higher Education from Vocation to Funding*, 2021, 288pp. ISBN 978-2-88931-389-1

Co-publications & Other

Kenneth R. Ross, *Mission Rediscovered: Transforming Disciples*, 2020, 138pp. ISBN 978-2-88931-369-3

Obiora Ike, Amélé Adamavi-Aho Ekué, Anja Andriamay, Lucy Howe López (Eds.), *Who Cares About Ethics?* 2020, 352pp. ISBN 978-2-88931-381-5

This is only selection of our latest publications, to view our full collection please visit:

www.globethics.net/publications